D A R K A R K
AFTER THE FLOOD

CULLEN BUNN

JUAN DOE

JESUS HERVAS

ANTONIO FUSO

JUANCHO!

STEFANO SIMEONE

DAVE SHARPE

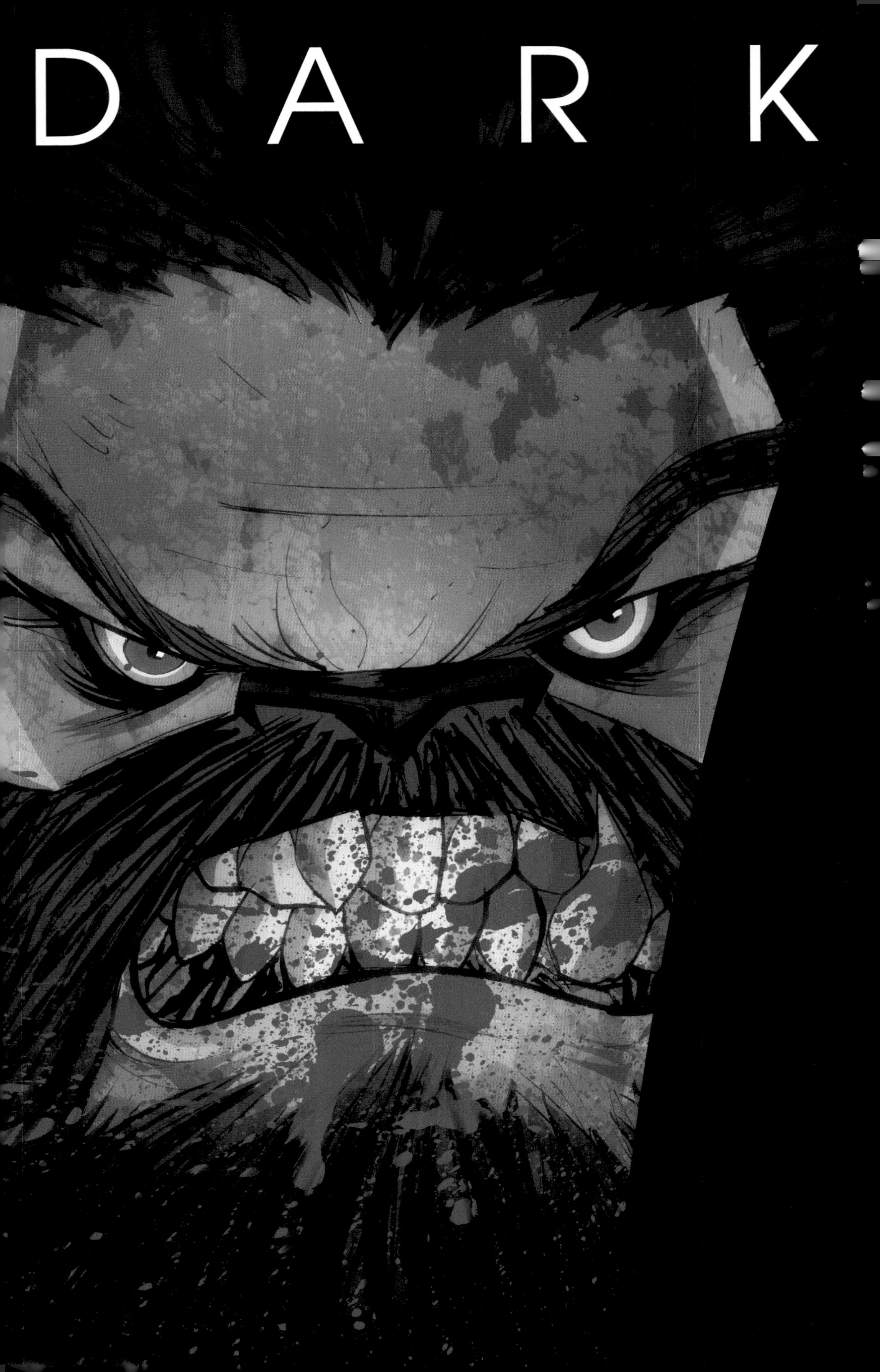
DARK

A R K

AFTER THE FLOOD

CULLEN BUNN writer
JUAN DOE artist (issues #1 & 2)
JESUS HERVAS artist (issues #3 - 5)
JUANCHO! colorist (issues #3 - 5)
DAVE SHARPE letterer

INSTINCT

CULLEN BUNN writer
ANTONIO FUSO artist
STEFANO SIMEONE colorist
DAVE SHARPE letterer

JUAN DOE front & original covers
ANDREI BRESSAN, JUAN DOE, FRANCESCO FRANCAVILLA, NAT JONES, LEILA LEIZ w/ **EDGY ZIANE, ARMANDO RAMIREZ** and **MIKE ROOTH** variant covers

JOHN J. HILL logo designer
COREY BREEN book designer
MIKE MARTS editor

created by **CULLEN BUNN**

AFTERSHOCK™

MIKE MARTS - Editor-in-Chief • JOE PRUETT - Publisher/CCO • LEE KRAMER - President • JON KRAMER - Chief Executive Officer
STEVE ROTTERDAM - SVP, Sales & Marketing • DAN SHIRES - VP, Film & Television UK • CHRISTINA HARRINGTON - Managing Editor
MARC HAMMOND - Sr. Retail Sales Development Manager • RUTHANN THOMPSON - Sr. Retailer Relations Manager • KATHERINE JAMISON - Marketing Manager
BLAKE STOCKER - Director of Finance • AARON MARION - Publicist • LISA MOODY - Finance • RYAN CARROLL - Development Coordinator
JAWAD QURESHI - Technology Advisor/Strategist • RACHEL PINNELAS - Social Community Manager • CHARLES PRITCHETT - Design & Production Manager
COREY BREEN - Collections Production • TEDDY LEO - Editorial Assistant • STEPHANIE CASEBIER & SARAH PRUETT - Publishing Assistants

AfterShock Logo Design by COMICRAFT
Publicity: contact AARON MARION (aaron@publichausagency.com) & RYAN CROY (ryan@publichausagency.com) at PUBLICHAUS
Special thanks to: ATOM! FREEMAN, IRA KURGAN, MARINE KSADZHIKYAN & ANTONIA LIANOS

AFTERSHOCKCOMICS.COM Follow us on social media

I N T R O D U C T I O N

What are you going to do when the sky starts to fall?

Because it will start to fall.

I'm betting you don't need me to tell you that. Not right now. If ever the fates conspired to remind us that the sky is held together with ever-weakening glue, it's right now. So, you know it. I know it. The question remains, of course.

What are you going to do?

The humans and monsters and ghosts of DARK ARK: AFTER THE FLOOD have endured the deluge. The sky fell for them. In buckets. In buckets flung down by the Almighty Himself. Some of our "heroes" made it through in better shape than others. Few of them made it through unchanged. And Khalee, who committed an unthinkable act to rise to her position as shepherd of monsters, knows that there is more calamity on the horizon.

When God tries to drown you, well, that calls for some introspection.

With this chapter of the DARK ARK saga, I wanted to play with the expectations readers might have for Khalee and Shrae...and the demonic powers that drive them...and even God to some degree. The story of Shrae's Ark did not come to an end when the rains stopped falling and land was discovered. And it didn't start when Shrae started building his vessel. It started with a different calamity long ago. And it ends—

I'm not telling just yet.

But with her actions in this story, Khalee is taking a massive hammer to the fragile sky. She shatters it. It was just a matter of time before it collapsed anyway. It always does.
And what is Khalee going to do?

Persevere.

Maybe there are other options, but not for Khalee. Not for me. And I hope not for you. You assess the situation, look into the "eyes" of your enemy—even if that enemy is the Devil, even if that enemy is the Almighty—and you fight for all your worth.

Will Khalee prevail? Maybe, maybe not.

But I bet that enemy of hers will know they've been in a helluva scrap.

CULLEN BUNN
September 2020

1

INSTINCT

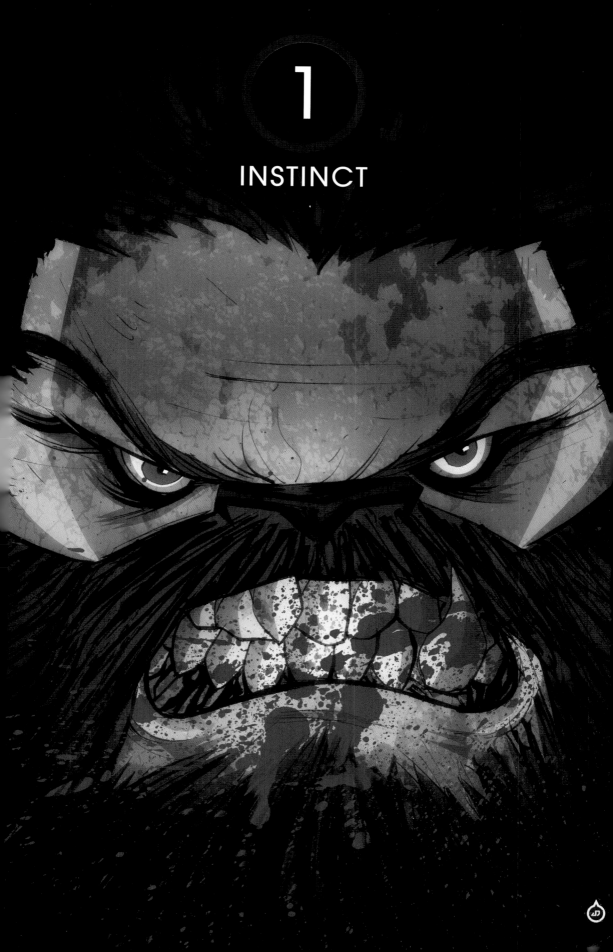

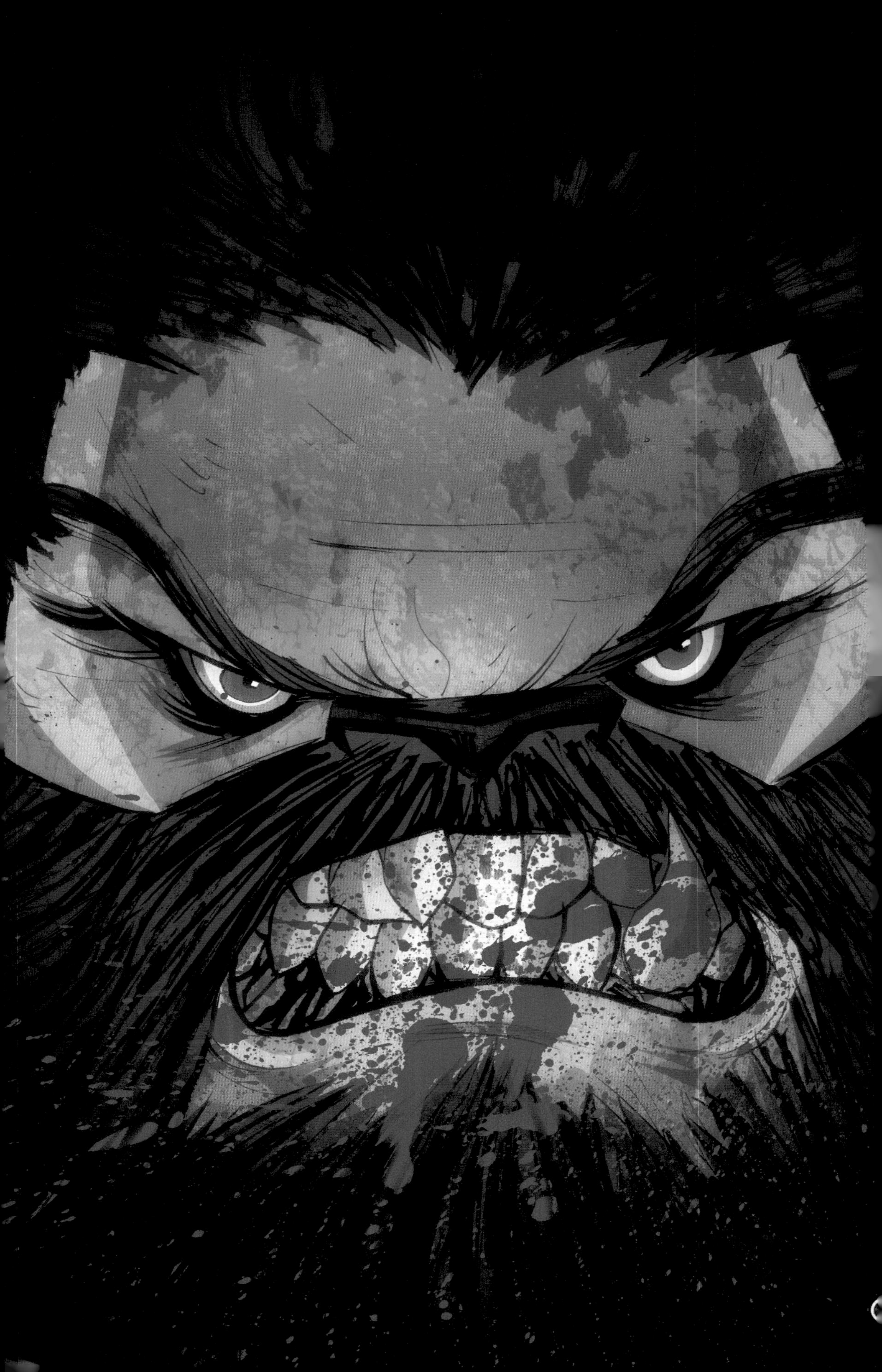

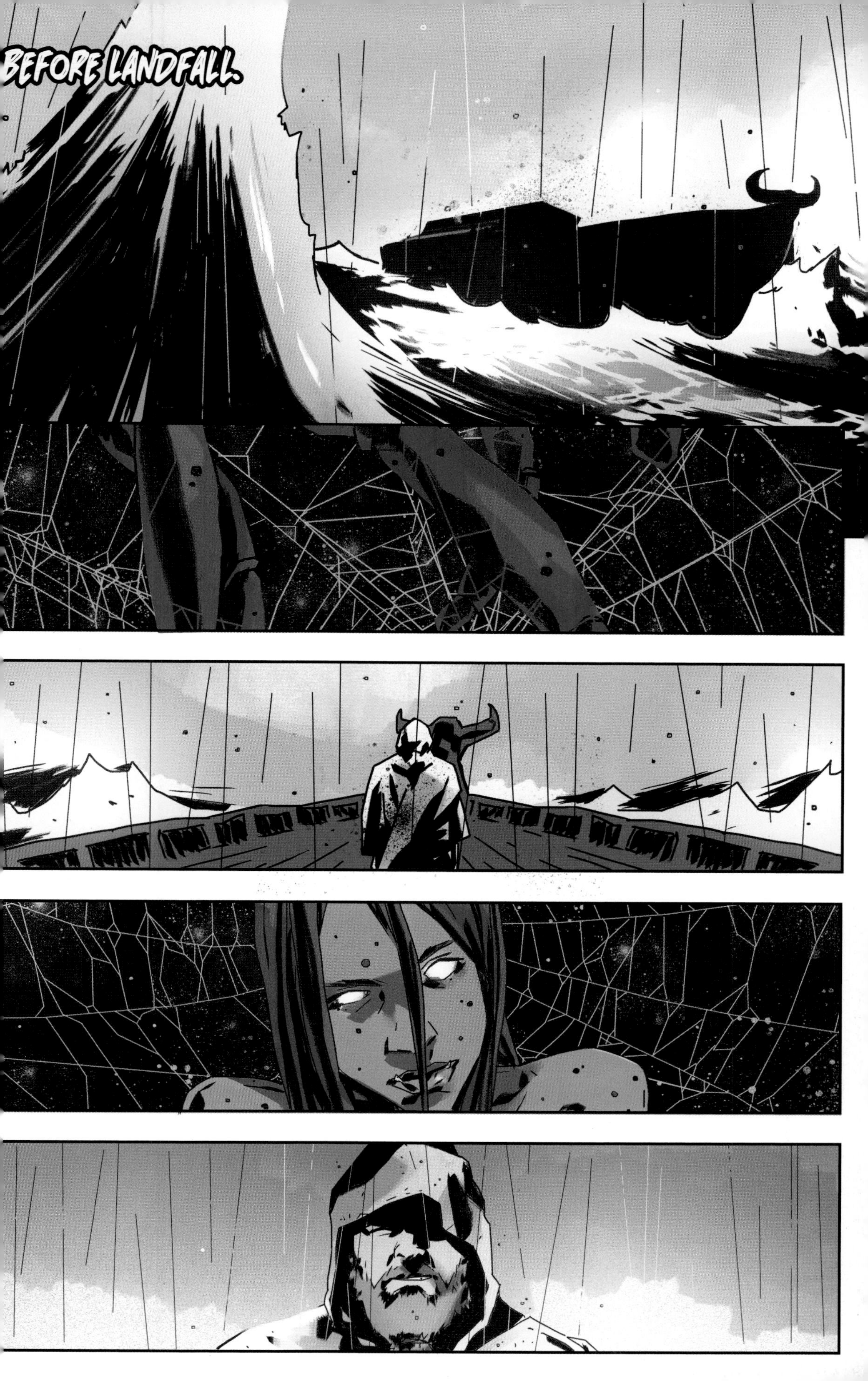
BEFORE LANDFALL.

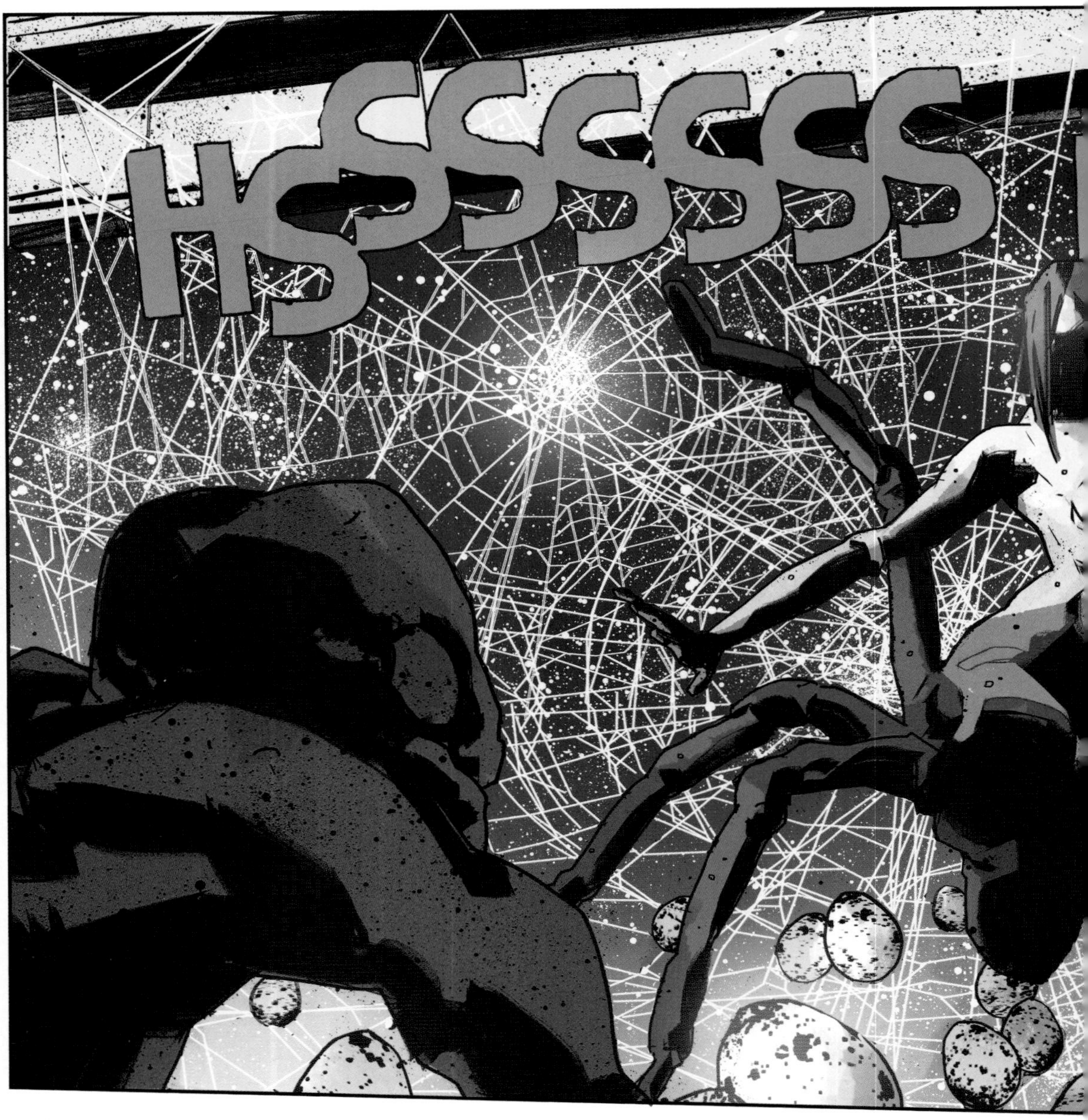
HSSSSSSS

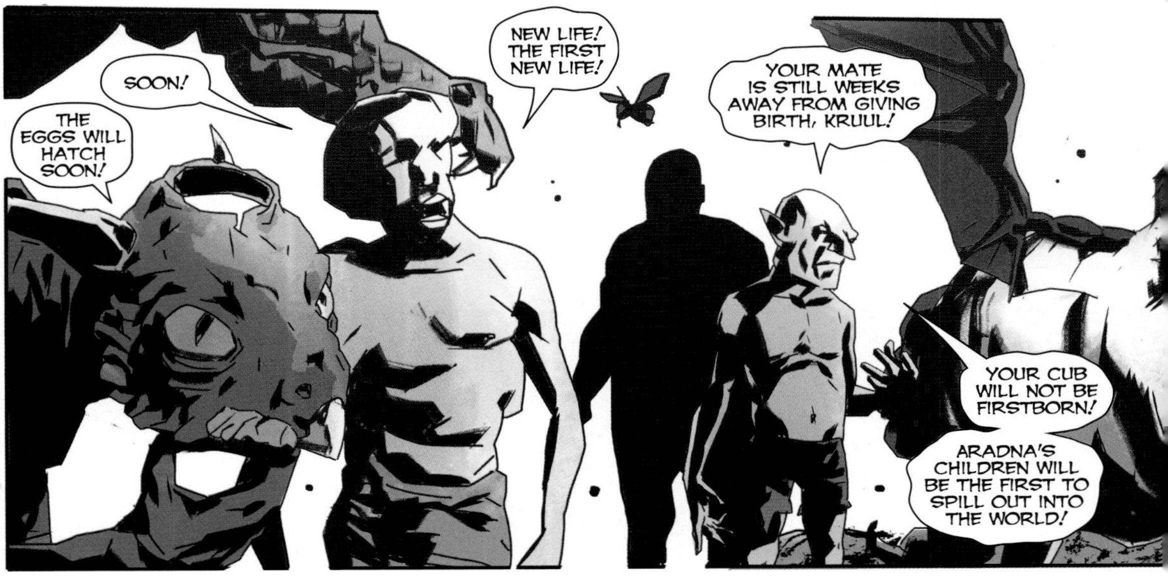
THE EGGS WILL HATCH SOON!
SOON!
NEW LIFE! THE FIRST NEW LIFE!
YOUR MATE IS STILL WEEKS AWAY FROM GIVING BIRTH, KRUUL!
YOUR CUB WILL NOT BE FIRSTBORN!
ARADNA'S CHILDREN WILL BE THE FIRST TO SPILL OUT INTO THE WORLD!

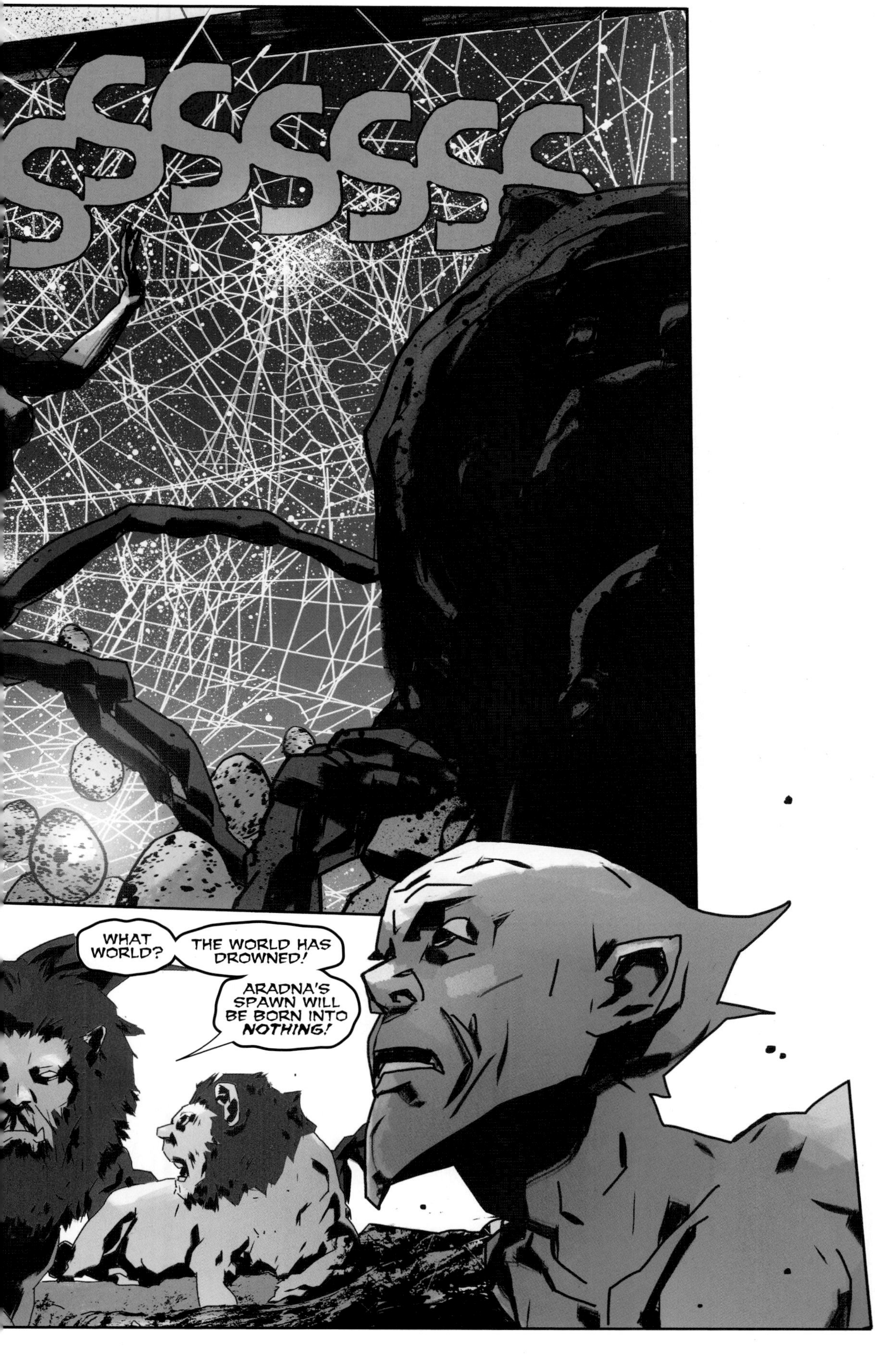
SSSSSS
WHAT WORLD?
THE WORLD HAS DROWNED!
ARADNA'S SPAWN WILL BE BORN INTO *NOTHING!*

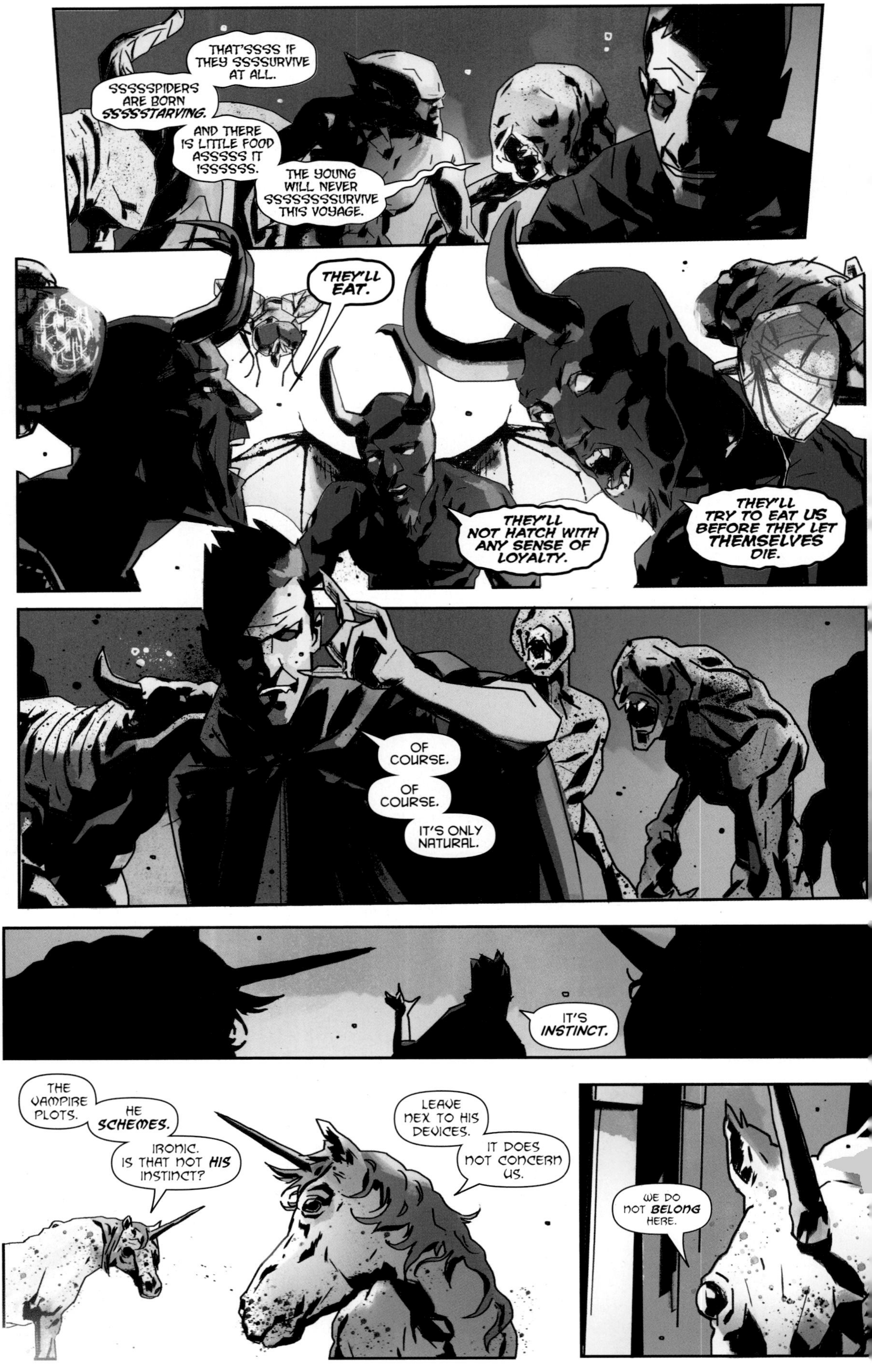
SSSSSPIDERS ARE BORN SSSSSTARVING.
THAT'SSSS IF THEY SSSSURVIVE AT ALL.
AND THERE IS LITTLE FOOD ASSSSS IT ISSSSSS.
THE YOUNG WILL NEVER SSSSSSSSURVIVE THIS VOYAGE.
THEY'LL EAT.
THEY'LL NOT HATCH WITH ANY SENSE OF LOYALTY.
THEY'LL TRY TO EAT US BEFORE THEY LET THEMSELVES DIE.
OF COURSE.
OF COURSE.
IT'S ONLY NATURAL.
IT'S INSTINCT.
THE VAMPIRE PLOTS.
HE SCHEMES.
IRONIC. IS THAT NOT HIS INSTINCT?
LEAVE NEX TO HIS DEVICES.
IT DOES NOT CONCERN US.
WE DO NOT BELONG HERE.

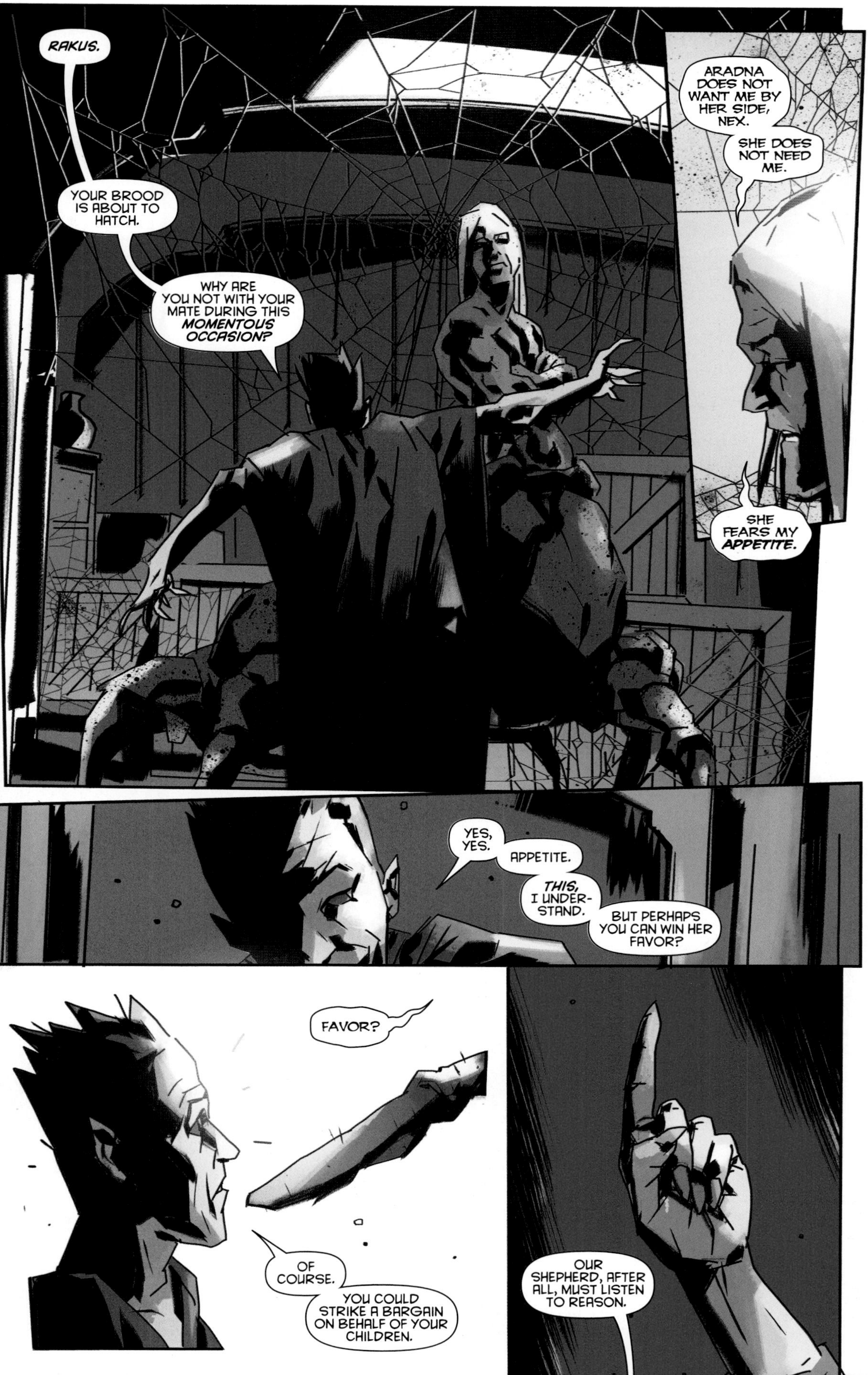
RAKUS.
YOUR BROOD IS ABOUT TO HATCH.
WHY ARE YOU NOT WITH YOUR MATE DURING THIS MOMENTOUS OCCASION?
ARADNA DOES NOT WANT ME BY HER SIDE, NEX.
SHE DOES NOT NEED ME.
SHE FEARS MY APPETITE.
YES, YES.
APPETITE.
THIS, I UNDER-STAND.
BUT PERHAPS YOU CAN WIN HER FAVOR?
FAVOR?
OF COURSE.
YOU COULD STRIKE A BARGAIN ON BEHALF OF YOUR CHILDREN.
OUR SHEPHERD, AFTER ALL, MUST LISTEN TO REASON.

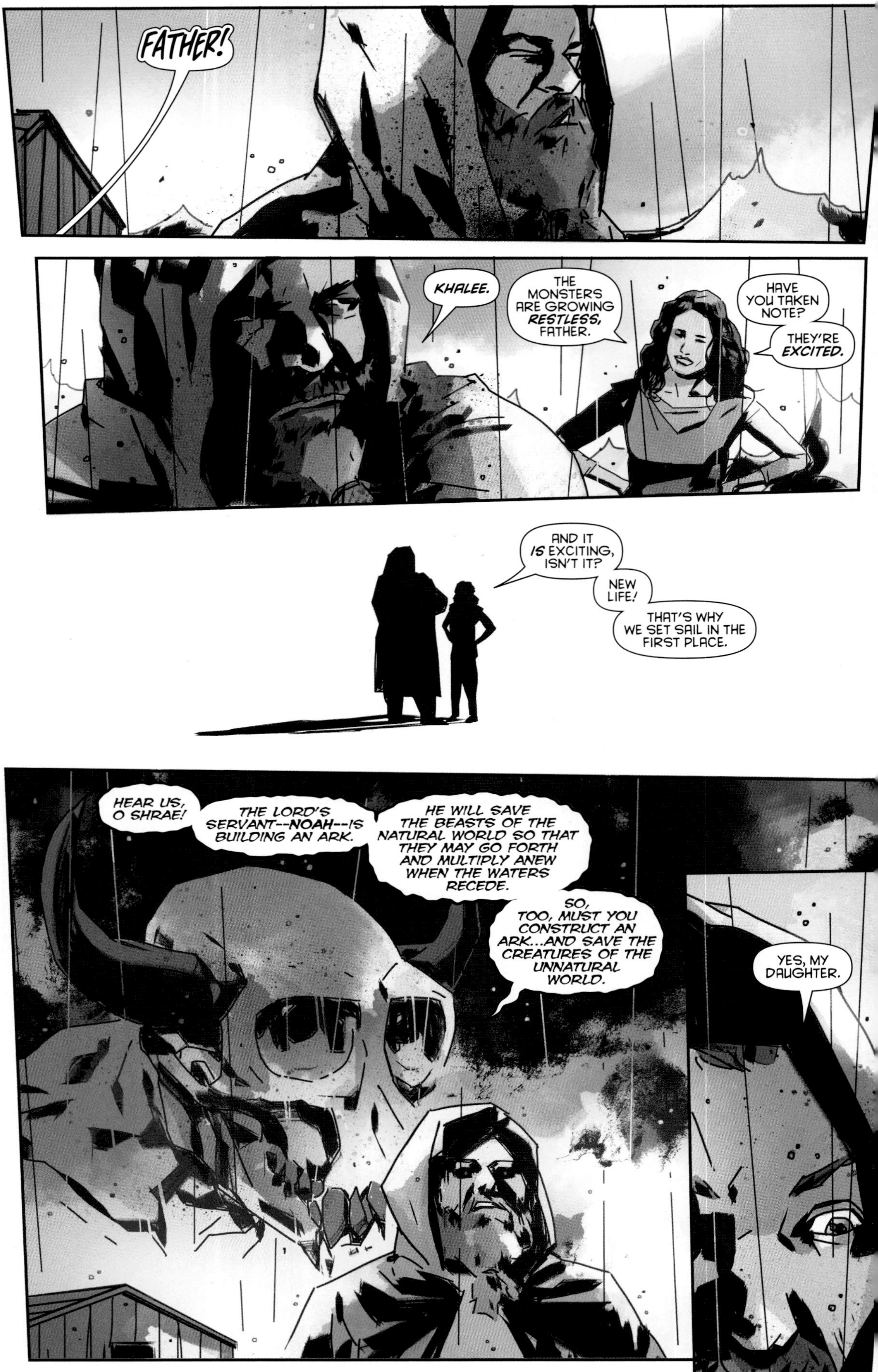
FATHER!
KHALEE.
THE MONSTERS ARE GROWING RESTLESS, FATHER.
HAVE YOU TAKEN NOTE?
THEY'RE EXCITED.
AND IT IS EXCITING, ISN'T IT?
NEW LIFE!
THAT'S WHY WE SET SAIL IN THE FIRST PLACE.
HEAR US, O SHRAE!
THE LORD'S SERVANT--NOAH--IS BUILDING AN ARK.
HE WILL SAVE THE BEASTS OF THE NATURAL WORLD SO THAT THEY MAY GO FORTH AND MULTIPLY ANEW WHEN THE WATERS RECEDE.
SO, TOO, MUST YOU CONSTRUCT AN ARK...AND SAVE THE CREATURES OF THE UNNATURAL WORLD.
YES, MY DAUGHTER.

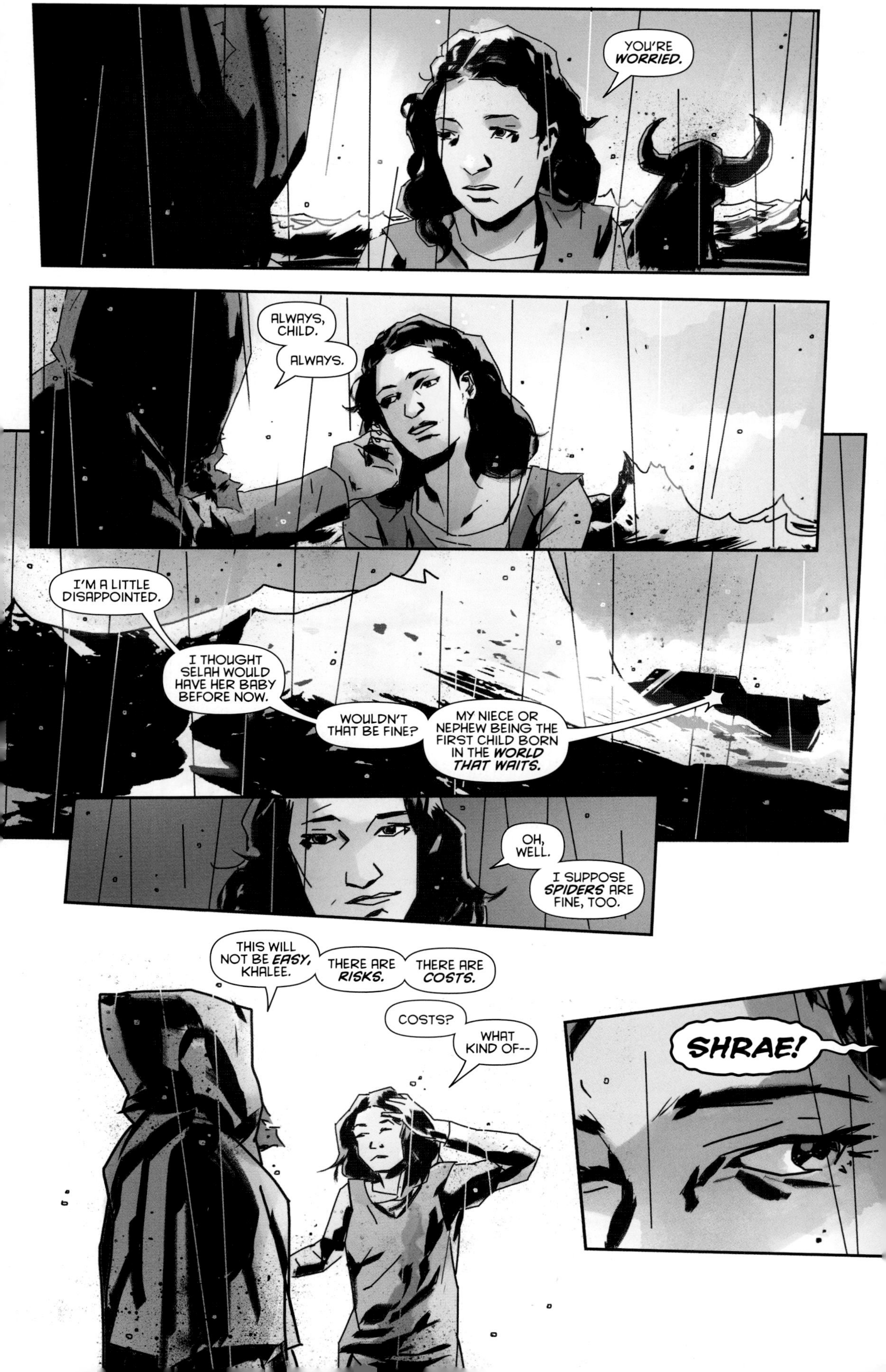
YOU'RE WORRIED.
ALWAYS, CHILD.
ALWAYS.
I'M A LITTLE DISAPPOINTED.
I THOUGHT SELAH WOULD HAVE HER BABY BEFORE NOW.
WOULDN'T THAT BE FINE?
MY NIECE OR NEPHEW BEING THE FIRST CHILD BORN IN THE WORLD THAT WAITS.
OH, WELL.
I SUPPOSE SPIDERS ARE FINE, TOO.
THIS WILL NOT BE EASY, KHALEE.
THERE ARE RISKS.
THERE ARE COSTS.
COSTS?
WHAT KIND OF--
SHRAE!

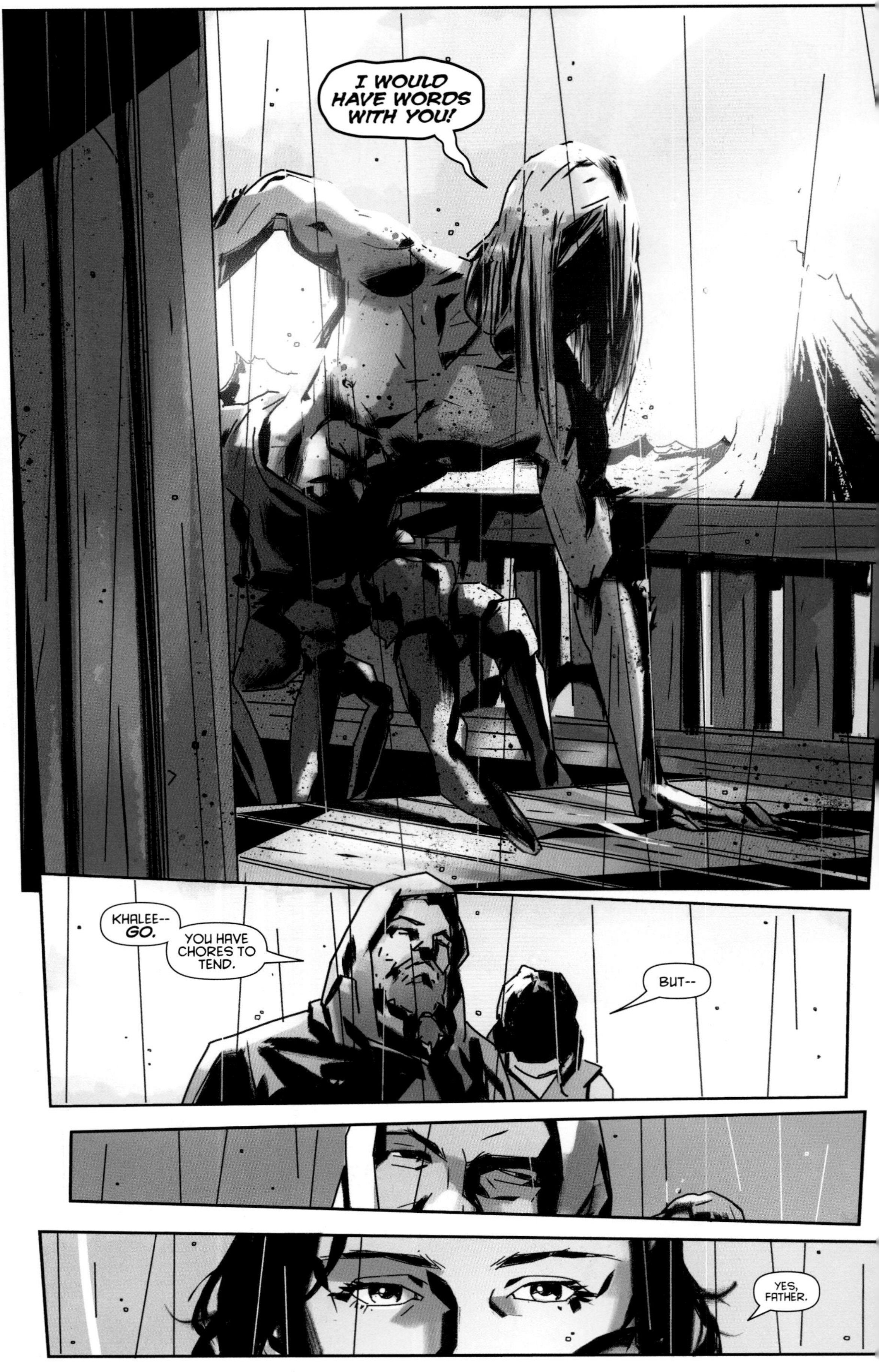
I WOULD HAVE WORDS WITH YOU!
KHALEE-- GO.
YOU HAVE CHORES TO TEND.
BUT--
YES, FATHER.

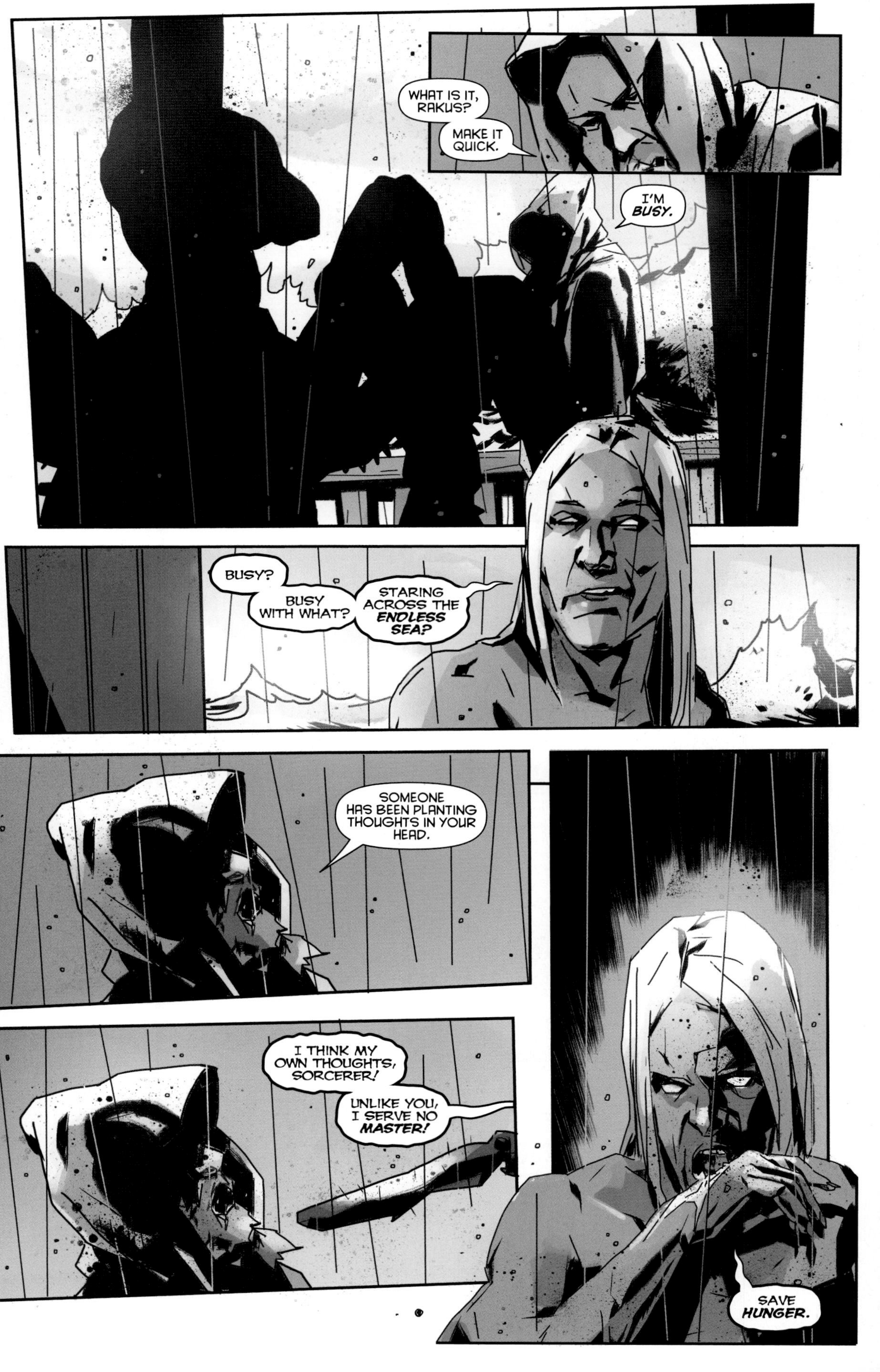

WHAT IS IT, RAKUS?
MAKE IT QUICK.
I'M *BUSY.*
BUSY?
BUSY WITH WHAT?
STARING ACROSS THE *ENDLESS SEA?*
SOMEONE HAS BEEN PLANTING THOUGHTS IN YOUR HEAD.
I THINK MY OWN THOUGHTS, SORCERER!
UNLIKE YOU, I SERVE NO *MASTER!*
SAVE *HUNGER.*

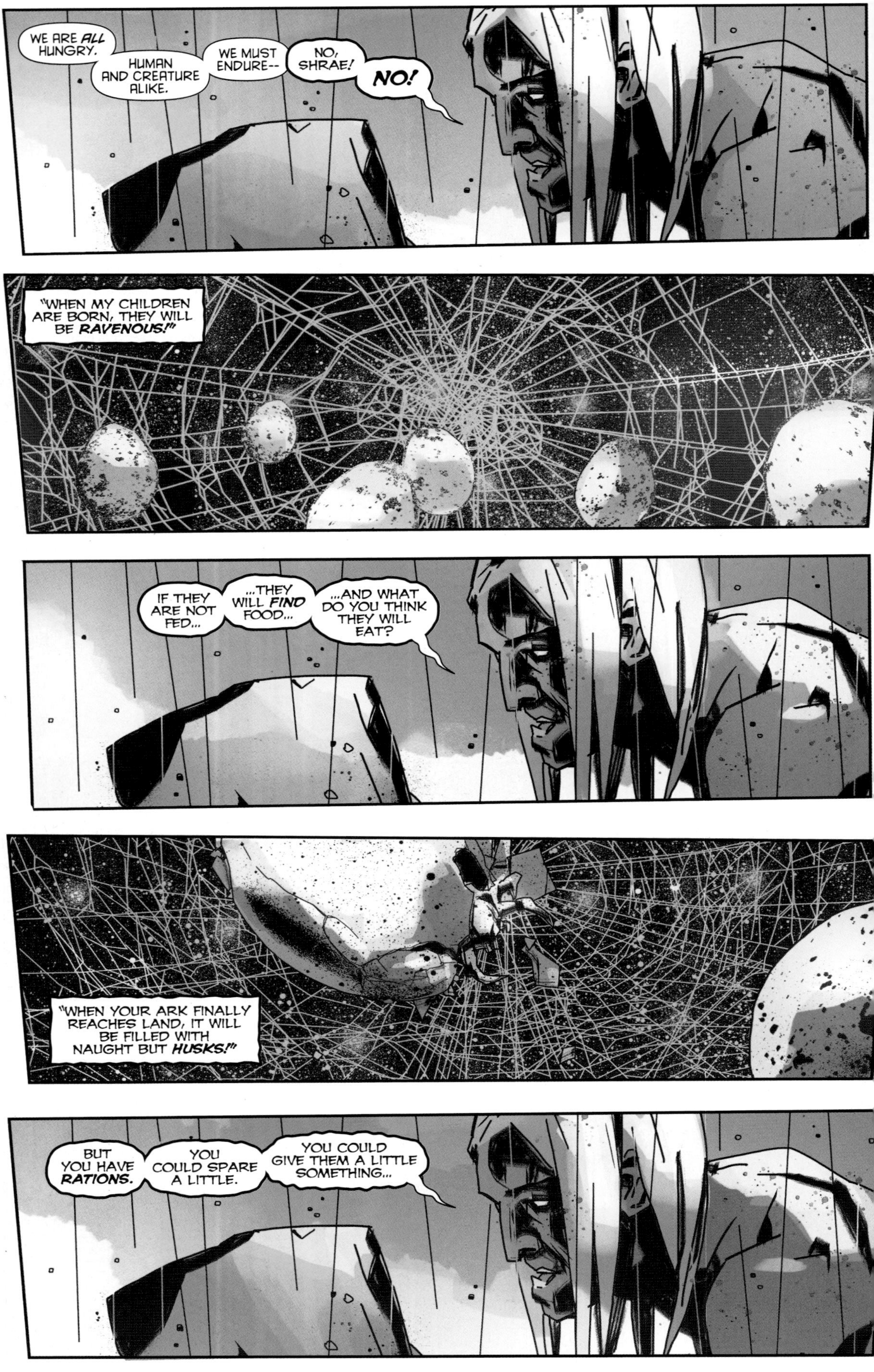
WE ARE ALL HUNGRY.
HUMAN AND CREATURE ALIKE.
WE MUST ENDURE--
NO, SHRAE!
NO!
"WHEN MY CHILDREN ARE BORN, THEY WILL BE RAVENOUS!"
IF THEY ARE NOT FED...
...THEY WILL FIND FOOD...
...AND WHAT DO YOU THINK THEY WILL EAT?
"WHEN YOUR ARK FINALLY REACHES LAND, IT WILL BE FILLED WITH NAUGHT BUT HUSKS!"
BUT YOU HAVE RATIONS.
YOU COULD SPARE A LITTLE.
YOU COULD GIVE THEM A LITTLE SOMETHING...

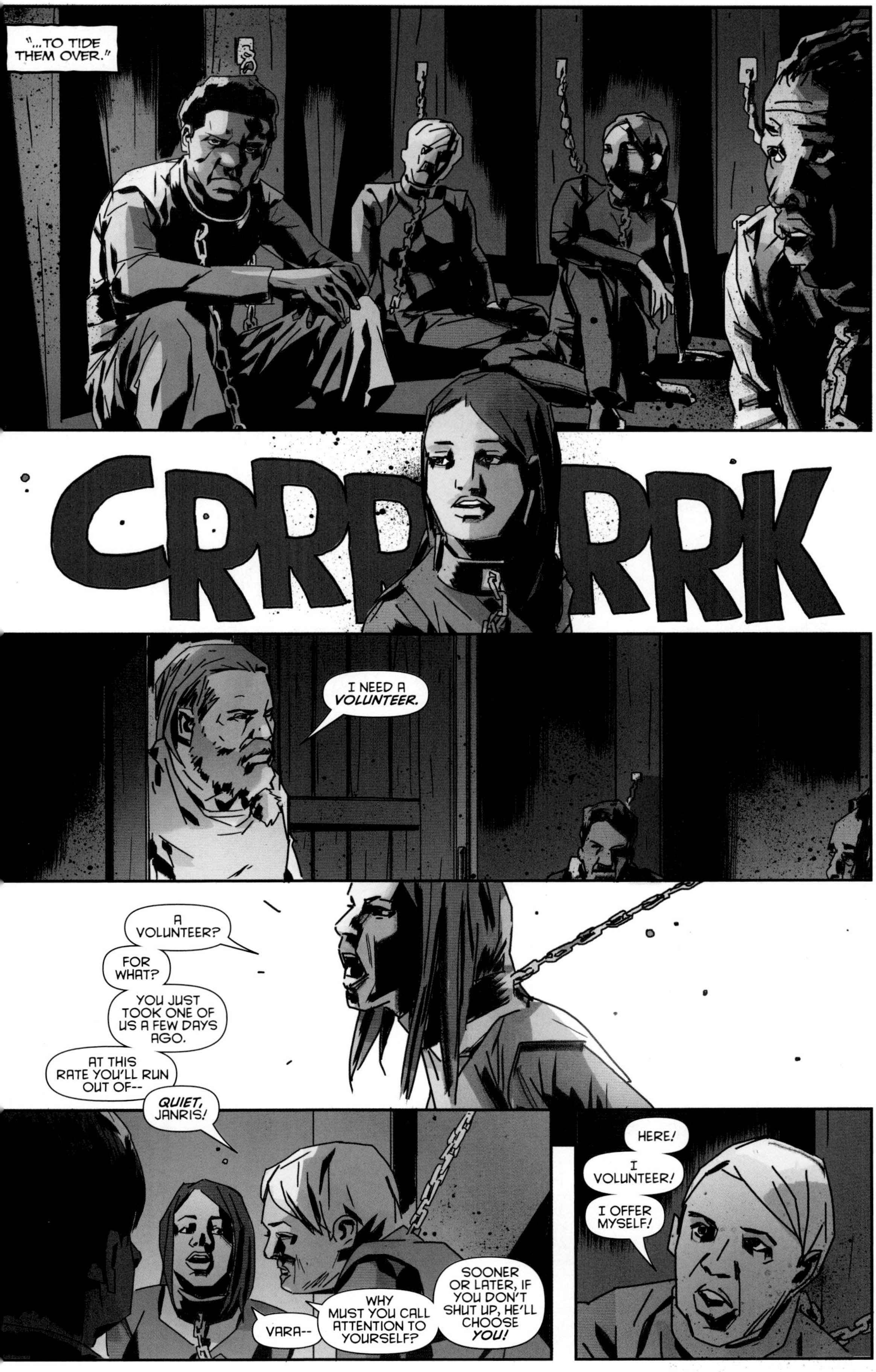
"...TO TIDE THEM OVER."
CRRRRRK
I NEED A *VOLUNTEER.*
A VOLUNTEER?
FOR WHAT?
YOU JUST TOOK ONE OF US A FEW DAYS AGO.
AT THIS RATE YOU'LL RUN OUT OF--
QUIET, JANRIS!
VARA--
WHY MUST YOU CALL ATTENTION TO YOURSELF?
SOONER OR LATER, IF YOU DON'T SHUT UP, HE'LL CHOOSE *YOU!*
HERE!
I VOLUNTEER!
I OFFER MYSELF!

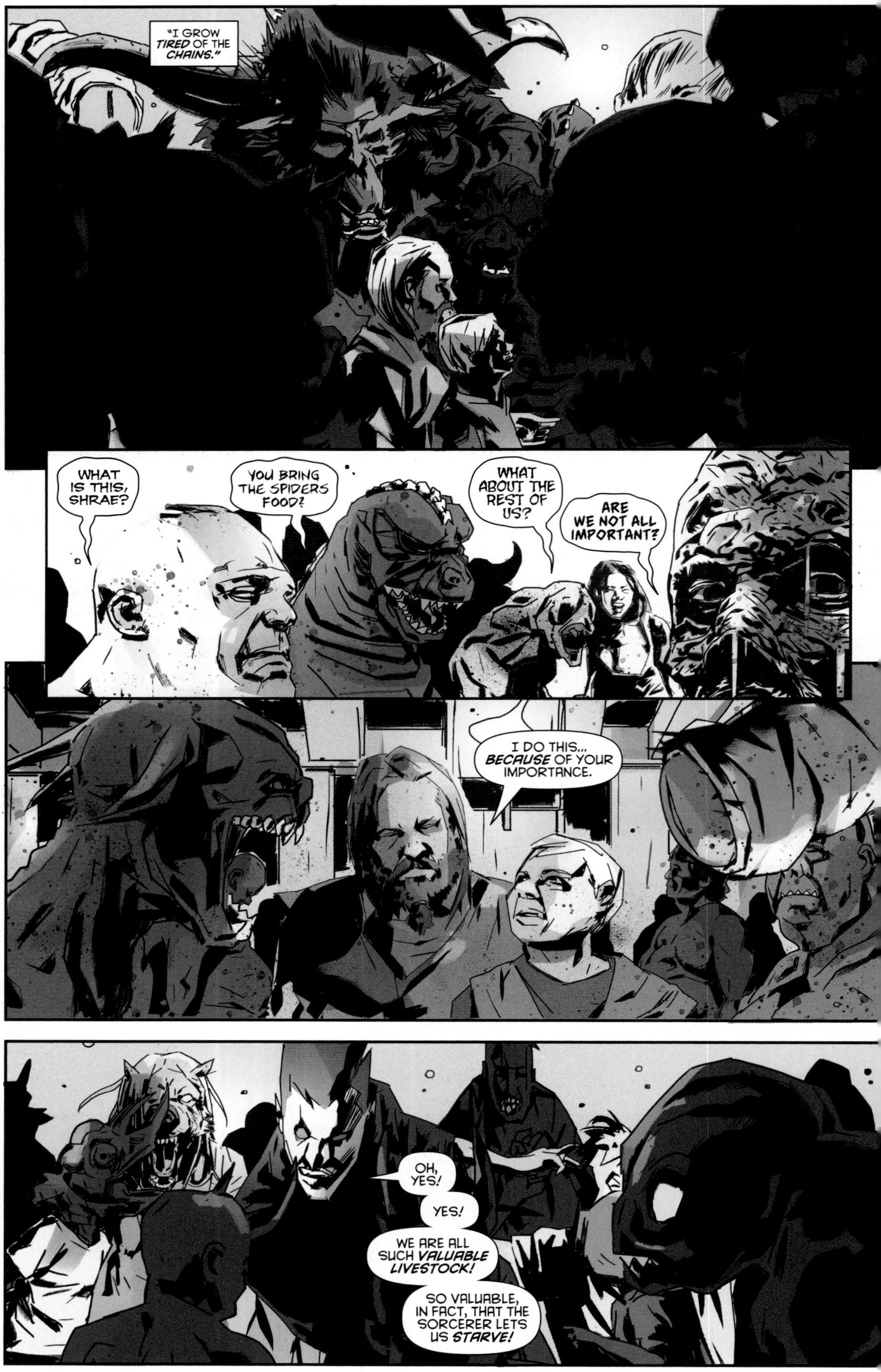

"I GROW TIRED OF THE CHAINS."
WHAT IS THIS, SHRAE?
YOU BRING THE SPIDERS FOOD?
WHAT ABOUT THE REST OF US?
ARE WE NOT ALL IMPORTANT?
I DO THIS... BECAUSE OF YOUR IMPORTANCE.
OH, YES!
YES!
WE ARE ALL SUCH VALUABLE LIVESTOCK!
SO VALUABLE, IN FACT, THAT THE SORCERER LETS US STARVE!

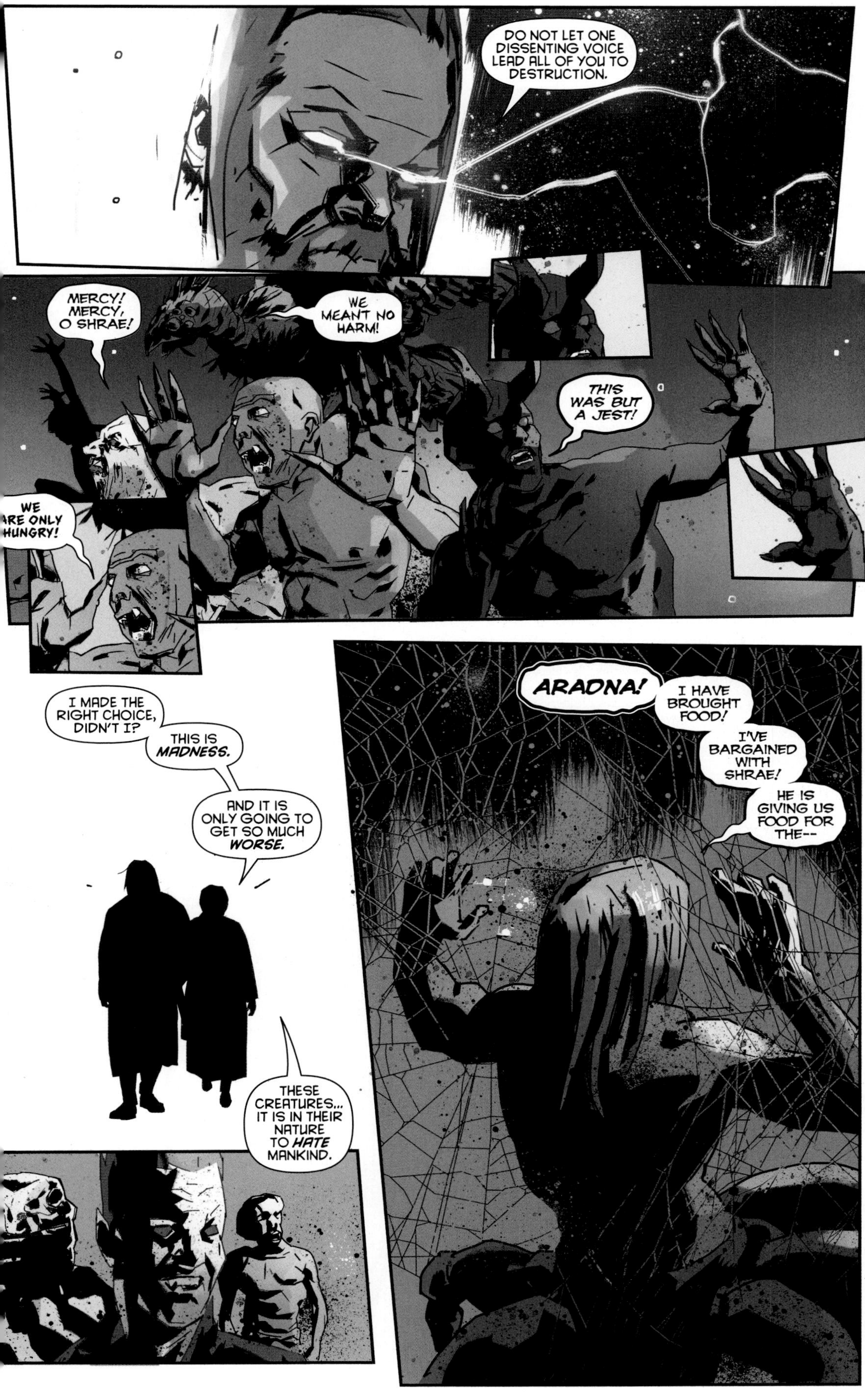
DO NOT LET ONE DISSENTING VOICE LEAD ALL OF YOU TO DESTRUCTION.
MERCY! MERCY, O SHRAE!
WE MEANT NO HARM!
THIS WAS BUT A JEST!
WE ARE ONLY HUNGRY!
I MADE THE RIGHT CHOICE, DIDN'T I?
THIS IS MADNESS.
AND IT IS ONLY GOING TO GET SO MUCH WORSE.
THESE CREATURES... IT IS IN THEIR NATURE TO HATE MANKIND.
ARADNA!
I HAVE BROUGHT FOOD!
I'VE BARGAINED WITH SHRAE!
HE IS GIVING US FOOD FOR THE--

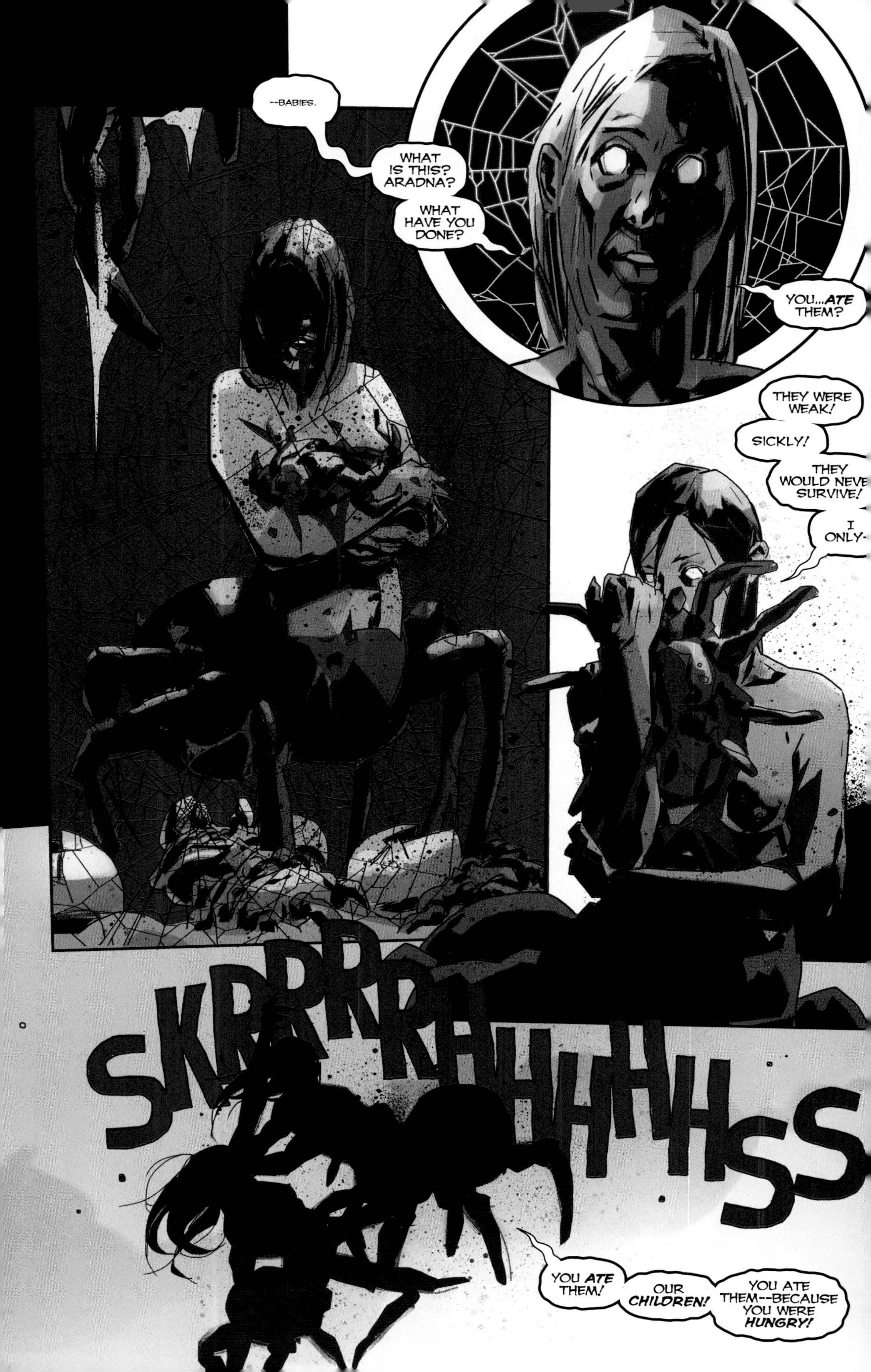
--BABIES.
WHAT IS THIS? ARADNA?
WHAT HAVE YOU DONE?
YOU...ATE THEM?
THEY WERE WEAK!
SICKLY!
THEY WOULD NEVE SURVIVE!
I ONLY-
SKRRRRAHHHHHSS
YOU ATE THEM!
OUR CHILDREN!
YOU ATE THEM--BECAUSE YOU WERE HUNGRY!

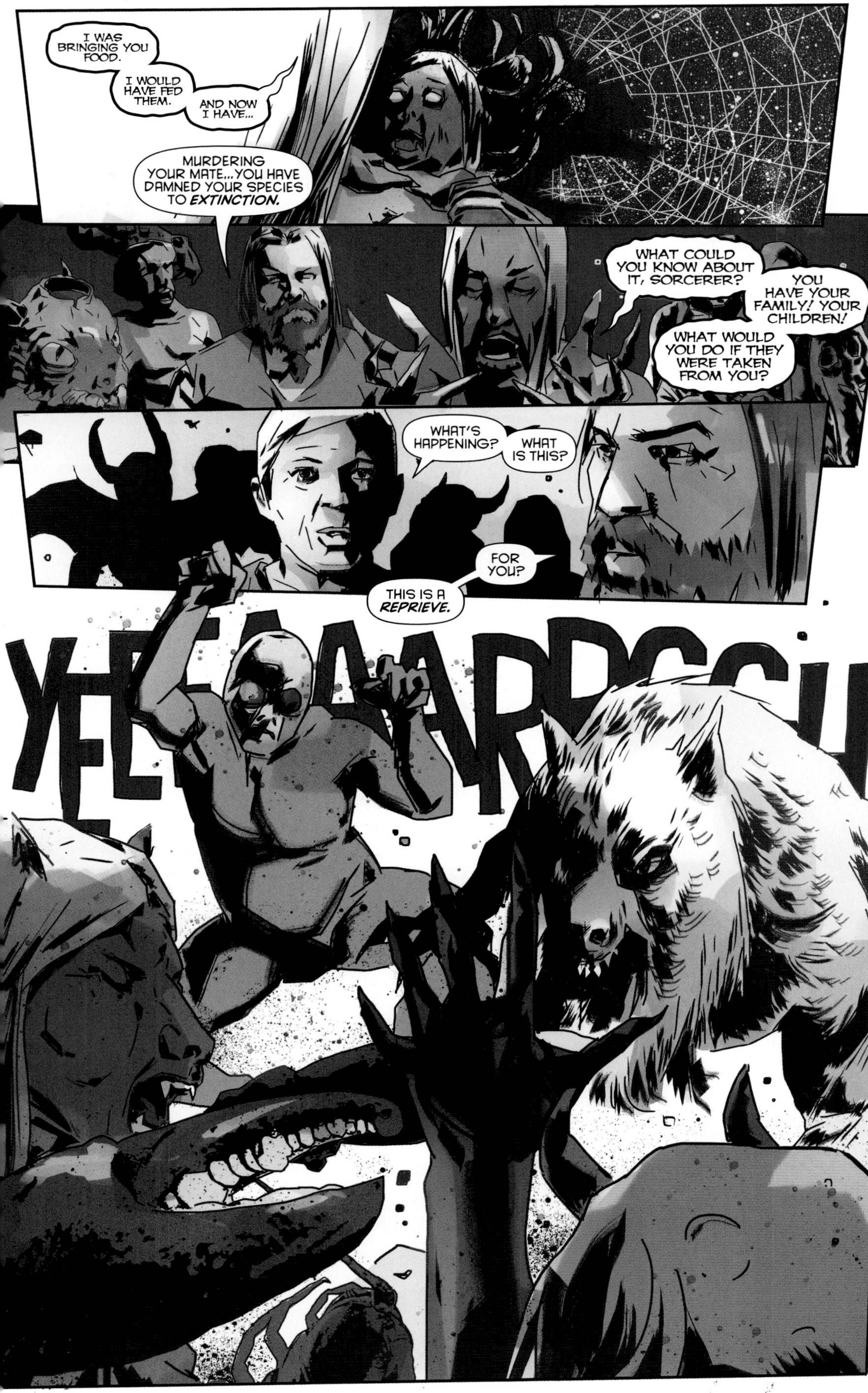
I WAS BRINGING YOU FOOD.
I WOULD HAVE FED THEM.
AND NOW I HAVE...
MURDERING YOUR MATE...YOU HAVE DAMNED YOUR SPECIES TO *EXTINCTION.*
WHAT COULD YOU KNOW ABOUT IT, SORCERER?
YOU HAVE YOUR FAMILY! YOUR CHILDREN!
WHAT WOULD YOU DO IF THEY WERE TAKEN FROM YOU?
WHAT'S HAPPENING?
WHAT IS THIS?
FOR YOU?
THIS IS A *REPRIEVE.*

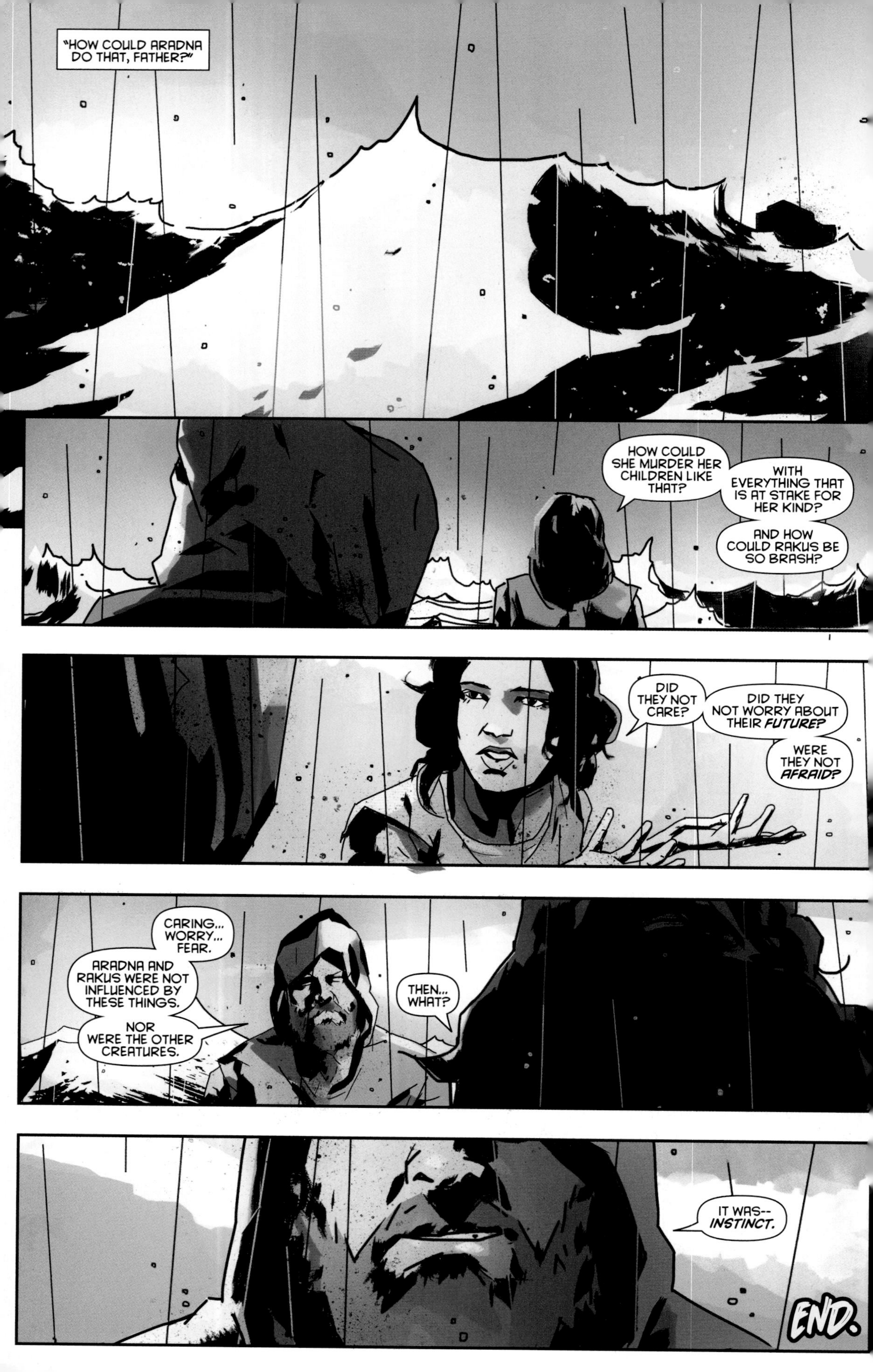
"HOW COULD ARADNA DO THAT, FATHER?"
HOW COULD SHE MURDER HER CHILDREN LIKE THAT?
WITH EVERYTHING THAT IS AT STAKE FOR HER KIND?
AND HOW COULD RAKUS BE SO BRASH?
DID THEY NOT CARE?
DID THEY NOT WORRY ABOUT THEIR *FUTURE?*
WERE THEY NOT *AFRAID?*
CARING... WORRY... FEAR.
ARADNA AND RAKUS WERE NOT INFLUENCED BY THESE THINGS.
NOR WERE THE OTHER CREATURES.
THEN... WHAT?
IT WAS-- *INSTINCT.*
END.

2

OBLIGATIONS

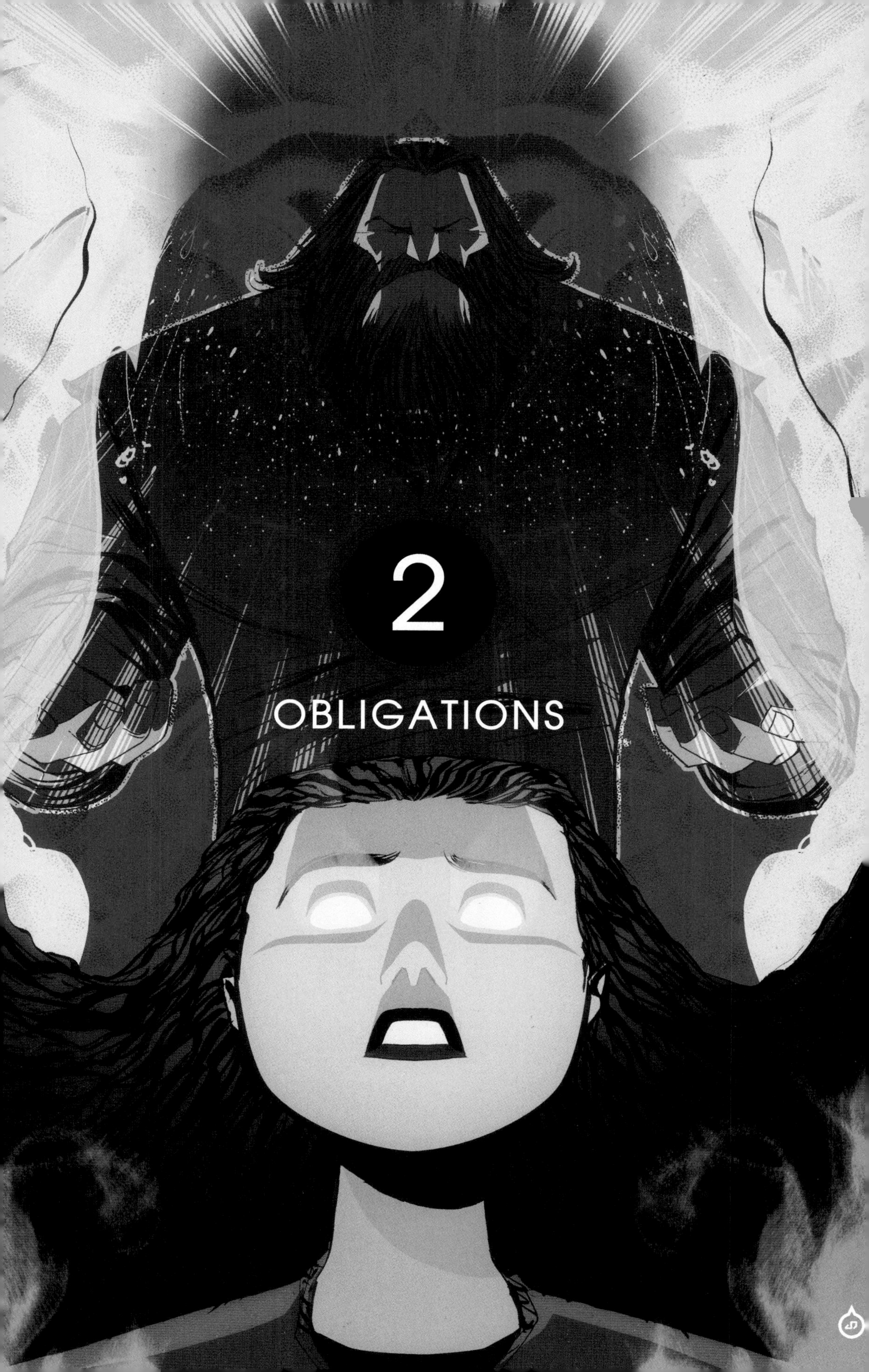

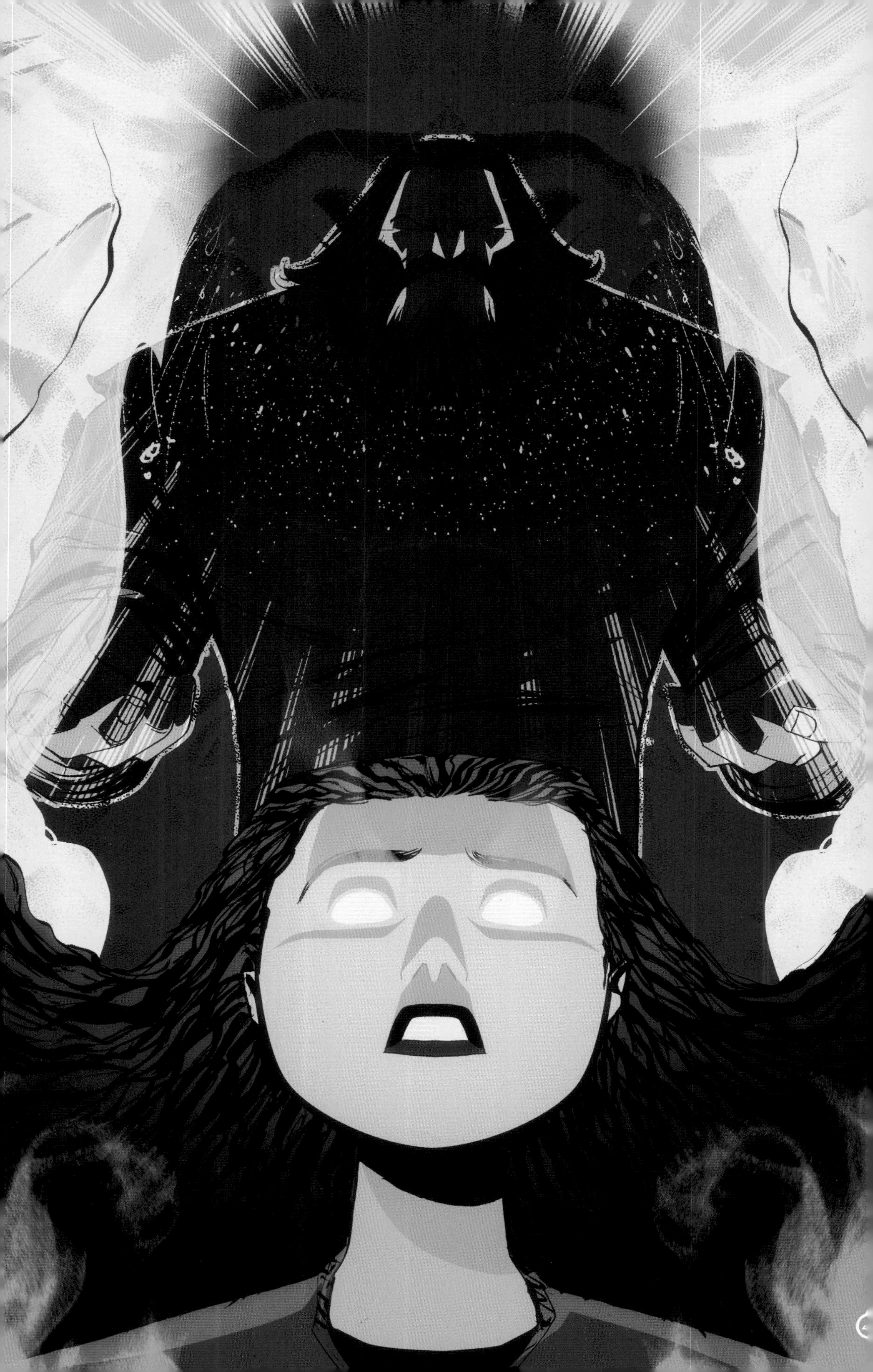

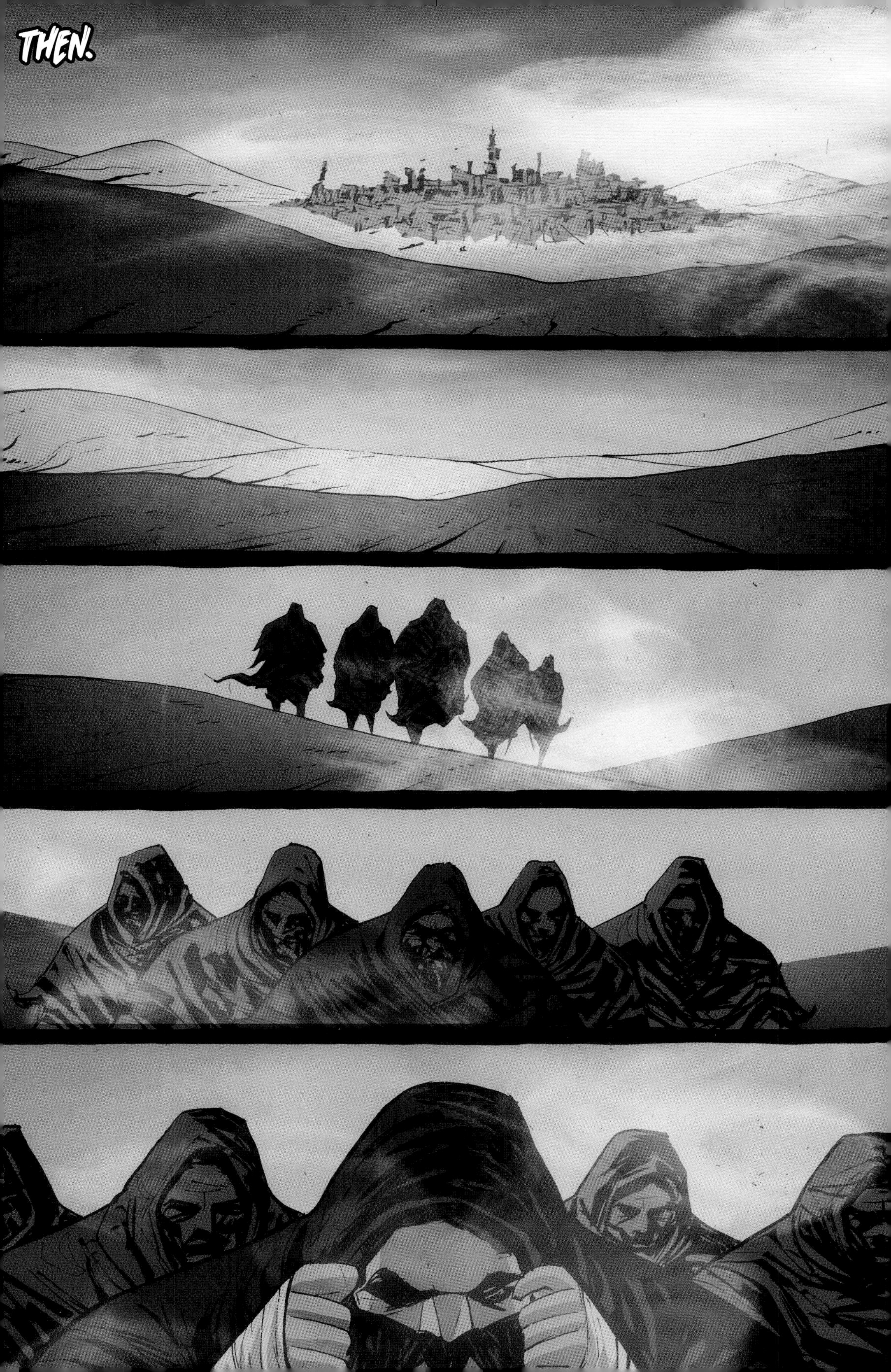
THEN.

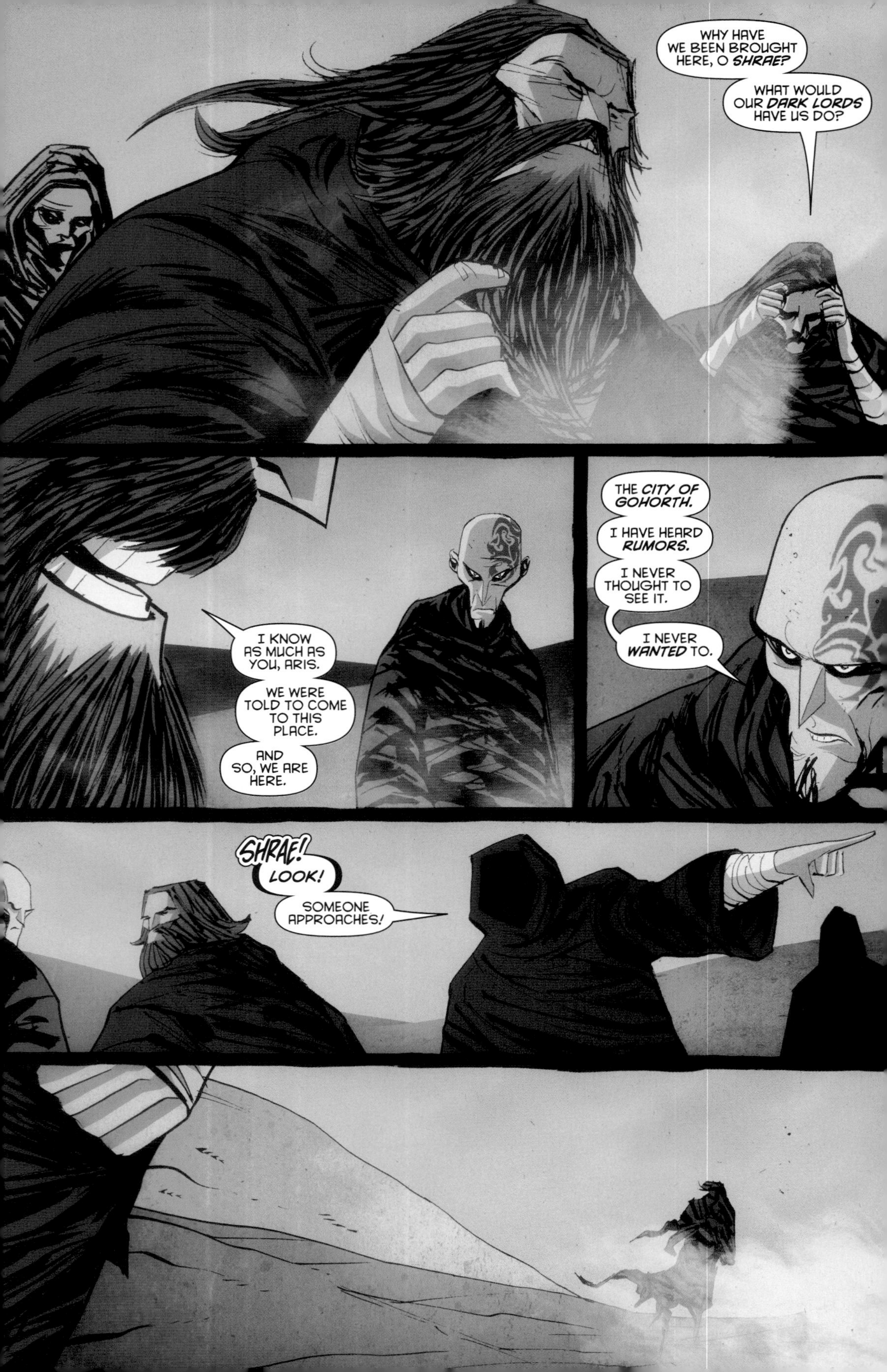
WHY HAVE WE BEEN BROUGHT HERE, O SHRAE?
WHAT WOULD OUR DARK LORDS HAVE US DO?
I KNOW AS MUCH AS YOU, ARIS.
WE WERE TOLD TO COME TO THIS PLACE.
AND SO, WE ARE HERE.
THE CITY OF GOHORTH.
I HAVE HEARD RUMORS.
I NEVER THOUGHT TO SEE IT.
I NEVER WANTED TO.
SHRAE!
LOOK!
SOMEONE APPROACHES!

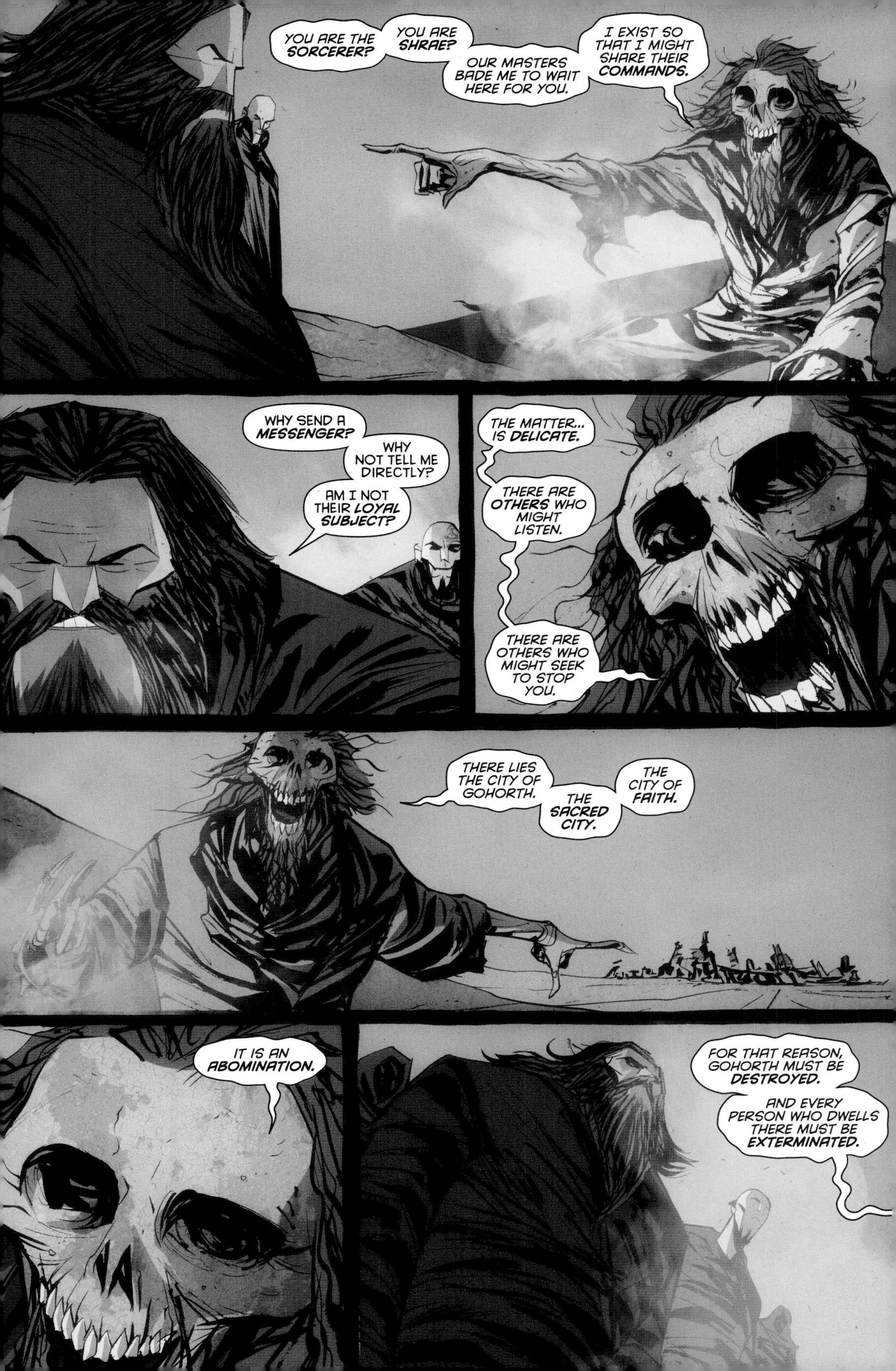
YOU ARE THE SORCERER?
YOU ARE SHRAE?
OUR MASTERS BADE ME TO WAIT HERE FOR YOU.
I EXIST SO THAT I MIGHT SHARE THEIR COMMANDS.
WHY SEND A MESSENGER?
WHY NOT TELL ME DIRECTLY?
AM I NOT THEIR LOYAL SUBJECT?
THE MATTER... IS DELICATE.
THERE ARE OTHERS WHO MIGHT LISTEN.
THERE ARE OTHERS WHO MIGHT SEEK TO STOP YOU.
THERE LIES THE CITY OF GOHORTH.
THE SACRED CITY.
THE CITY OF FAITH.
IT IS AN ABOMINATION.
FOR THAT REASON, GOHORTH MUST BE DESTROYED.
AND EVERY PERSON WHO DWELLS THERE MUST BE EXTERMINATED.

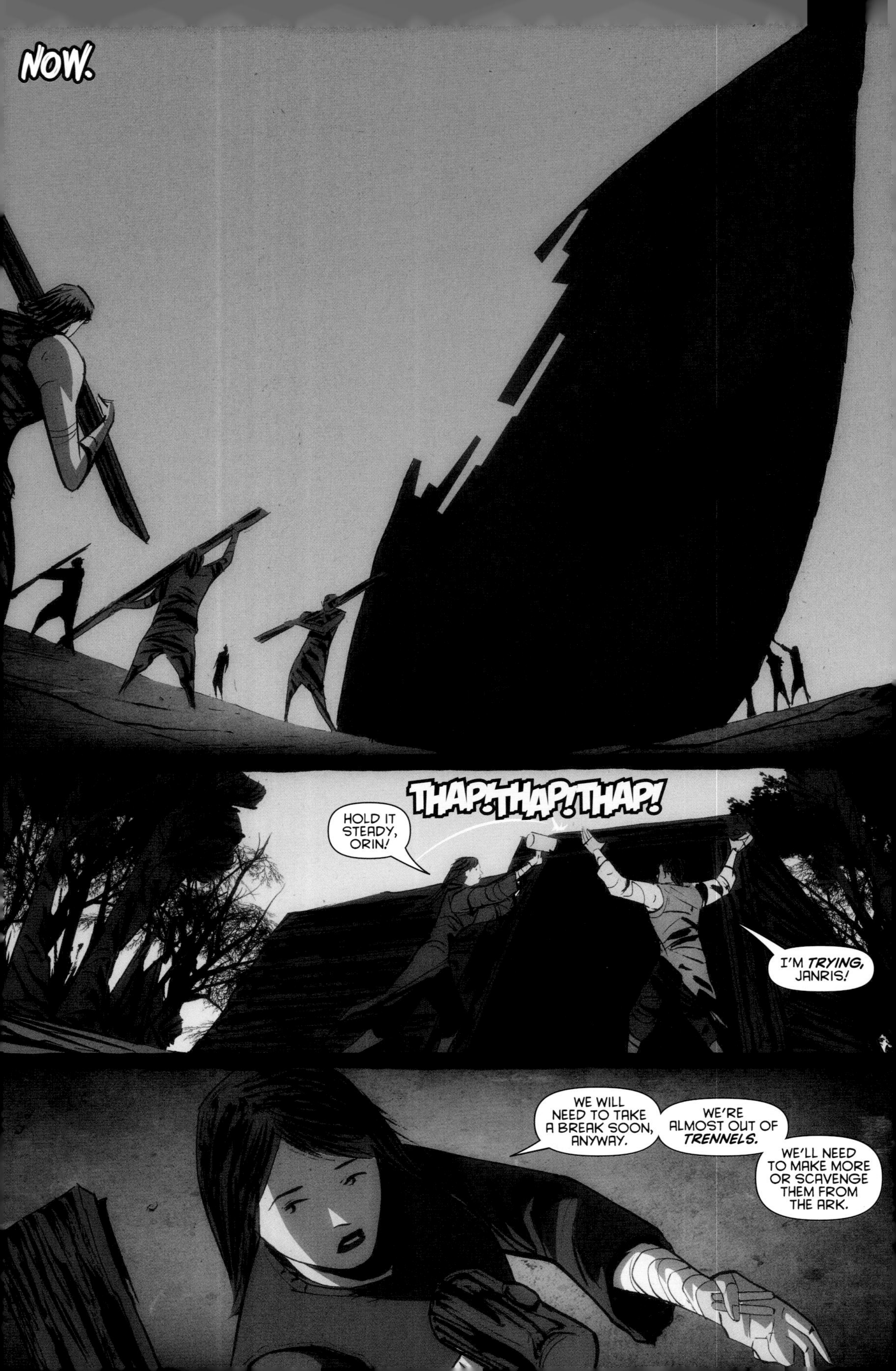
NOW.
THAP! THAP! THAP!
HOLD IT STEADY, ORIN!
I'M *TRYING,* JANRIS!
WE WILL NEED TO TAKE A BREAK SOON, ANYWAY.
WE'RE ALMOST OUT OF *TRENNELS.*
WE'LL NEED TO MAKE MORE OR SCAVENGE THEM FROM THE ARK.

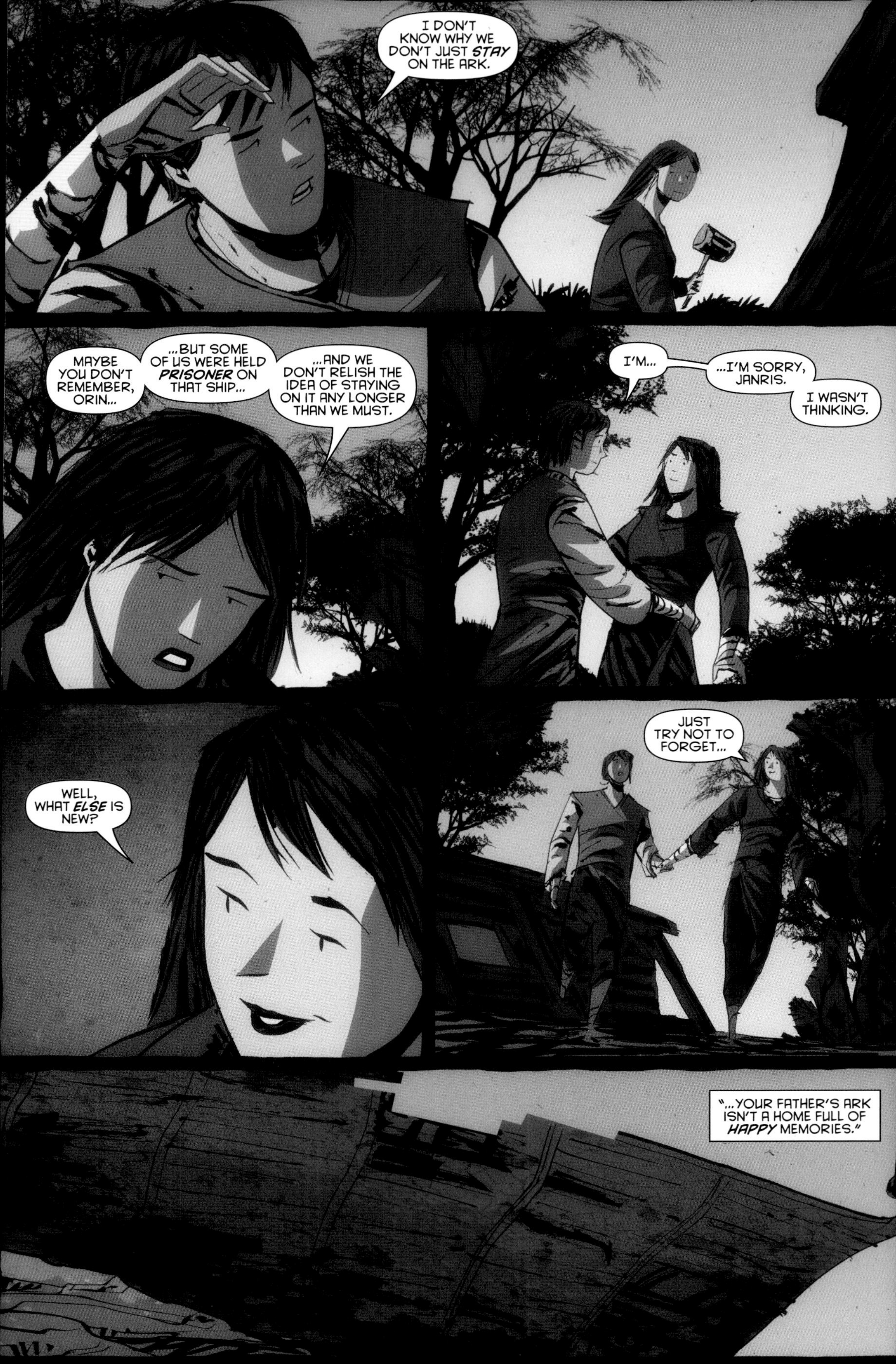
I DON'T KNOW WHY WE DON'T JUST STAY ON THE ARK.
MAYBE YOU DON'T REMEMBER, ORIN...
...BUT SOME OF US WERE HELD PRISONER ON THAT SHIP...
...AND WE DON'T RELISH THE IDEA OF STAYING ON IT ANY LONGER THAN WE MUST.
I'M...
...I'M SORRY, JANRIS.
I WASN'T THINKING.
WELL, WHAT ELSE IS NEW?
JUST TRY NOT TO FORGET...
"...YOUR FATHER'S ARK ISN'T A HOME FULL OF HAPPY MEMORIES."

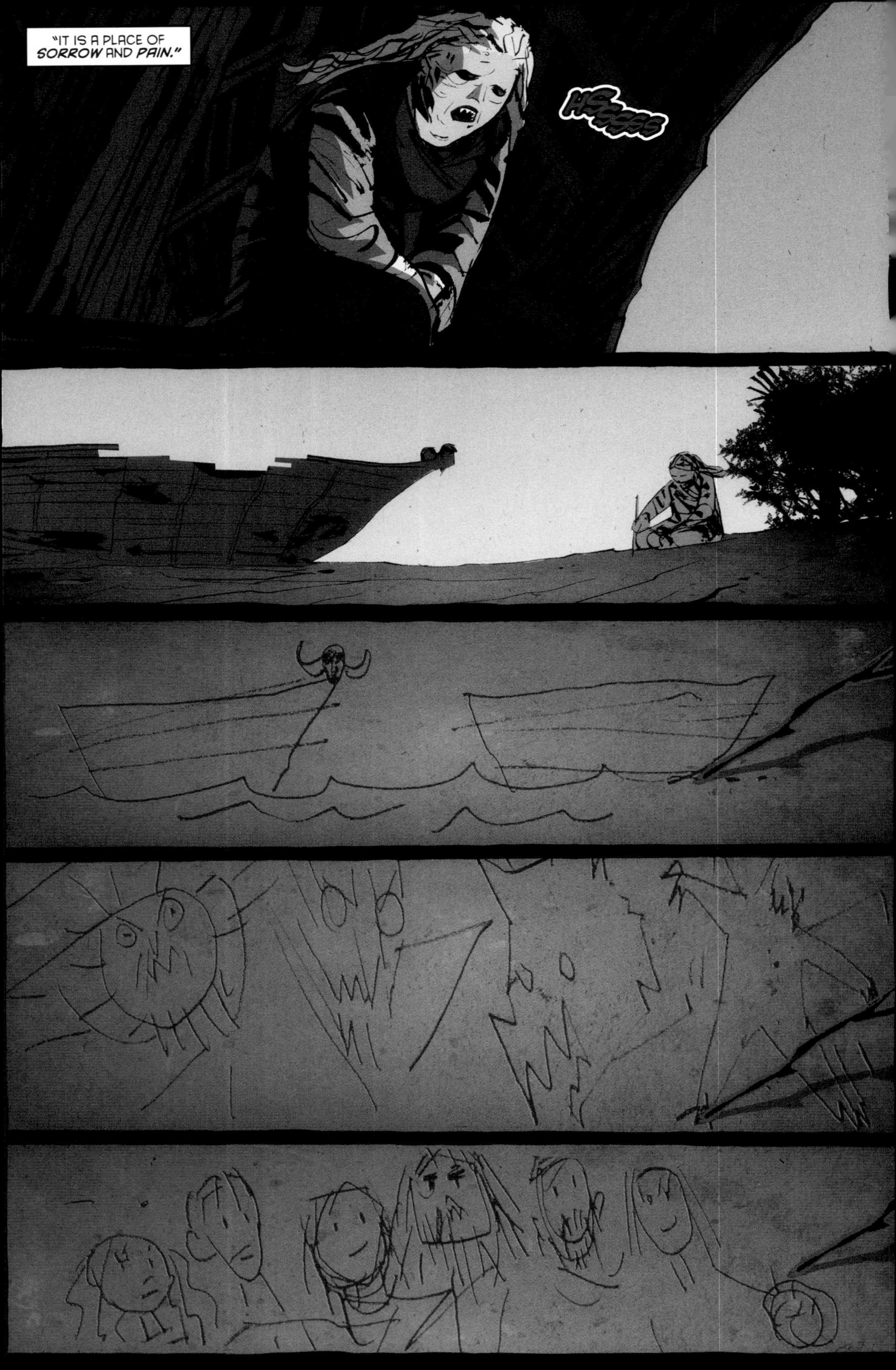
"IT IS A PLACE OF SORROW AND PAIN."
HSSSSSS

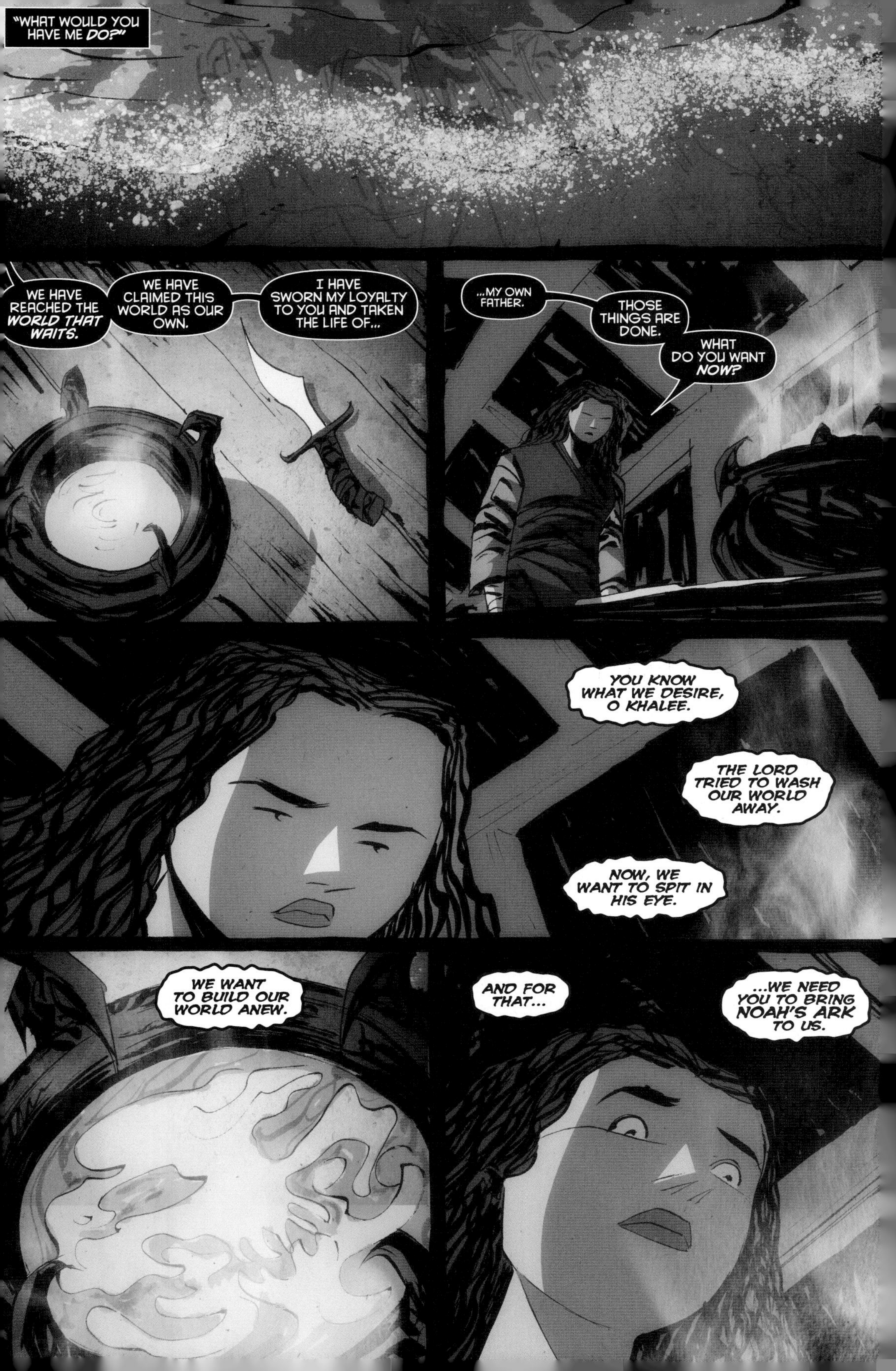

"WHAT WOULD YOU HAVE ME DO?"
WE HAVE REACHED THE WORLD THAT WAITS.
WE HAVE CLAIMED THIS WORLD AS OUR OWN.
I HAVE SWORN MY LOYALTY TO YOU AND TAKEN THE LIFE OF...
...MY OWN FATHER.
THOSE THINGS ARE DONE.
WHAT DO YOU WANT NOW?
YOU KNOW WHAT WE DESIRE, O KHALEE.
THE LORD TRIED TO WASH OUR WORLD AWAY.
NOW, WE WANT TO SPIT IN HIS EYE.
WE WANT TO BUILD OUR WORLD ANEW.
AND FOR THAT...
...WE NEED YOU TO BRING NOAH'S ARK TO US.

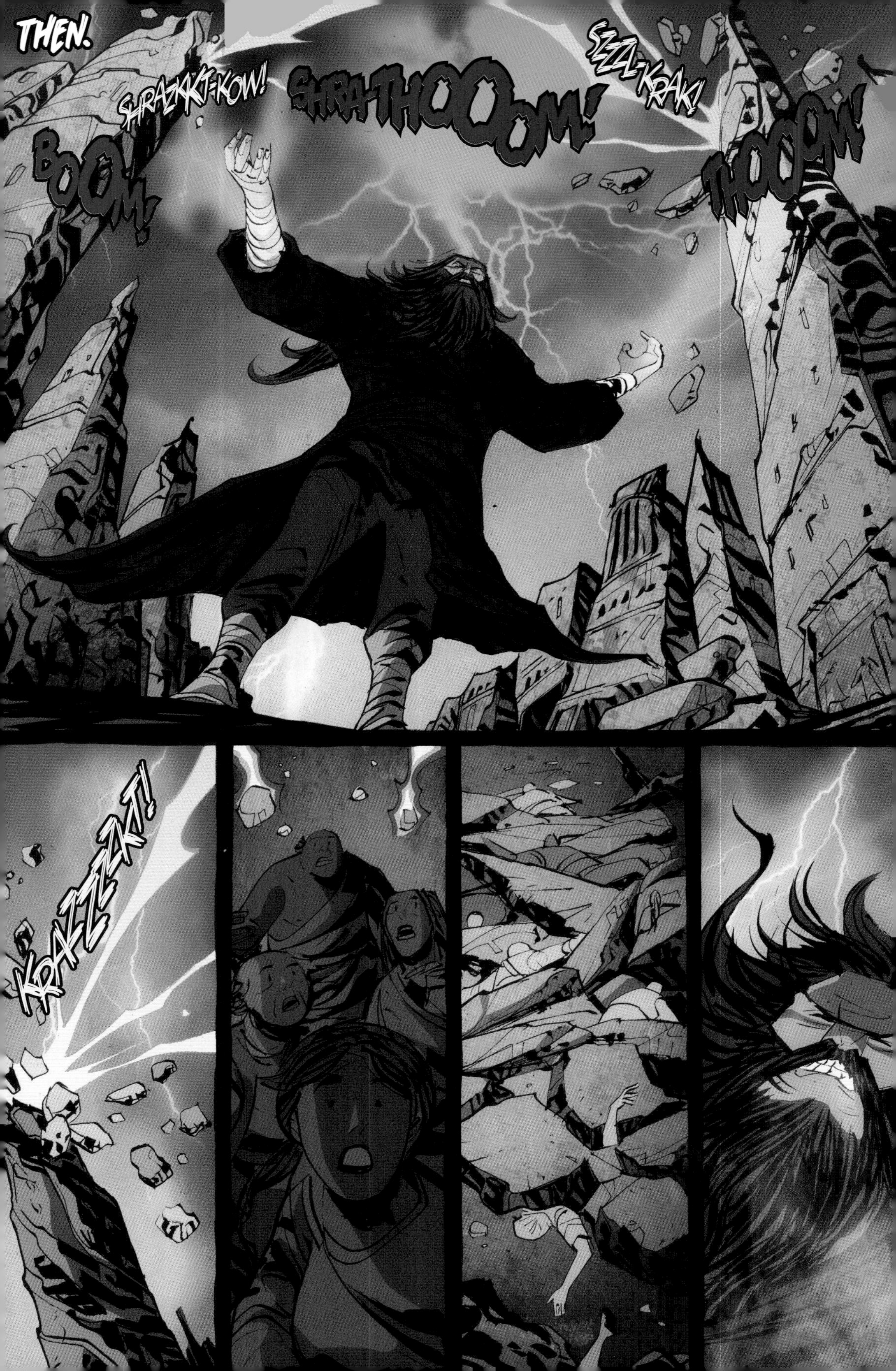
THEN.
SHRAZKKT-KOW!
BOOM!
SHRA-THOOOOM!
SZZZL-KRAK!
THOOOM!
KRAZZZZKT!

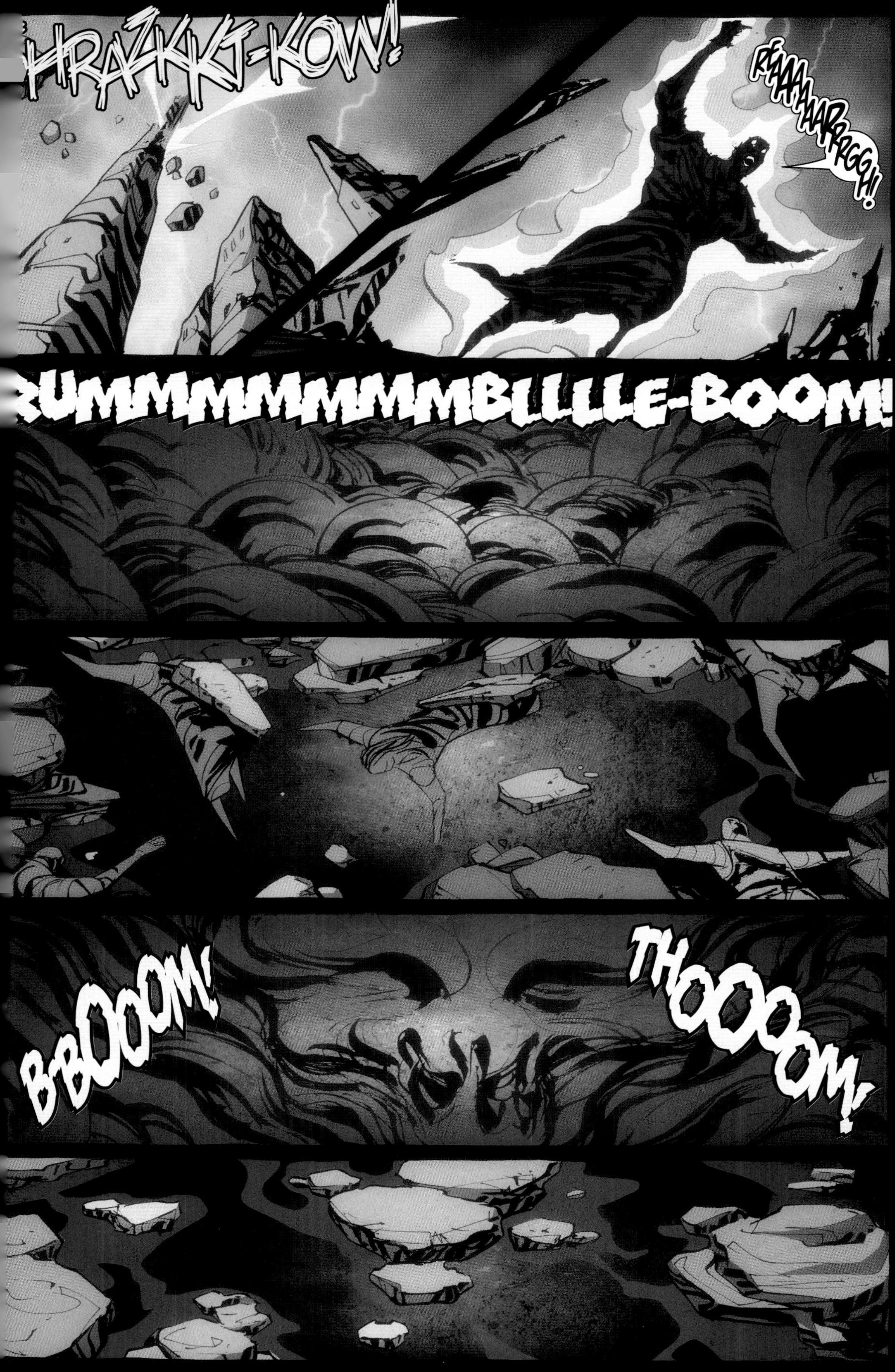
HRAZKKT-KOW!
REAAAAAARRGGH!
RUMMMMMMMMBLLLLE-BOOM!
BBOOOM!
THOOOOM!

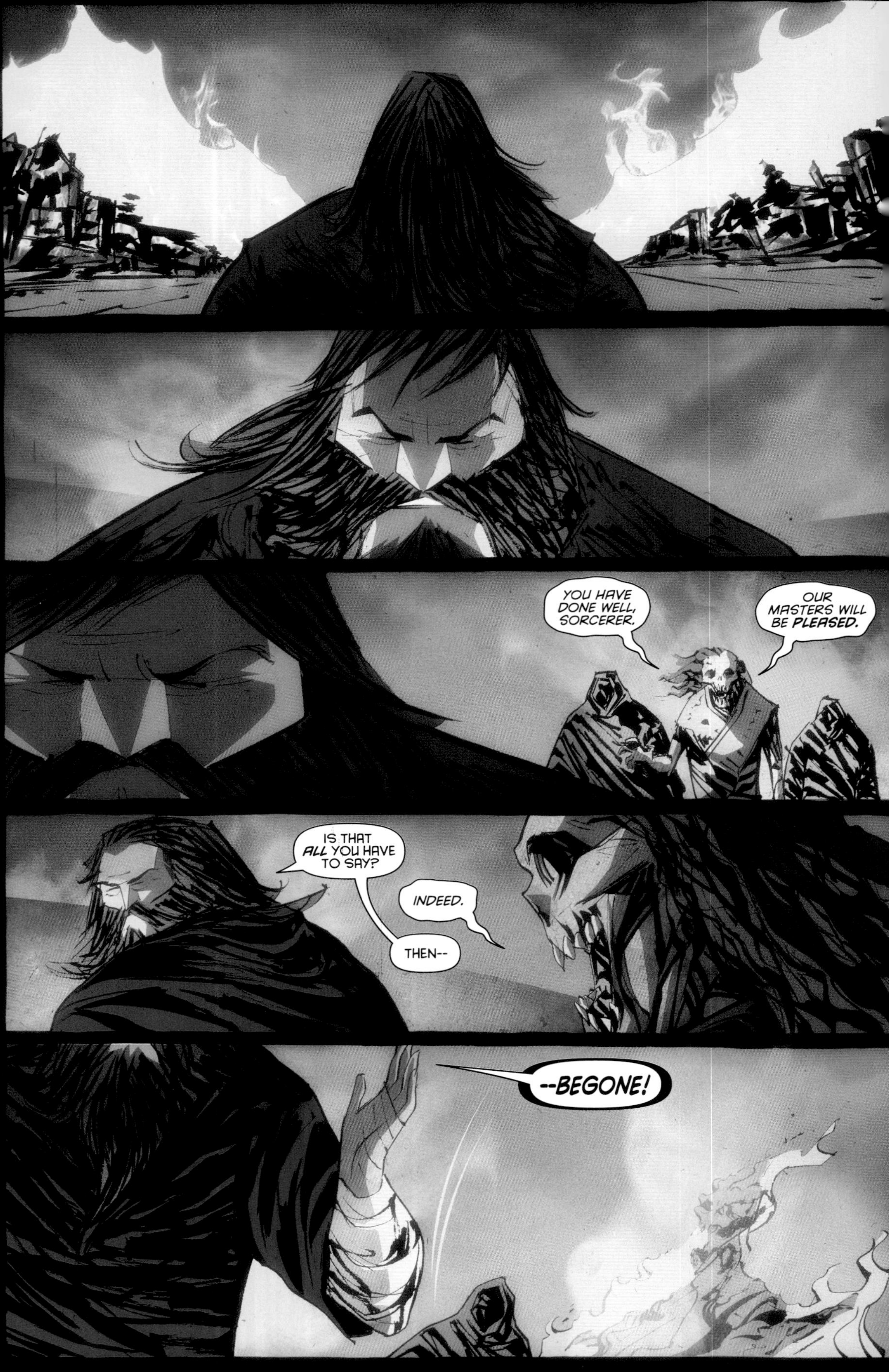
YOU HAVE DONE WELL, SORCERER.
OUR MASTERS WILL BE PLEASED.
IS THAT ALL YOU HAVE TO SAY?
INDEED.
THEN--
--BEGONE!

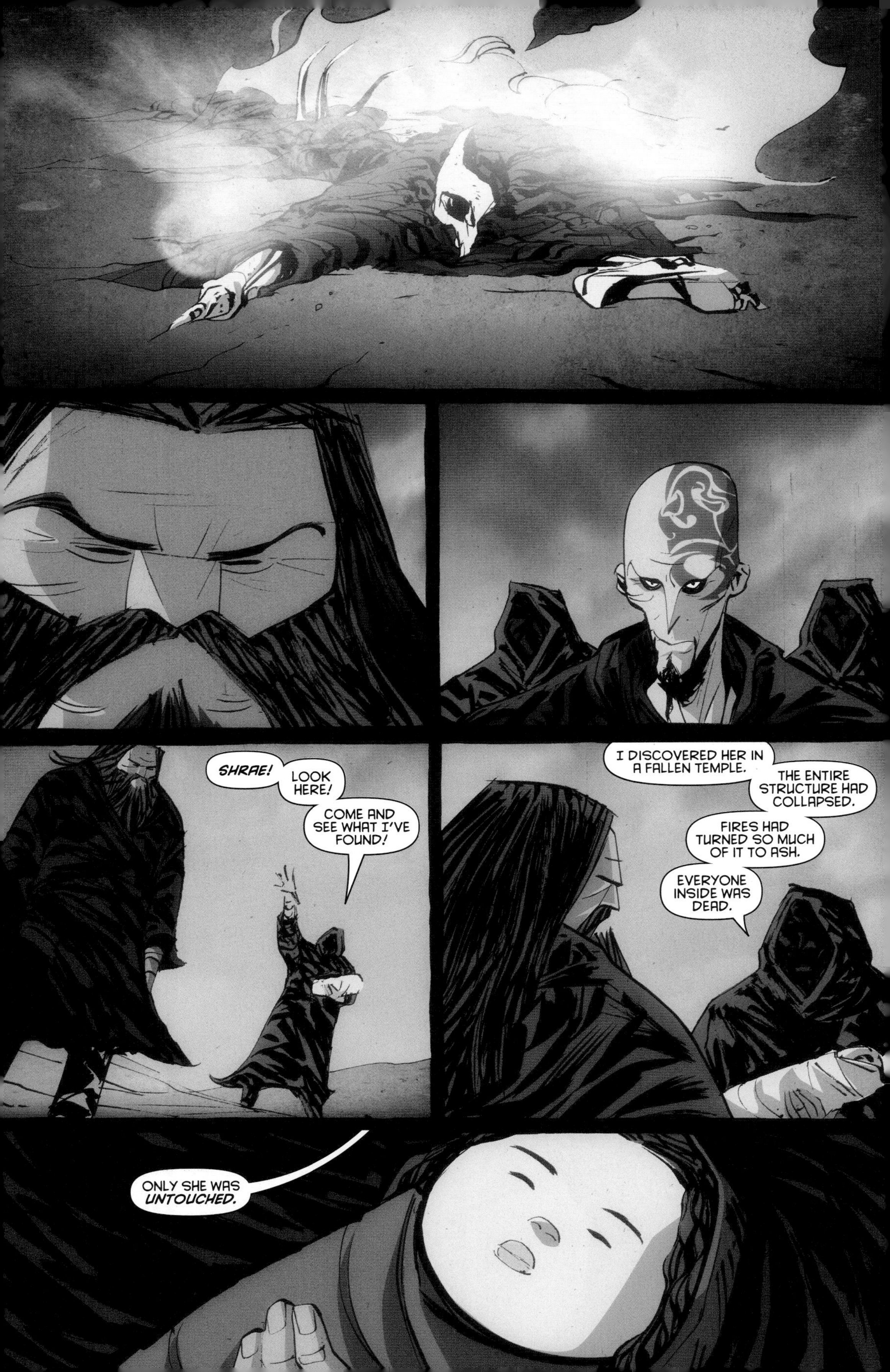
SHRAE!
LOOK HERE!
COME AND SEE WHAT I'VE FOUND!
I DISCOVERED HER IN A FALLEN TEMPLE.
THE ENTIRE STRUCTURE HAD COLLAPSED.
FIRES HAD TURNED SO MUCH OF IT TO ASH.
EVERYONE INSIDE WAS DEAD.
ONLY SHE WAS *UNTOUCHED*.

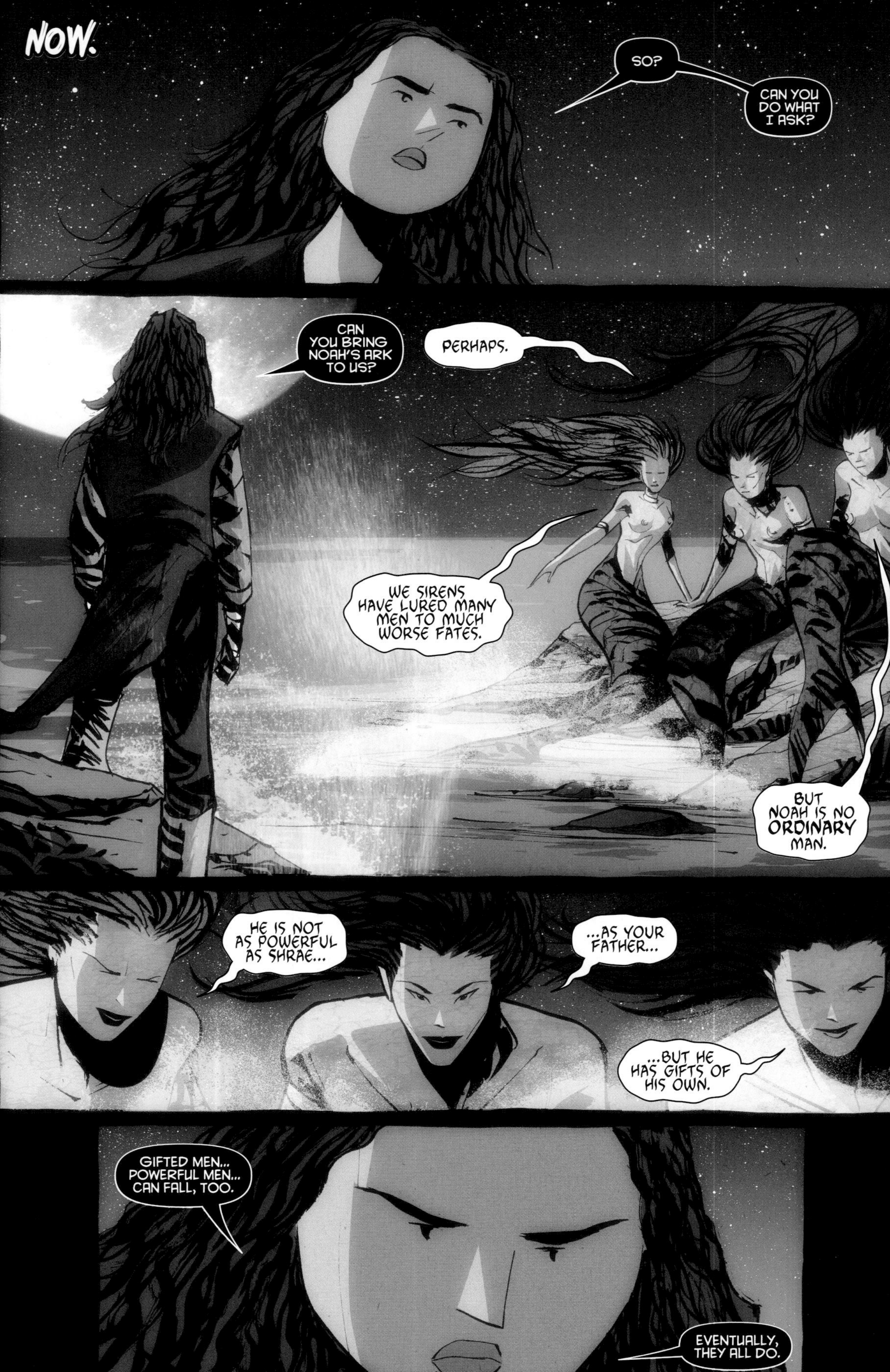
NOW.
SO?
CAN YOU DO WHAT I ASK?
CAN YOU BRING NOAH'S ARK TO US?
PERHAPS.
WE SIRENS HAVE LURED MANY MEN TO MUCH WORSE FATES.
BUT NOAH IS NO ORDINARY MAN.
HE IS NOT AS POWERFUL AS SHRAE...
...AS YOUR FATHER...
...BUT HE HAS GIFTS OF HIS OWN.
GIFTED MEN... POWERFUL MEN... CAN FALL, TOO.
EVENTUALLY, THEY ALL DO.

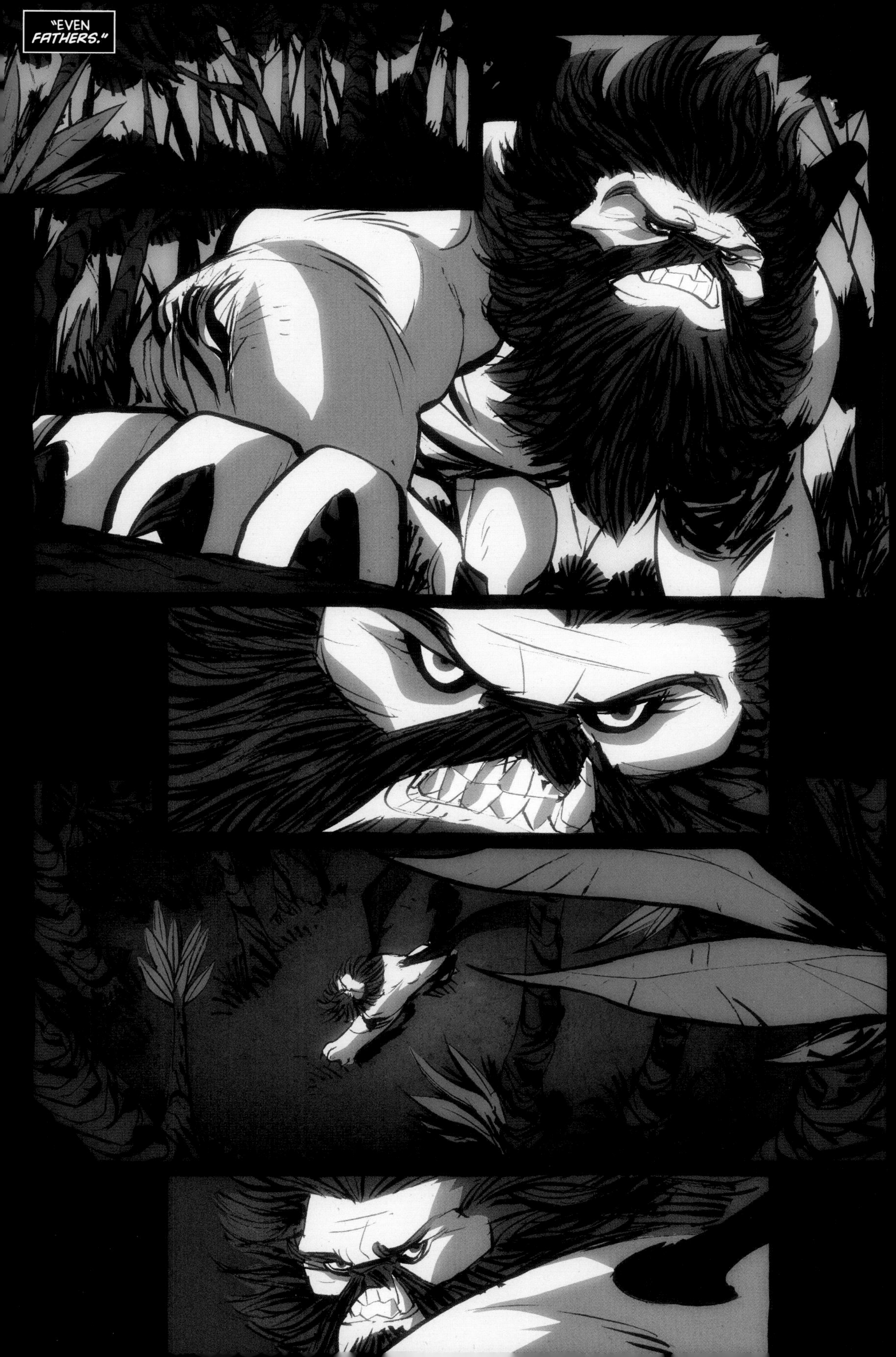
"EVEN *FATHERS.*"

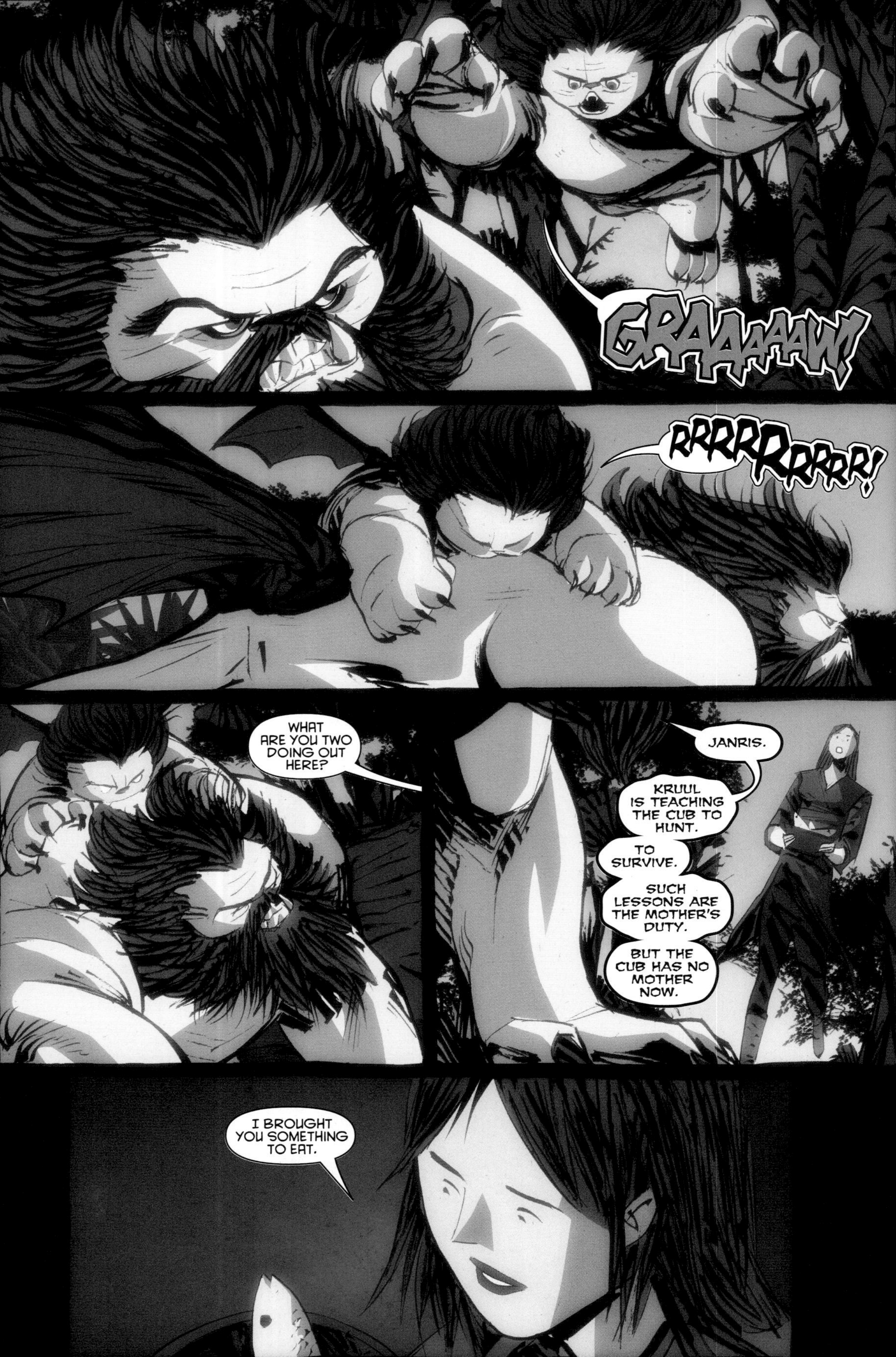
GRAAAAAAW!
RRRRRrrrr!
WHAT ARE YOU TWO DOING OUT HERE?
JANRIS.
KRUUL IS TEACHING THE CUB TO HUNT.
TO SURVIVE.
SUCH LESSONS ARE THE MOTHER'S DUTY.
BUT THE CUB HAS NO MOTHER NOW.
I BROUGHT YOU SOMETHING TO EAT.

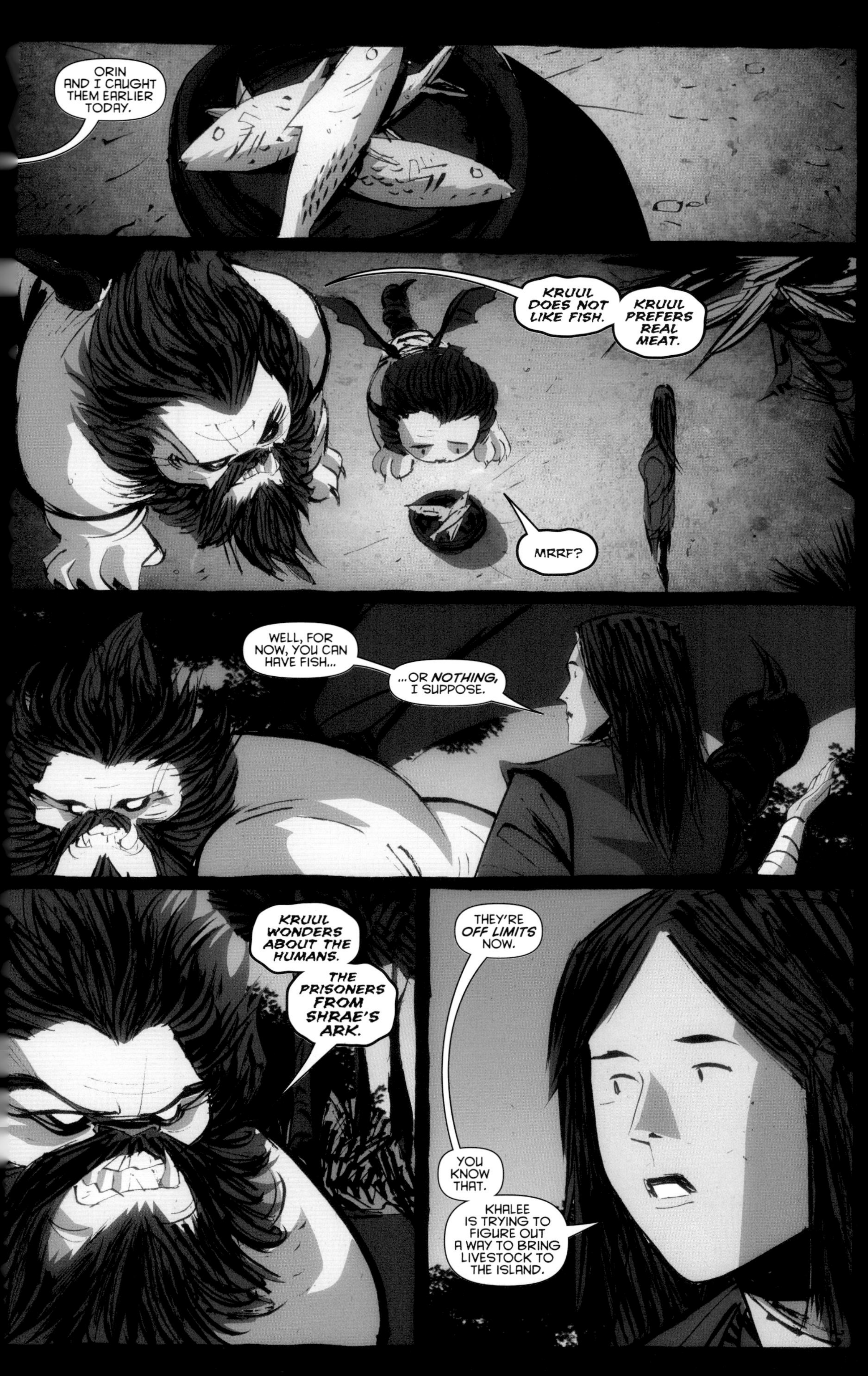
ORIN AND I CAUGHT THEM EARLIER TODAY.
KRUUL DOES NOT LIKE FISH.
KRUUL PREFERS REAL MEAT.
MRRF?
WELL, FOR NOW, YOU CAN HAVE FISH...
...OR NOTHING, I SUPPOSE.
KRUUL WONDERS ABOUT THE HUMANS.
THE PRISONERS FROM SHRAE'S ARK.
THEY'RE OFF LIMITS NOW.
YOU KNOW THAT.
KHALEE IS TRYING TO FIGURE OUT A WAY TO BRING LIVESTOCK TO THE ISLAND.

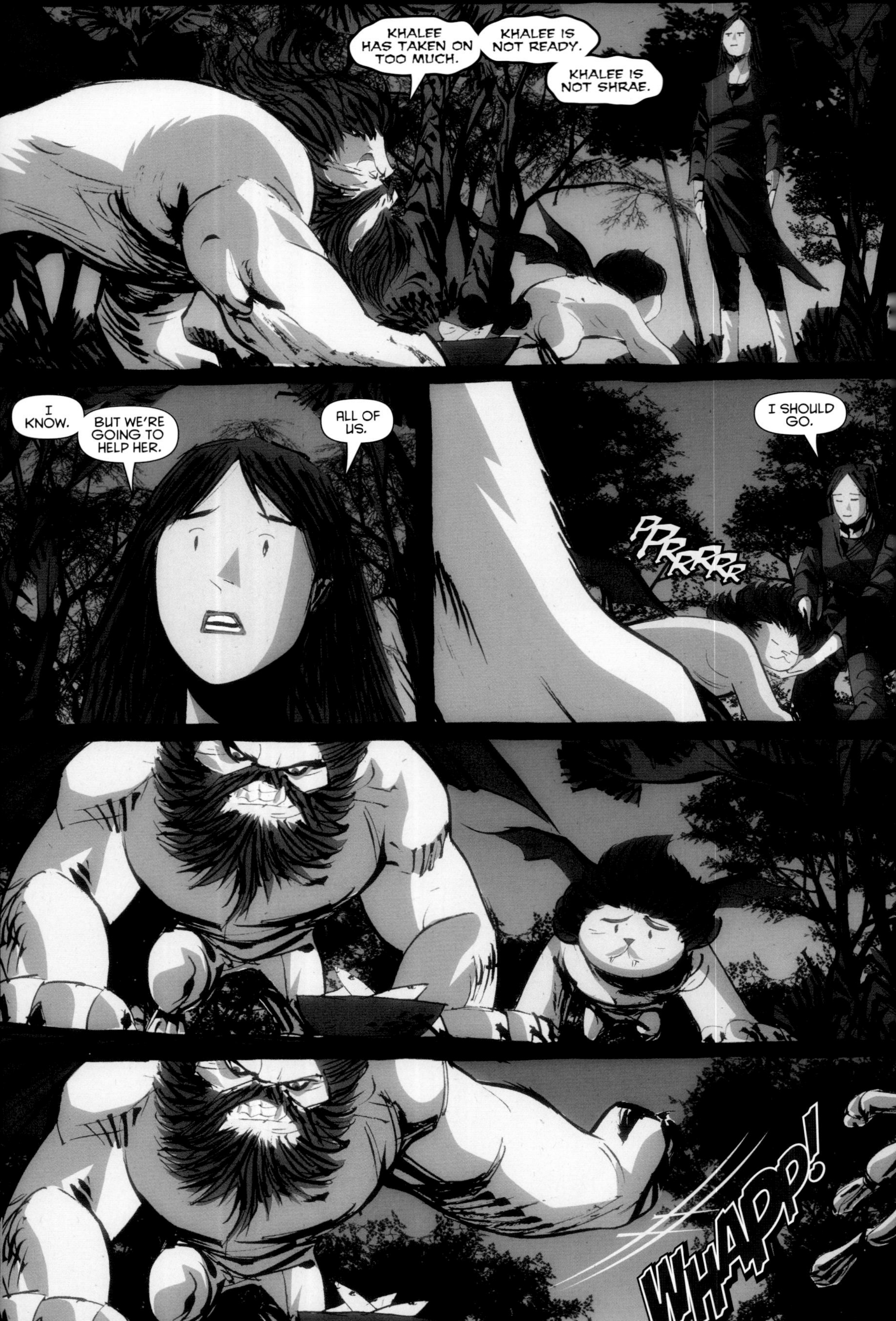
KHALEE HAS TAKEN ON TOO MUCH.
KHALEE IS NOT READY.
KHALEE IS NOT SHRAE.
I KNOW.
BUT WE'RE GOING TO HELP HER.
ALL OF US.
I SHOULD GO.
PPRRRRRR
WHAPP!

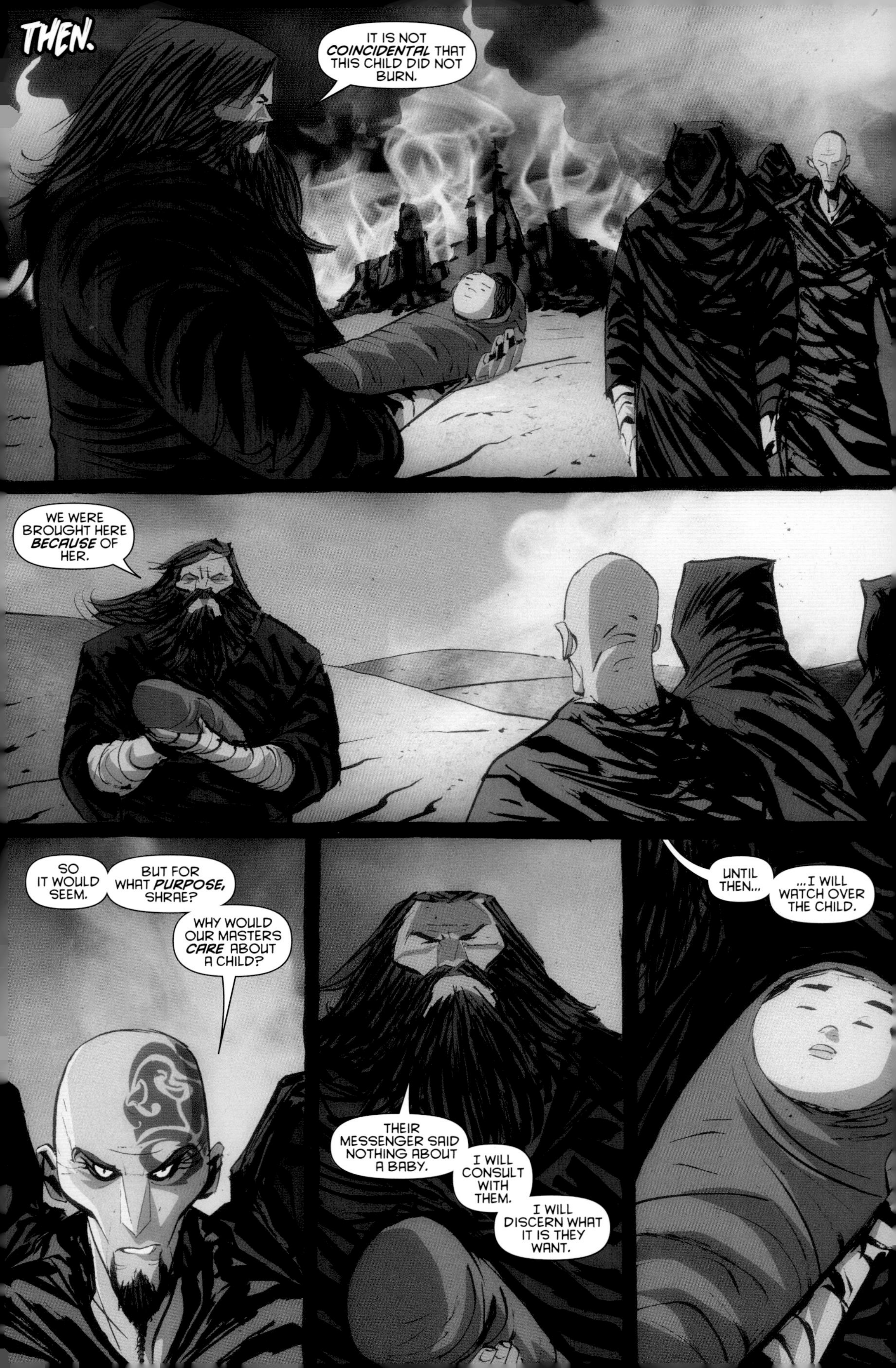
THEN.
IT IS NOT COINCIDENTAL THAT THIS CHILD DID NOT BURN.
WE WERE BROUGHT HERE BECAUSE OF HER.
SO IT WOULD SEEM.
BUT FOR WHAT PURPOSE, SHRAE?
WHY WOULD OUR MASTERS CARE ABOUT A CHILD?
THEIR MESSENGER SAID NOTHING ABOUT A BABY.
I WILL CONSULT WITH THEM.
I WILL DISCERN WHAT IT IS THEY WANT.
UNTIL THEN...
...I WILL WATCH OVER THE CHILD.

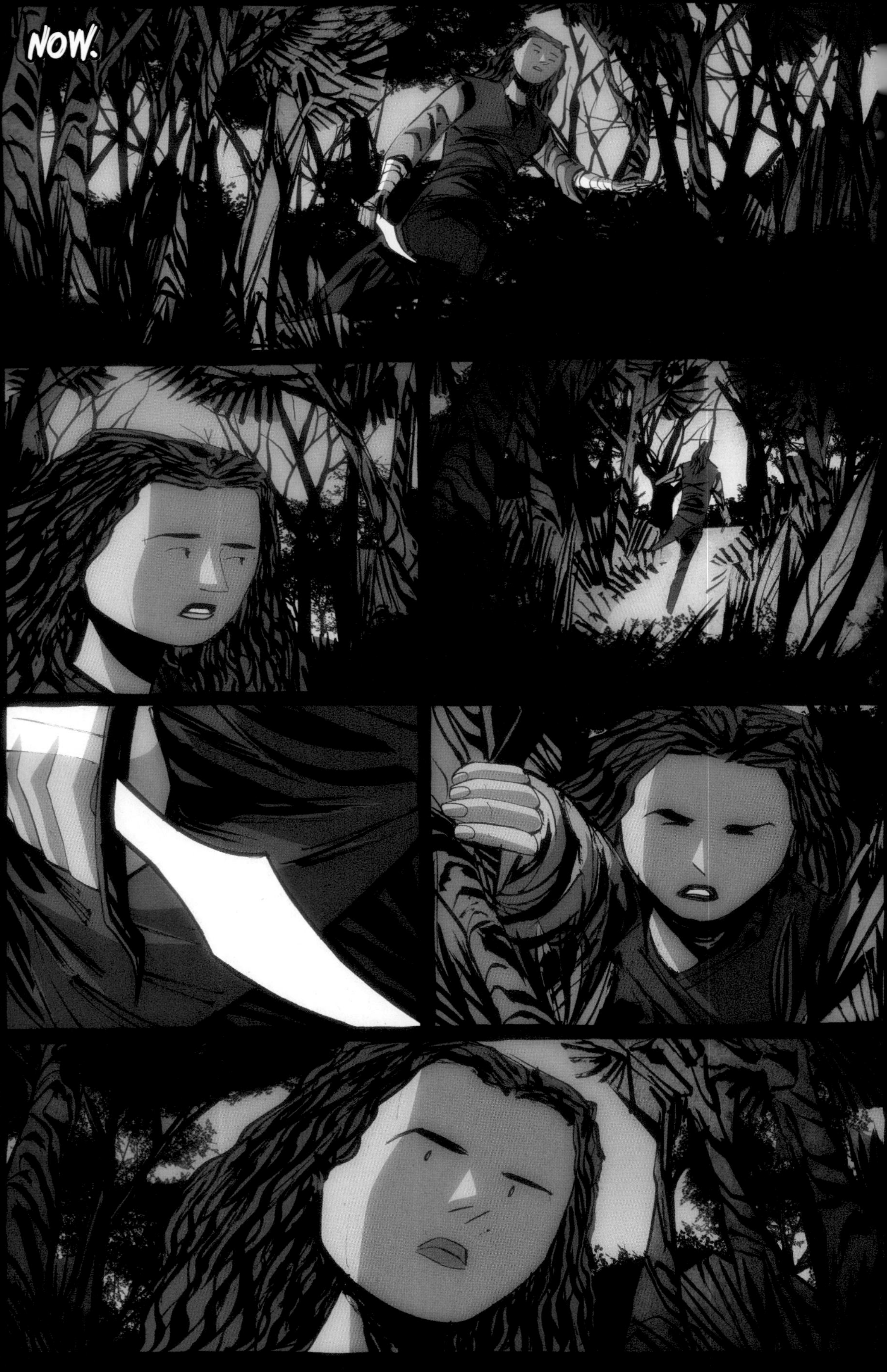
NOW.

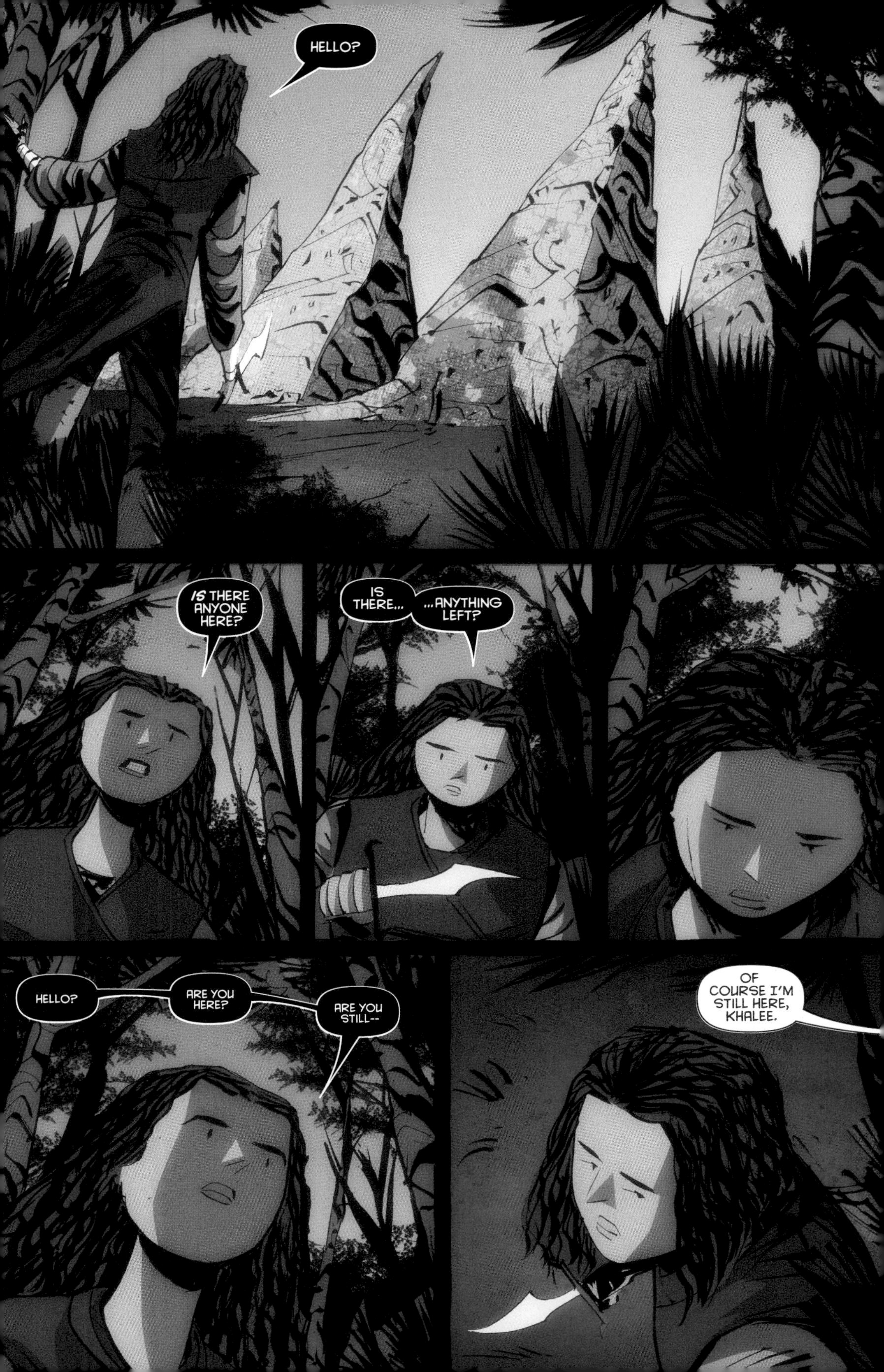
HELLO?
IS THERE ANYONE HERE?
IS THERE...
...ANYTHING LEFT?
HELLO?
ARE YOU HERE?
ARE YOU STILL--
OF COURSE I'M STILL HERE, KHALEE.

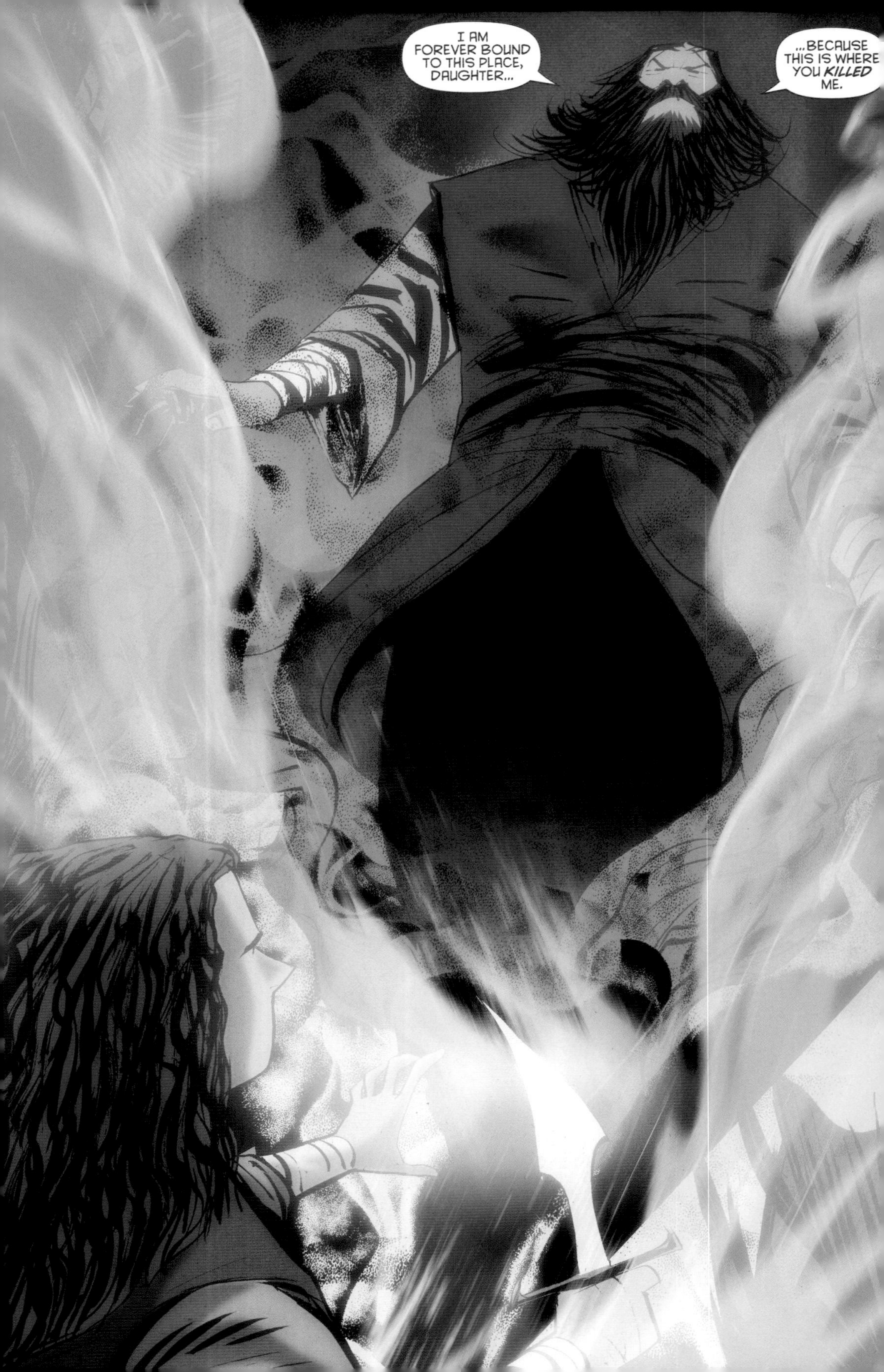
I AM FOREVER BOUND TO THIS PLACE, DAUGHTER...
...BECAUSE THIS IS WHERE YOU *KILLED* ME.

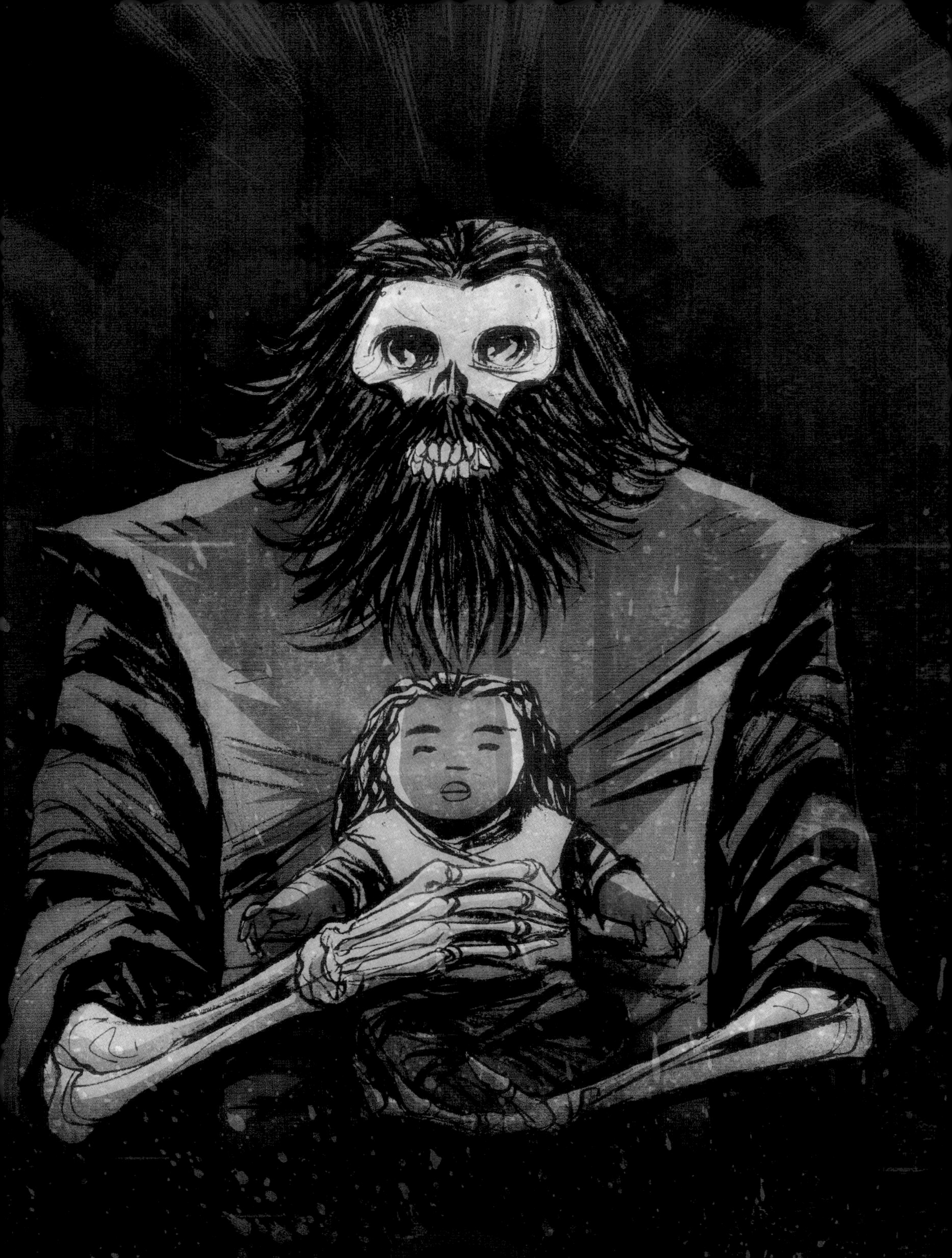

3

CALLINGS

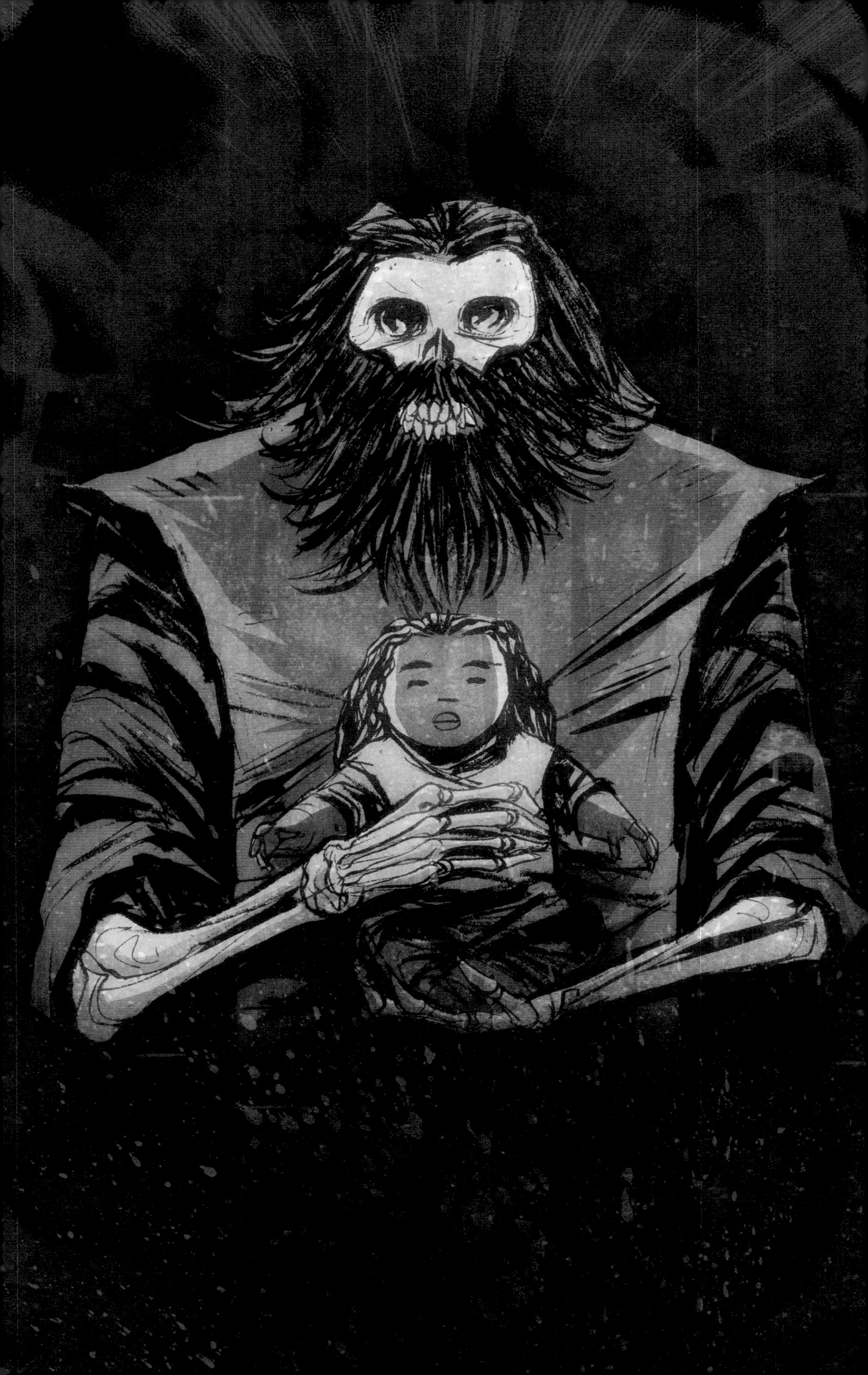

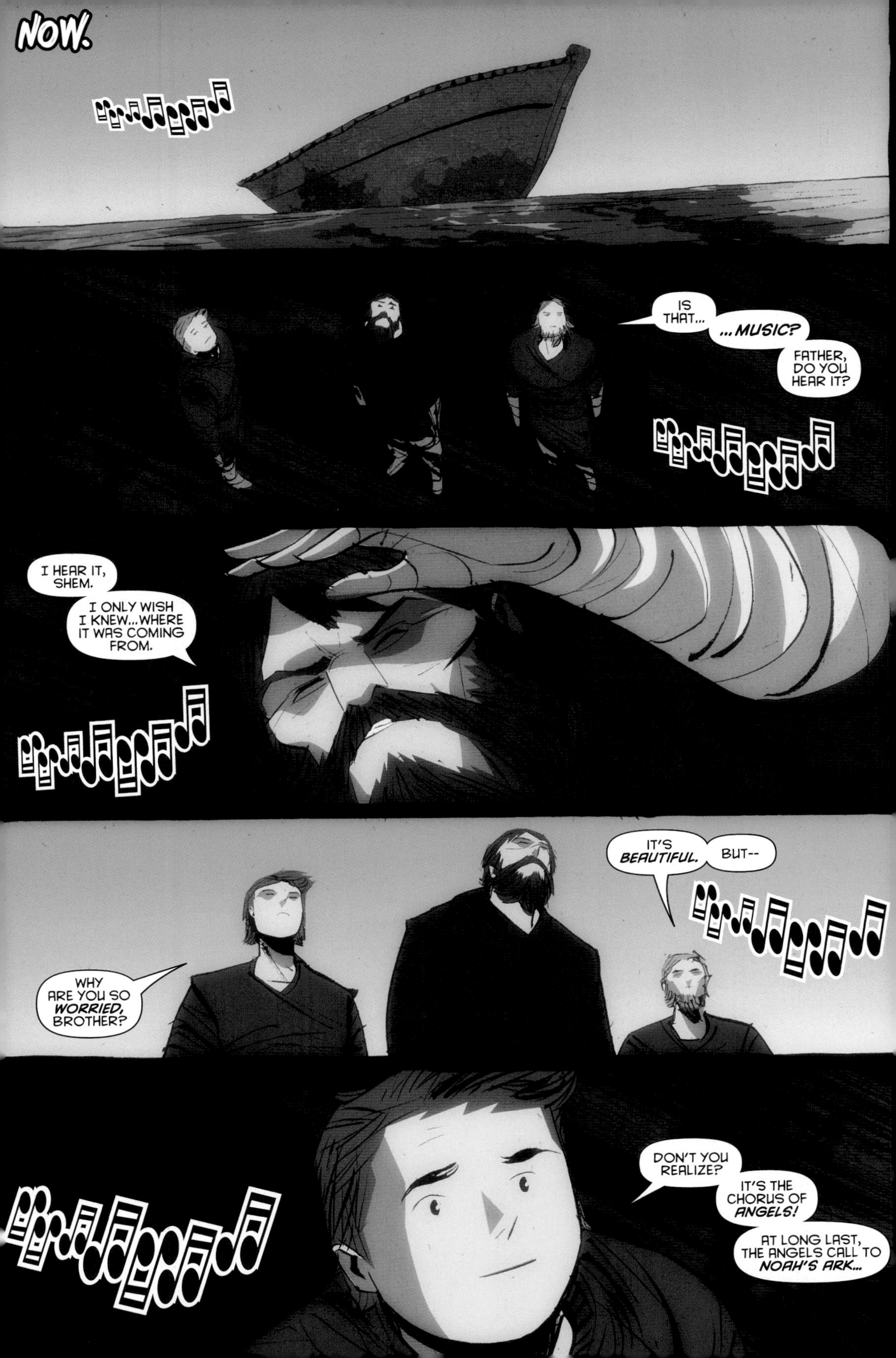
NOW.
IS THAT...
...MUSIC?
FATHER, DO YOU HEAR IT?
I HEAR IT, SHEM.
I ONLY WISH I KNEW...WHERE IT WAS COMING FROM.
IT'S BEAUTIFUL.
BUT--
WHY ARE YOU SO WORRIED, BROTHER?
DON'T YOU REALIZE?
IT'S THE CHORUS OF ANGELS!
AT LONG LAST, THE ANGELS CALL TO NOAH'S ARK...

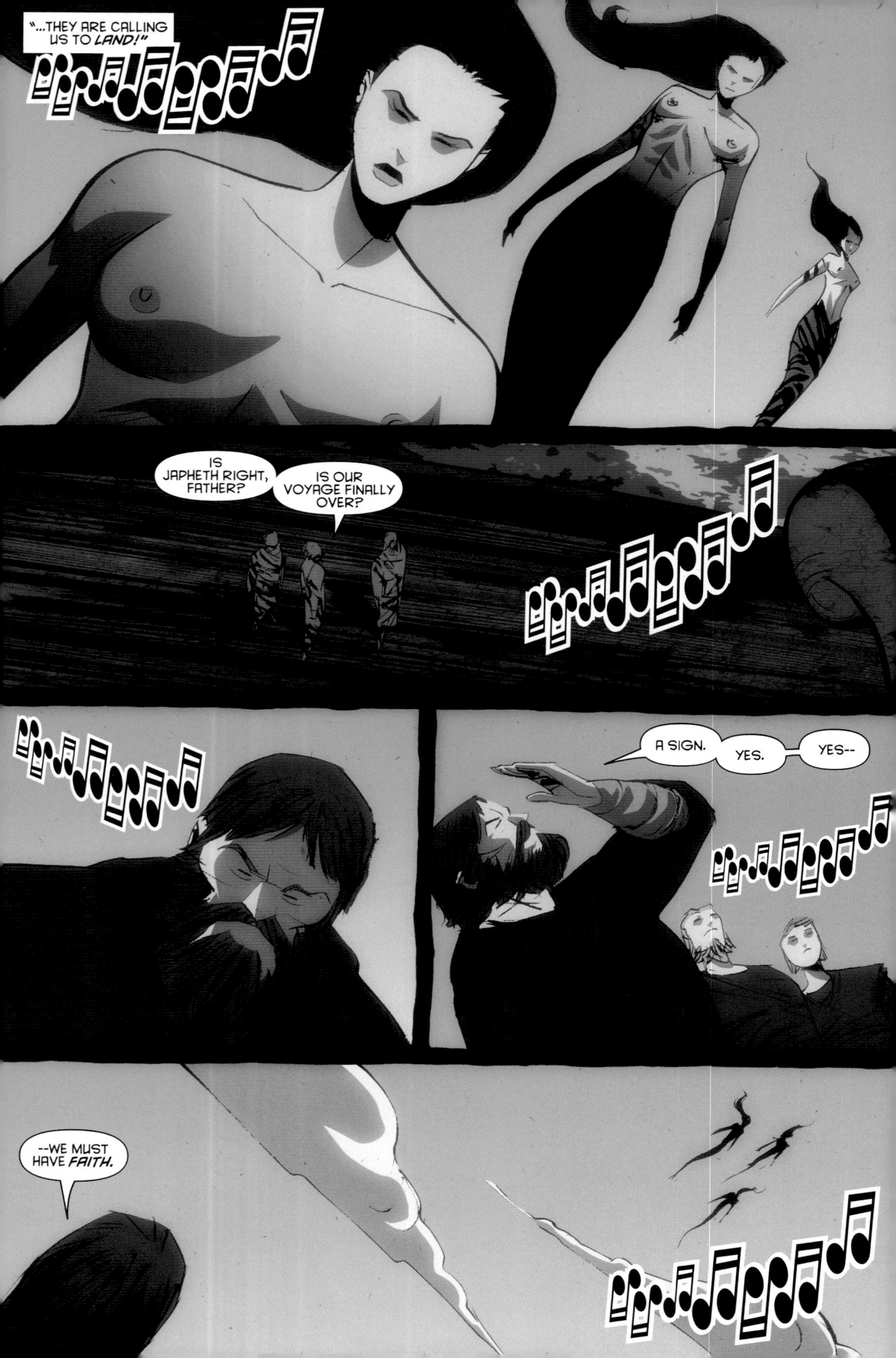
"...THEY ARE CALLING US TO LAND!"
IS JAPHETH RIGHT, FATHER?
IS OUR VOYAGE FINALLY OVER?
A SIGN.
YES.
YES--
--WE MUST HAVE FAITH.

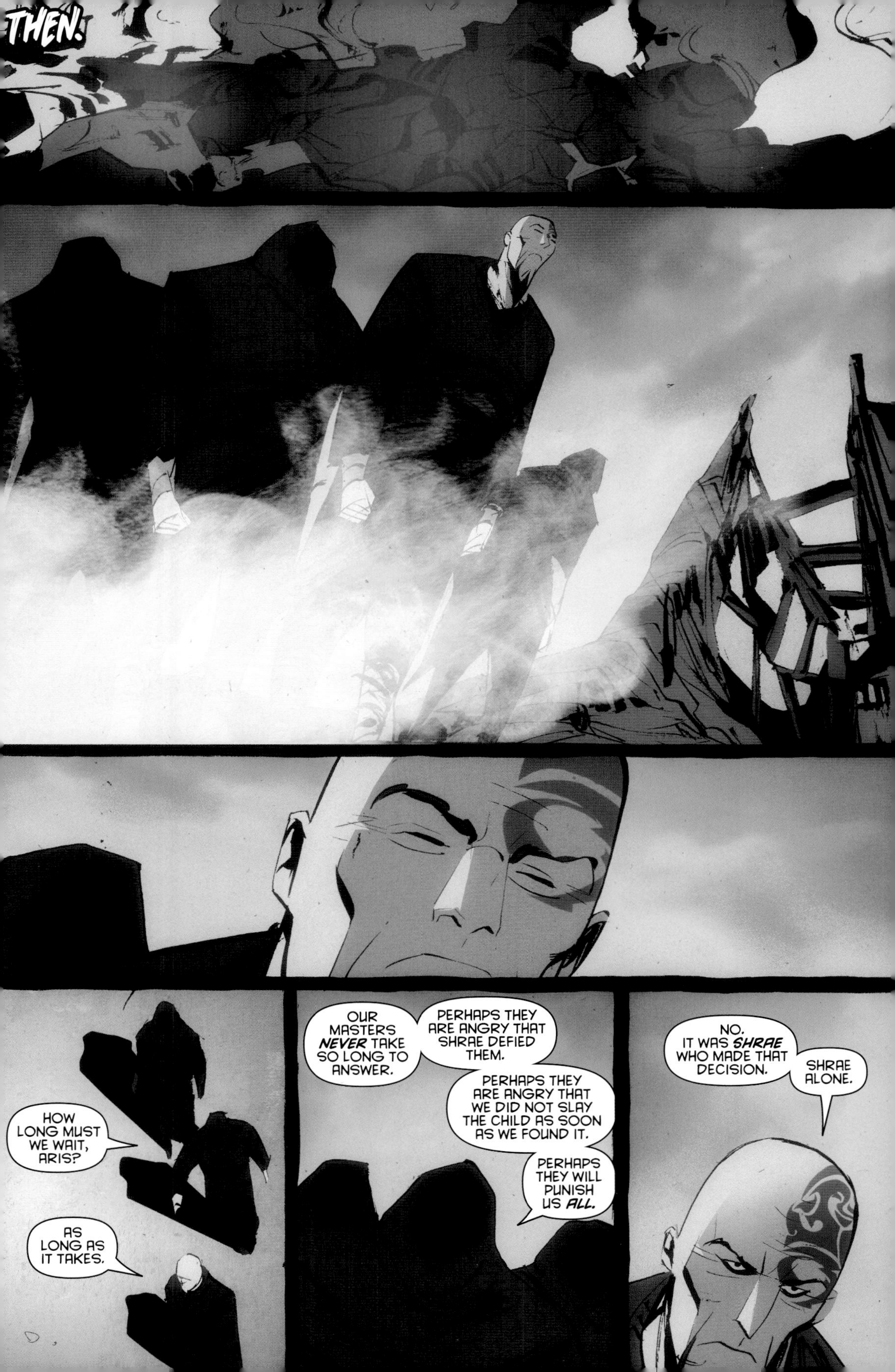
THEN.
HOW LONG MUST WE WAIT, ARIS?
AS LONG AS IT TAKES.
OUR MASTERS NEVER TAKE SO LONG TO ANSWER.
PERHAPS THEY ARE ANGRY THAT SHRAE DEFIED THEM.
PERHAPS THEY ARE ANGRY THAT WE DID NOT SLAY THE CHILD AS SOON AS WE FOUND IT.
PERHAPS THEY WILL PUNISH US ALL.
NO. IT WAS SHRAE WHO MADE THAT DECISION.
SHRAE ALONE.

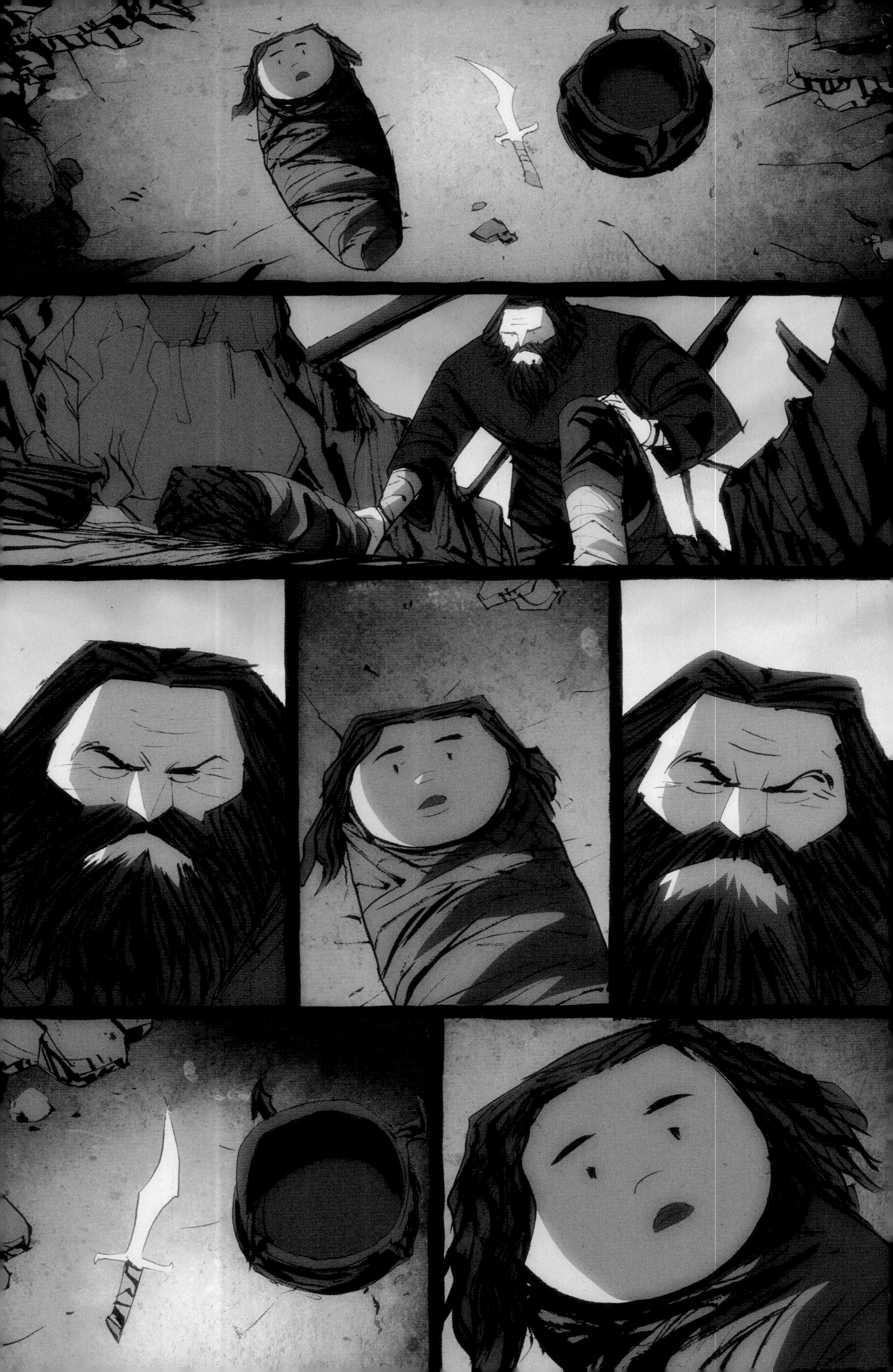

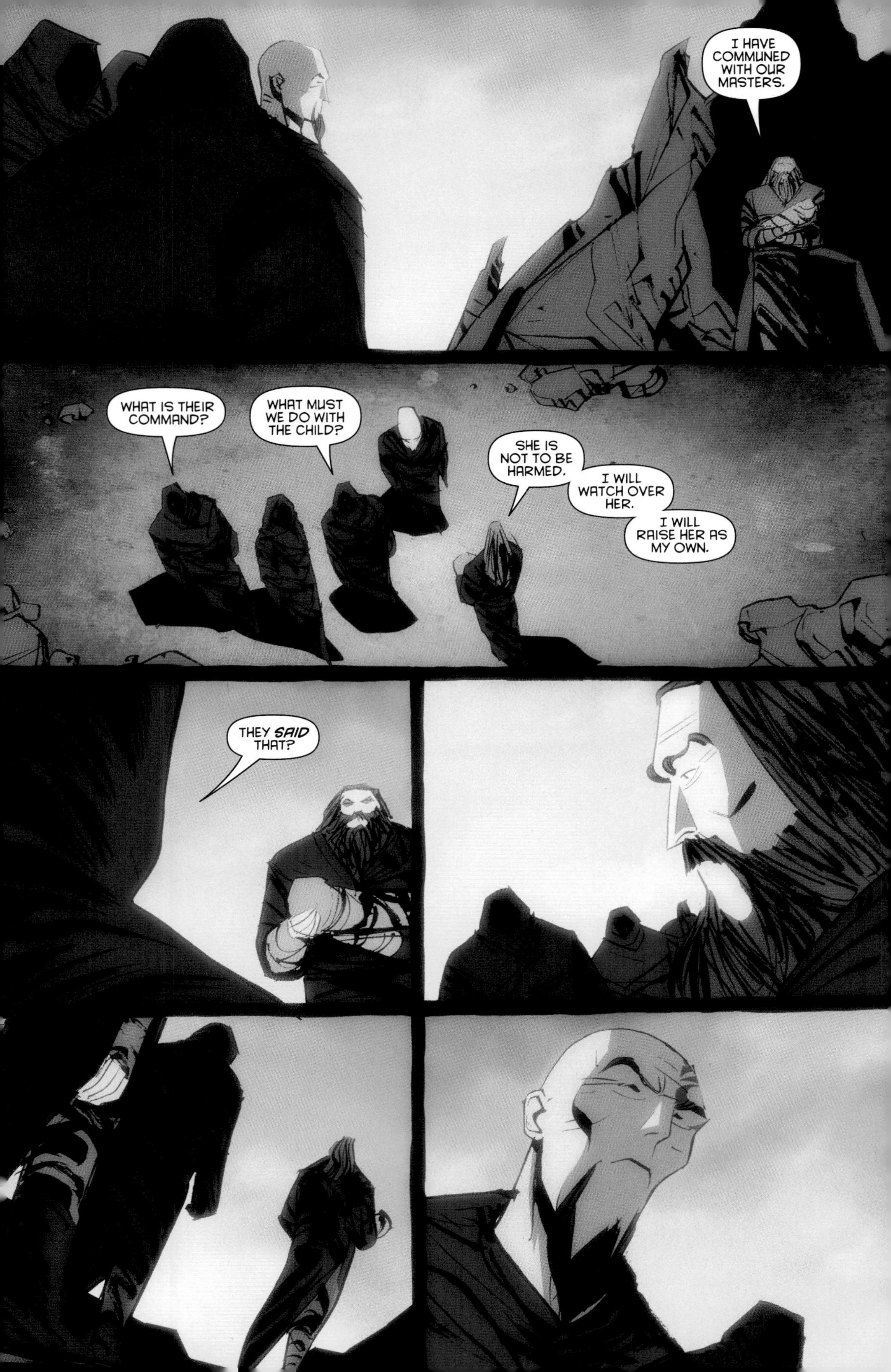
I HAVE COMMUNED WITH OUR MASTERS.
WHAT IS THEIR COMMAND?
WHAT MUST WE DO WITH THE CHILD?
SHE IS NOT TO BE HARMED.
I WILL WATCH OVER HER.
I WILL RAISE HER AS MY OWN.
THEY *SAID* THAT?

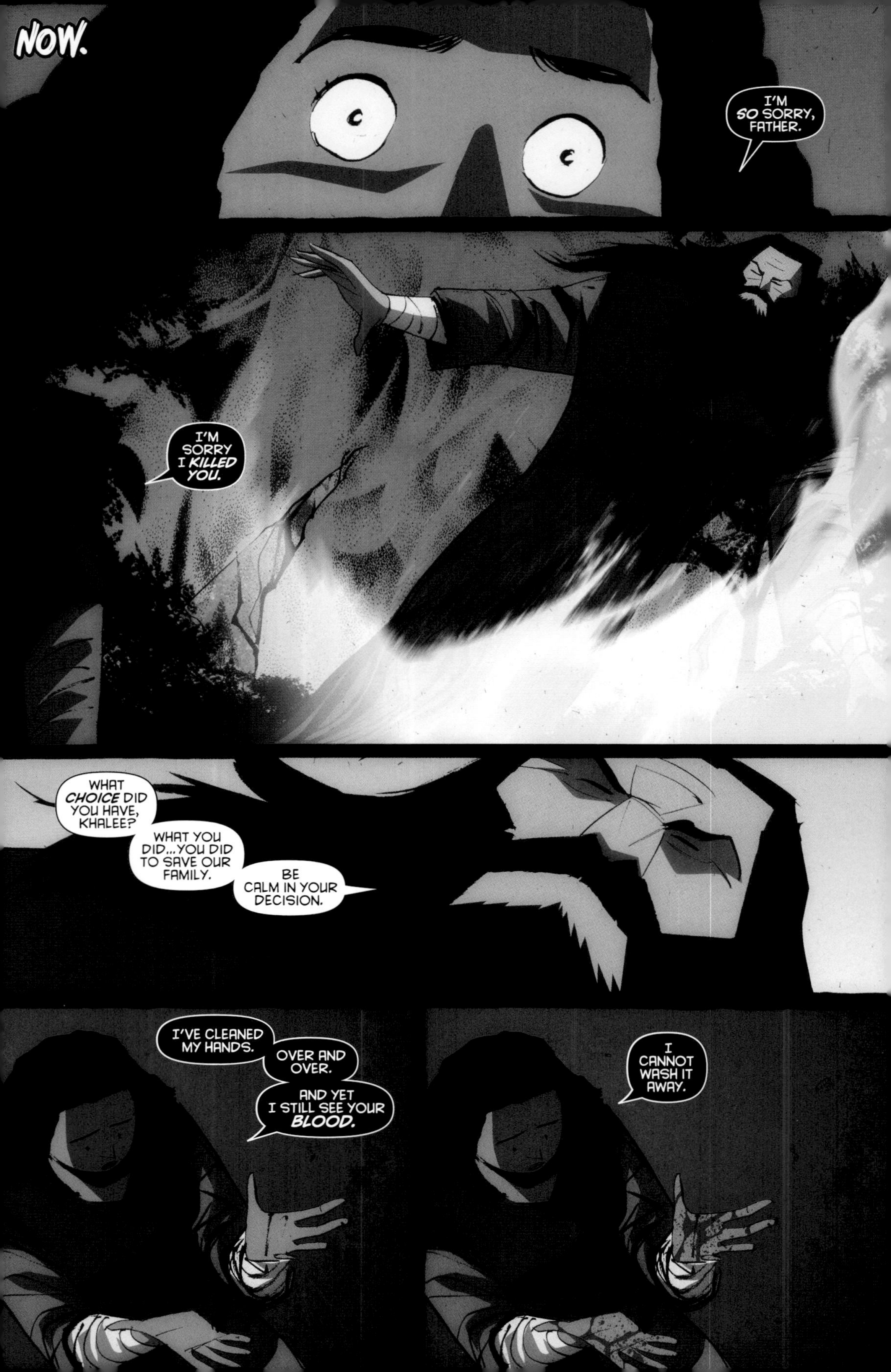
NOW.
I'M SO SORRY, FATHER.
I'M SORRY I KILLED YOU.
WHAT CHOICE DID YOU HAVE, KHALEE?
WHAT YOU DID...YOU DID TO SAVE OUR FAMILY.
BE CALM IN YOUR DECISION.
I'VE CLEANED MY HANDS.
OVER AND OVER.
AND YET I STILL SEE YOUR BLOOD.
I CANNOT WASH IT AWAY.

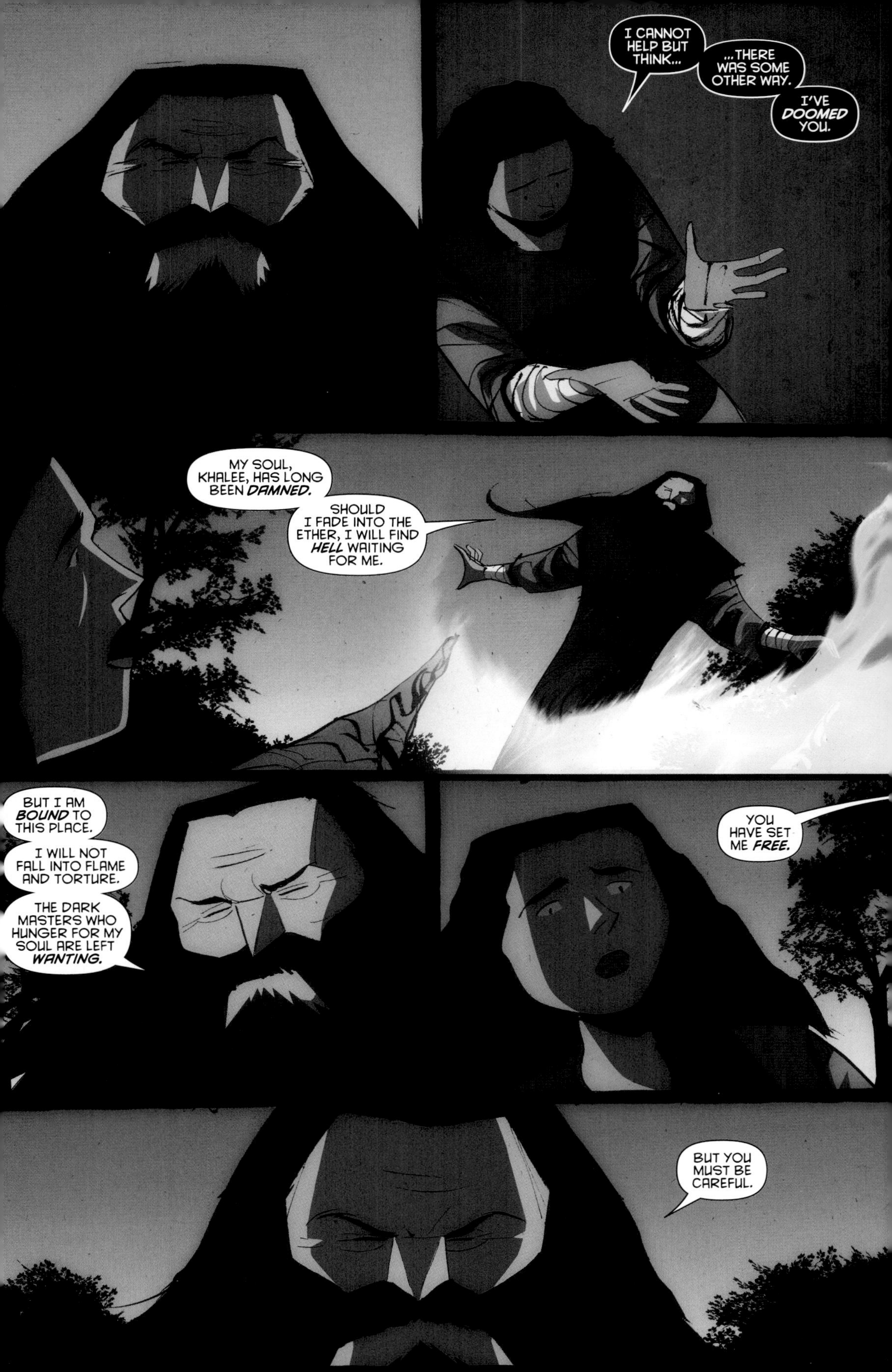
I CANNOT HELP BUT THINK...
...THERE WAS SOME OTHER WAY.
I'VE DOOMED YOU.
MY SOUL, KHALEE, HAS LONG BEEN DAMNED.
SHOULD I FADE INTO THE ETHER, I WILL FIND HELL WAITING FOR ME.
BUT I AM BOUND TO THIS PLACE.
I WILL NOT FALL INTO FLAME AND TORTURE.
THE DARK MASTERS WHO HUNGER FOR MY SOUL ARE LEFT WANTING.
YOU HAVE SET ME FREE.
BUT YOU MUST BE CAREFUL.

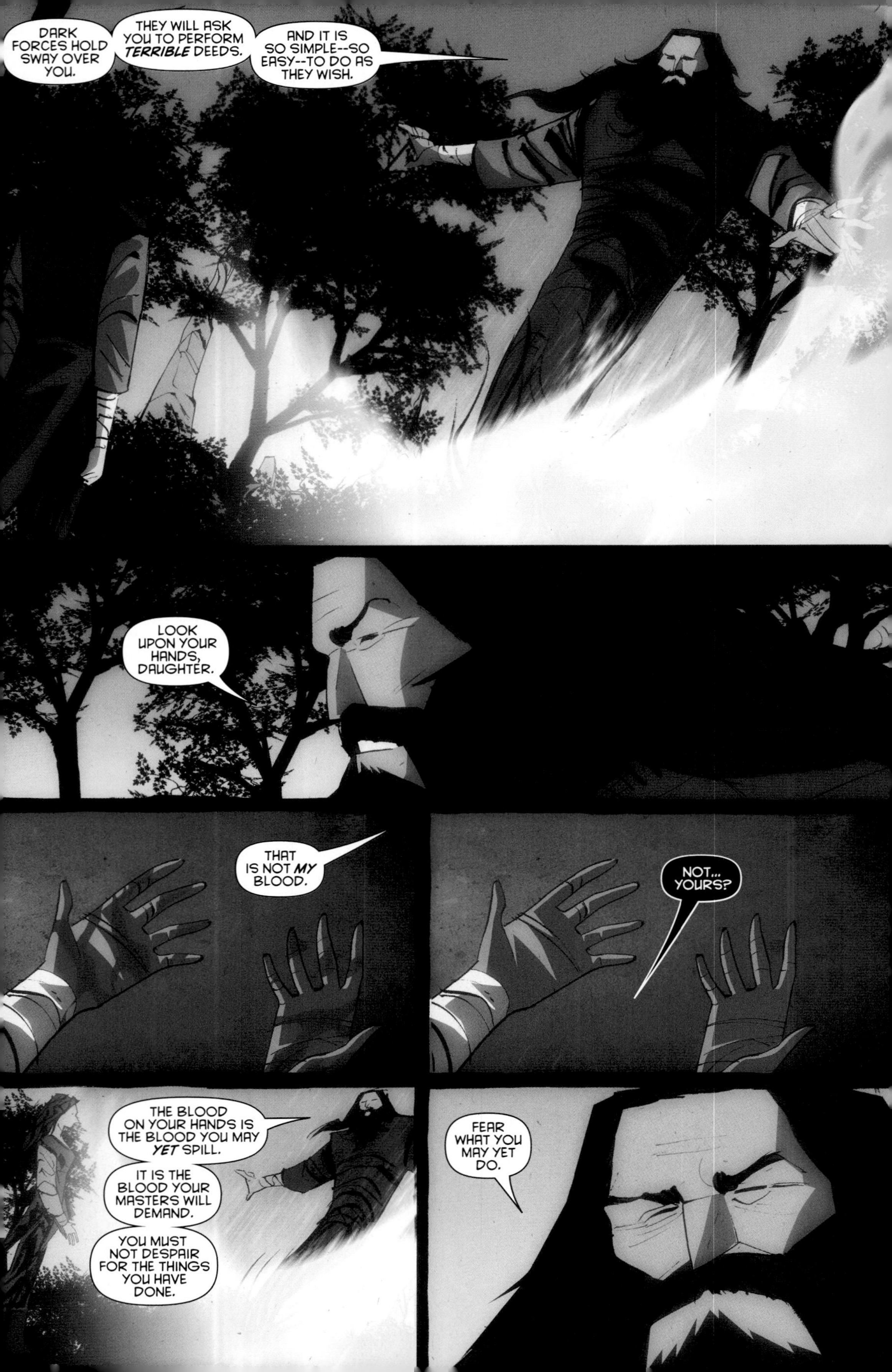
DARK FORCES HOLD SWAY OVER YOU.
THEY WILL ASK YOU TO PERFORM *TERRIBLE* DEEDS.
AND IT IS SO SIMPLE--SO EASY--TO DO AS THEY WISH.
LOOK UPON YOUR HANDS, DAUGHTER.
THAT IS NOT *MY* BLOOD.
NOT... YOURS?
THE BLOOD ON YOUR HANDS IS THE BLOOD YOU MAY *YET* SPILL.
IT IS THE BLOOD YOUR MASTERS WILL DEMAND.
YOU MUST NOT DESPAIR FOR THE THINGS YOU HAVE DONE.
FEAR WHAT YOU MAY YET DO.

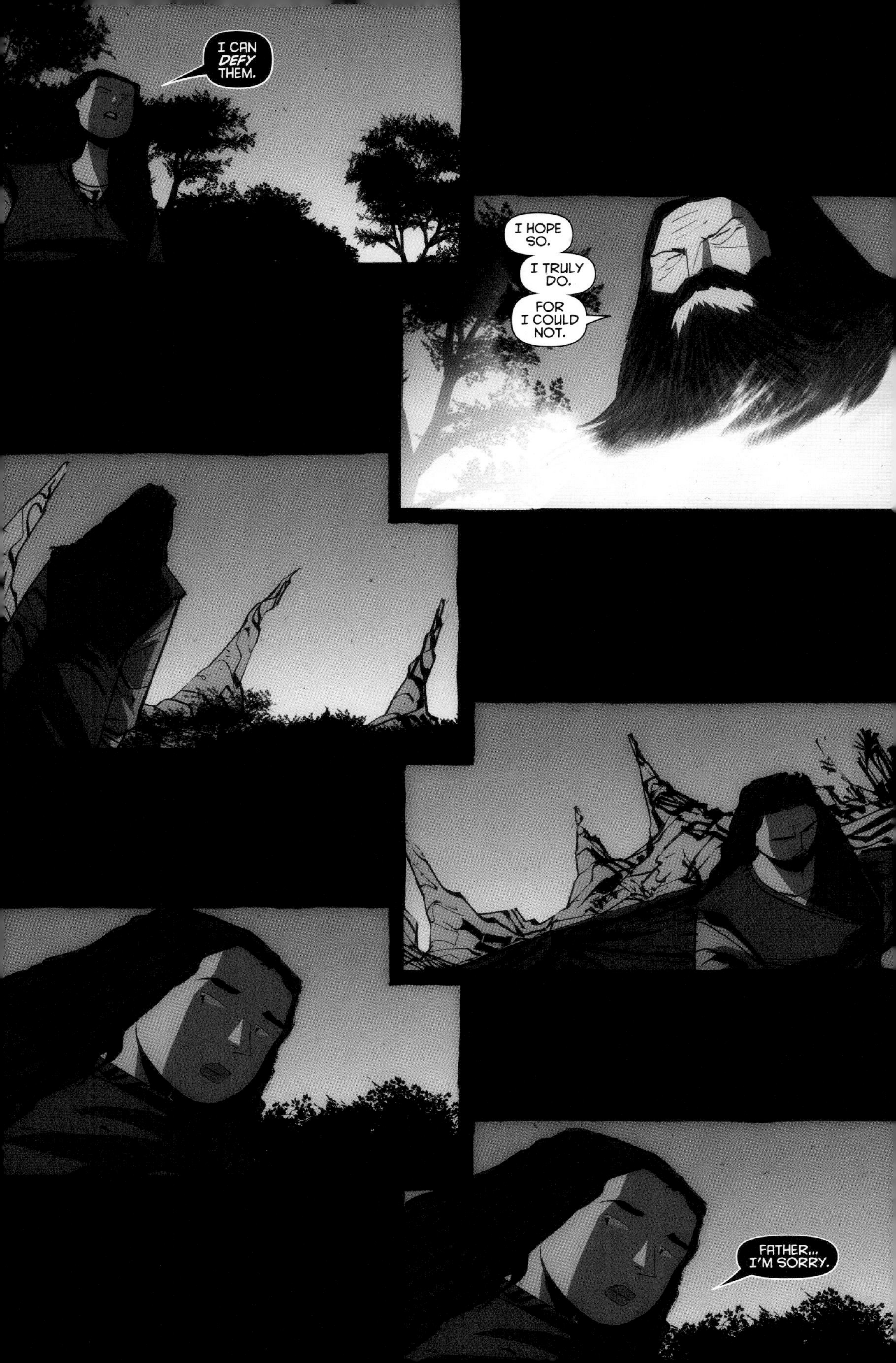
I CAN DEFY THEM.
I HOPE SO.
I TRULY DO.
FOR I COULD NOT.
FATHER... I'M SORRY.

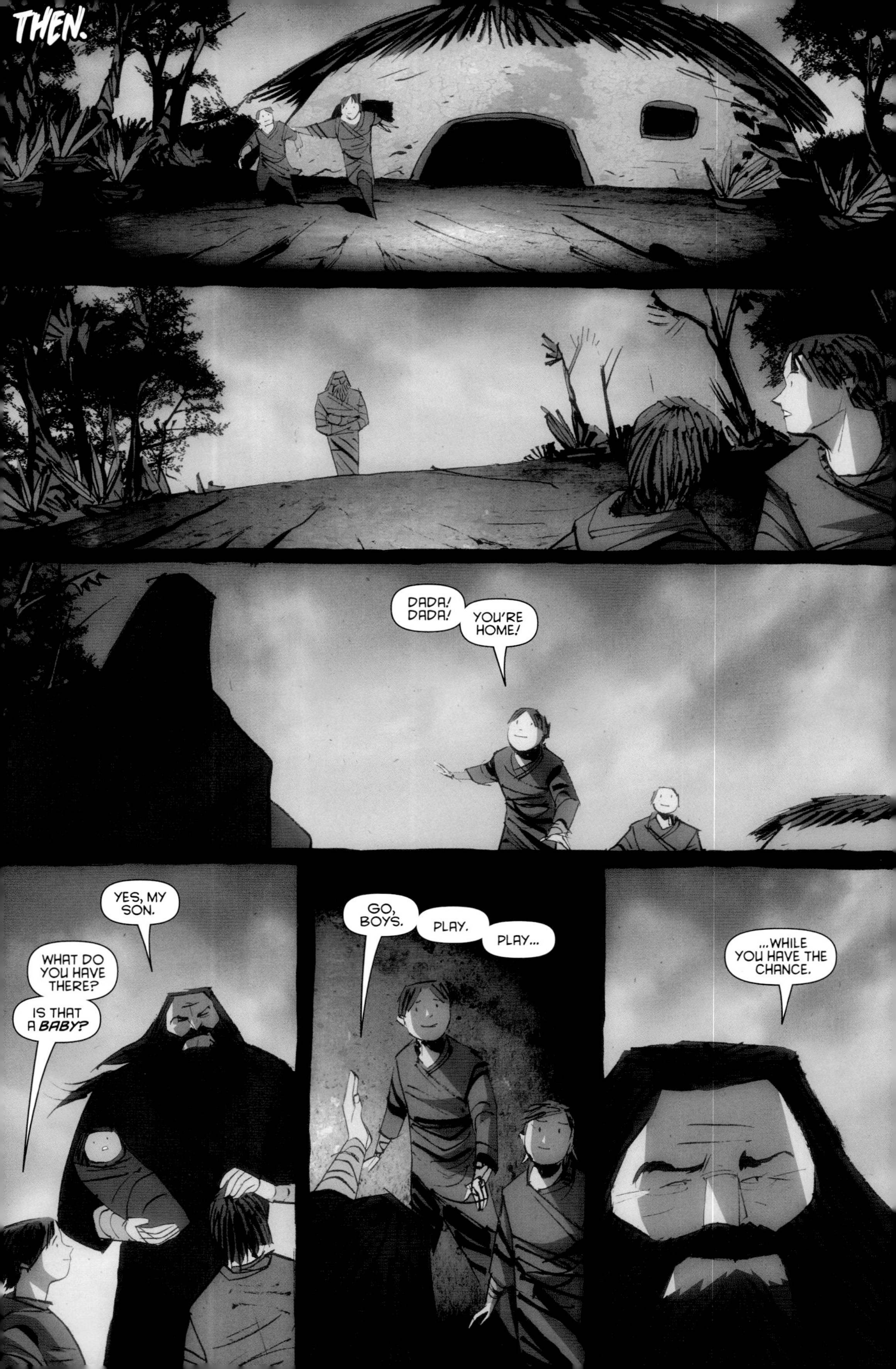
THEN.
DADA! DADA!
YOU'RE HOME!
YES, MY SON.
WHAT DO YOU HAVE THERE?
IS THAT A *BABY?*
GO, BOYS.
PLAY.
PLAY...
...WHILE YOU HAVE THE CHANCE.

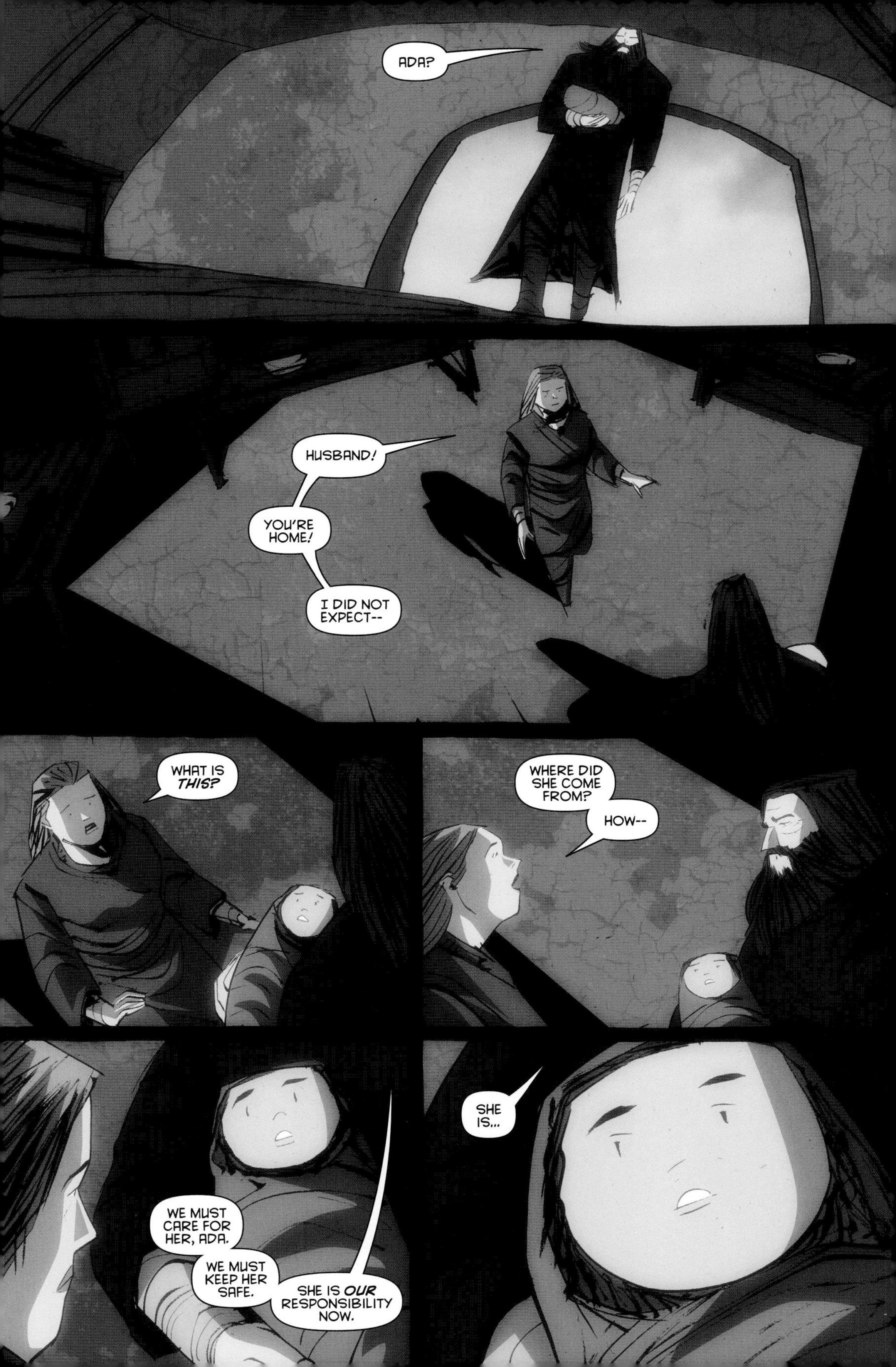

ADA?
HUSBAND!
YOU'RE HOME!
I DID NOT EXPECT--
WHAT IS *THIS?*
WHERE DID SHE COME FROM?
HOW--
WE MUST CARE FOR HER, ADA.
WE MUST KEEP HER SAFE.
SHE IS *OUR* RESPONSIBILITY NOW.
SHE IS...

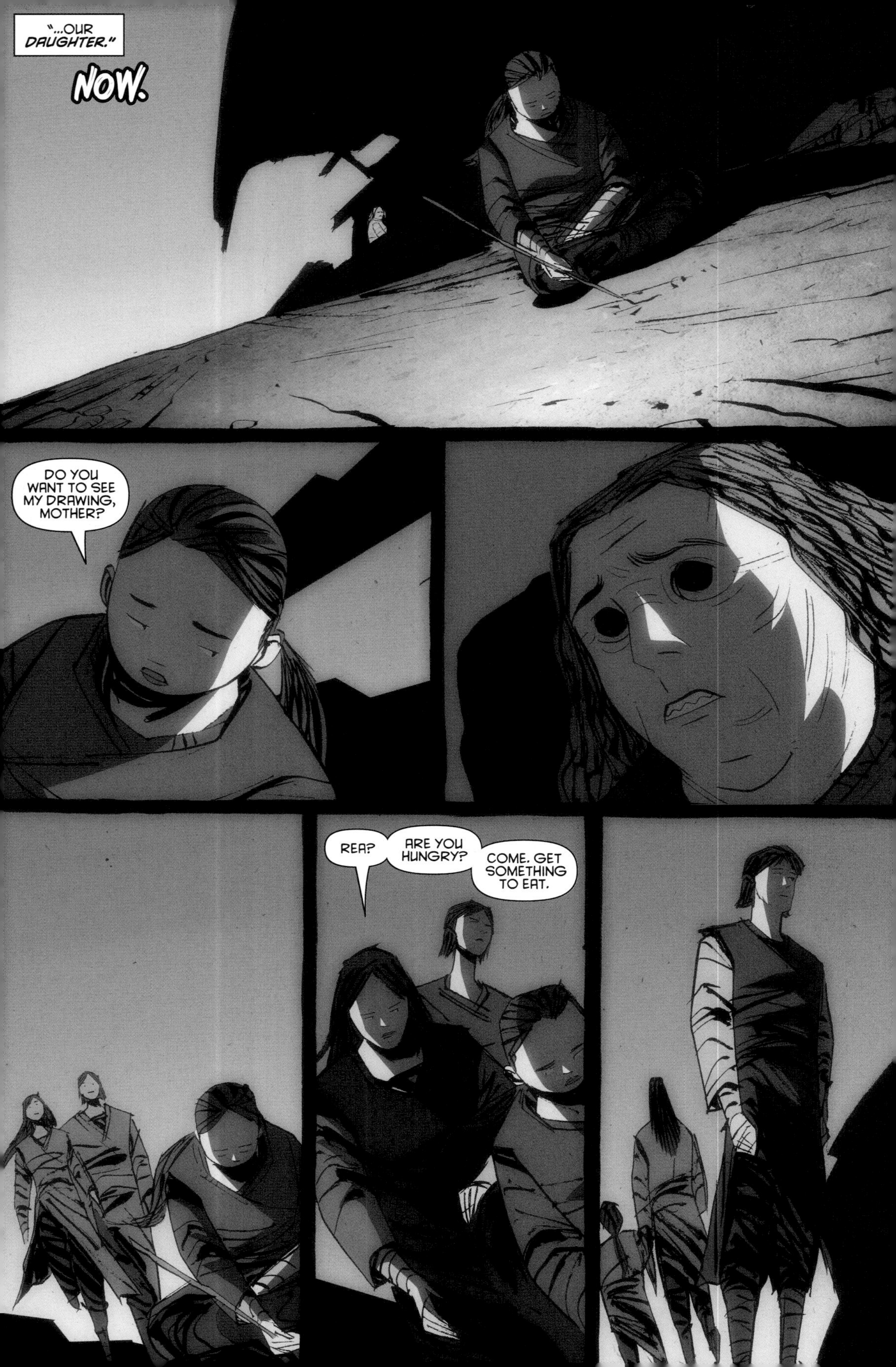
"...OUR DAUGHTER."
NOW.
DO YOU WANT TO SEE MY DRAWING, MOTHER?
REA?
ARE YOU HUNGRY?
COME. GET SOMETHING TO EAT.

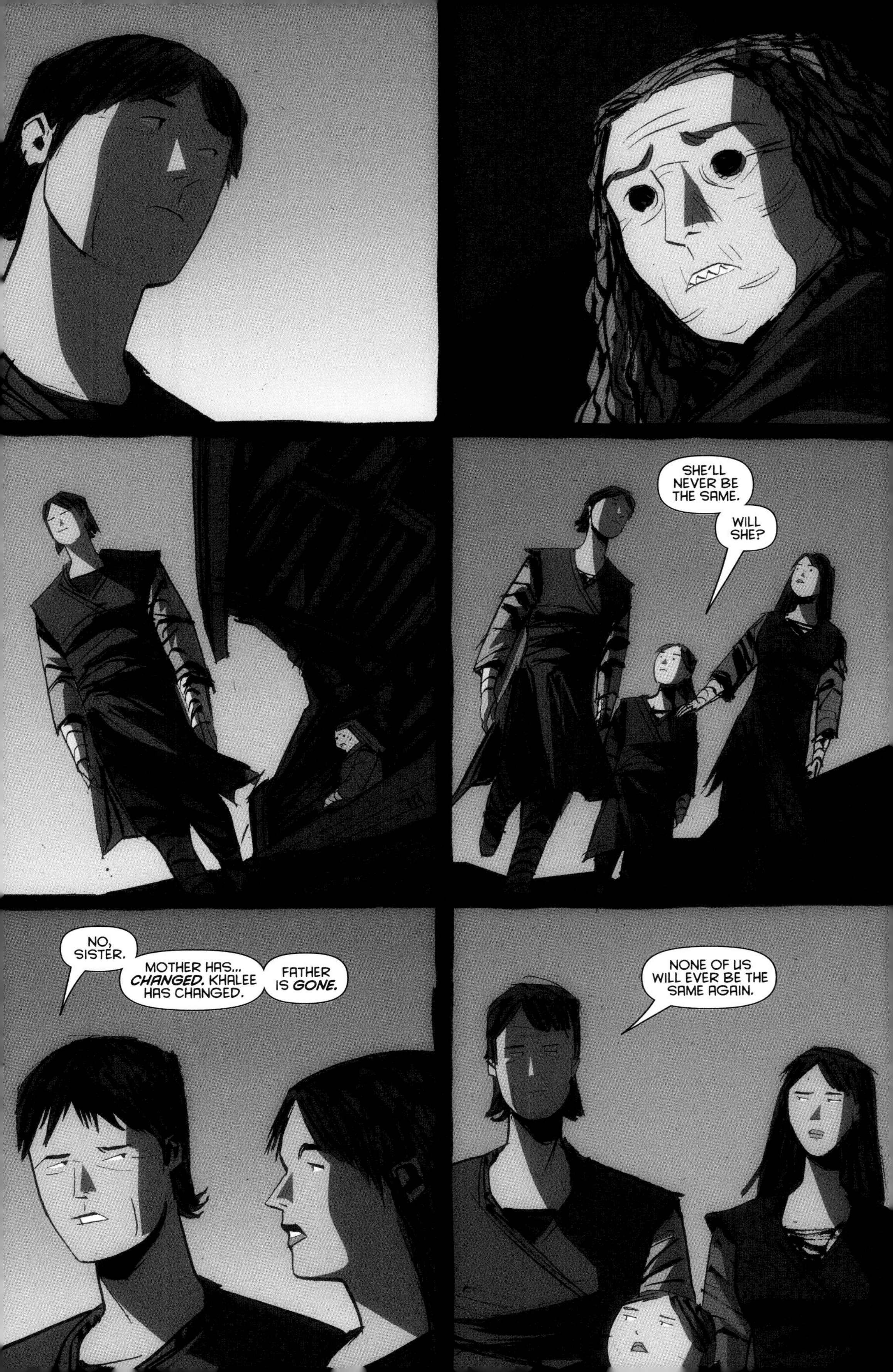
SHE'LL NEVER BE THE SAME.
WILL SHE?
NO, SISTER.
MOTHER HAS... CHANGED. KHALEE HAS CHANGED.
FATHER IS GONE.
NONE OF US WILL EVER BE THE SAME AGAIN.

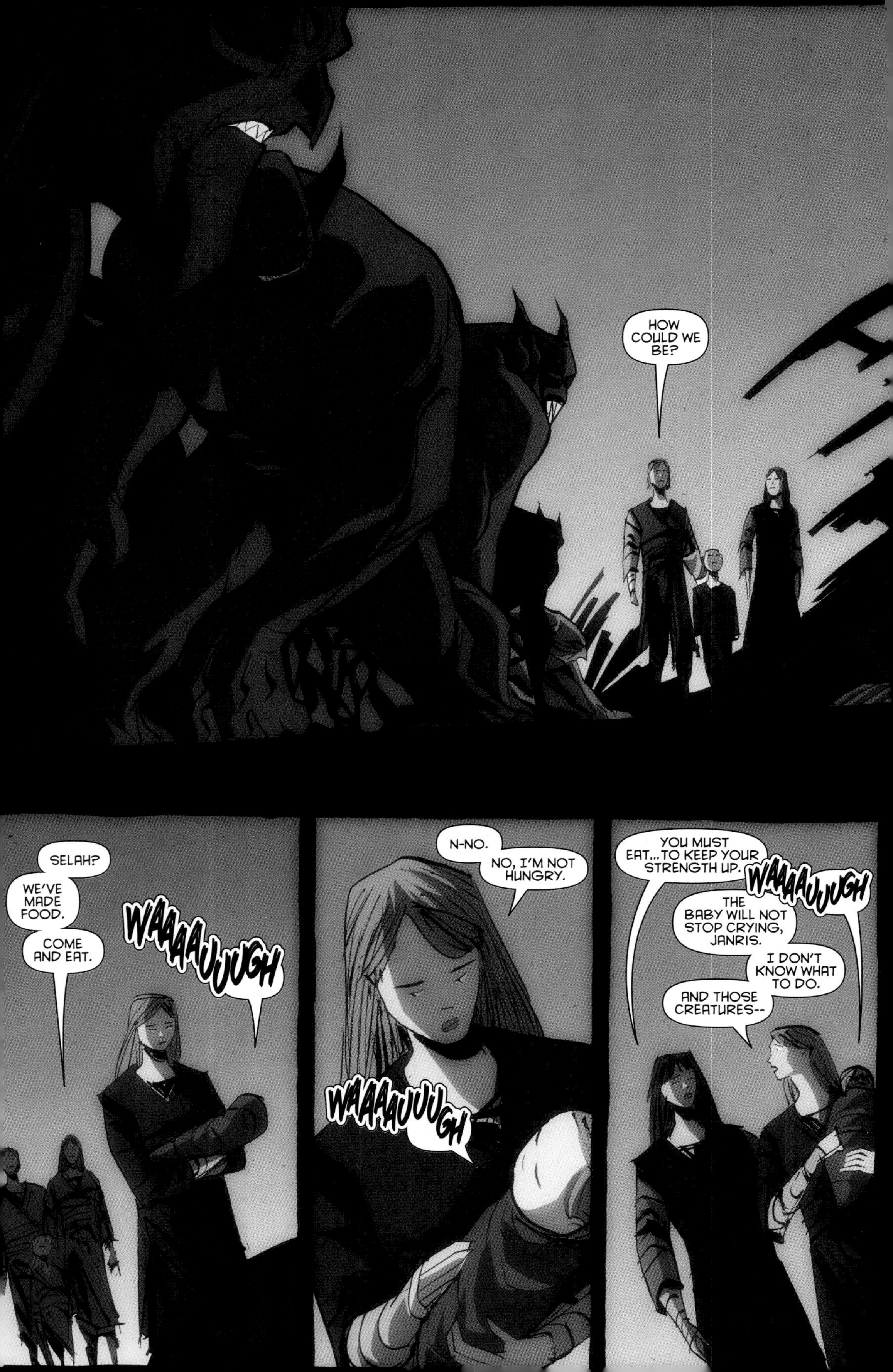
HOW COULD WE BE?
SELAH?
WE'VE MADE FOOD.
COME AND EAT.
WAAAAUUUGH
N-NO.
NO, I'M NOT HUNGRY.
WAAAAUUUGH
YOU MUST EAT... TO KEEP YOUR STRENGTH UP.
WAAAAUUUGH
THE BABY WILL NOT STOP CRYING, JANRIS.
I DON'T KNOW WHAT TO DO.
AND THOSE CREATURES--

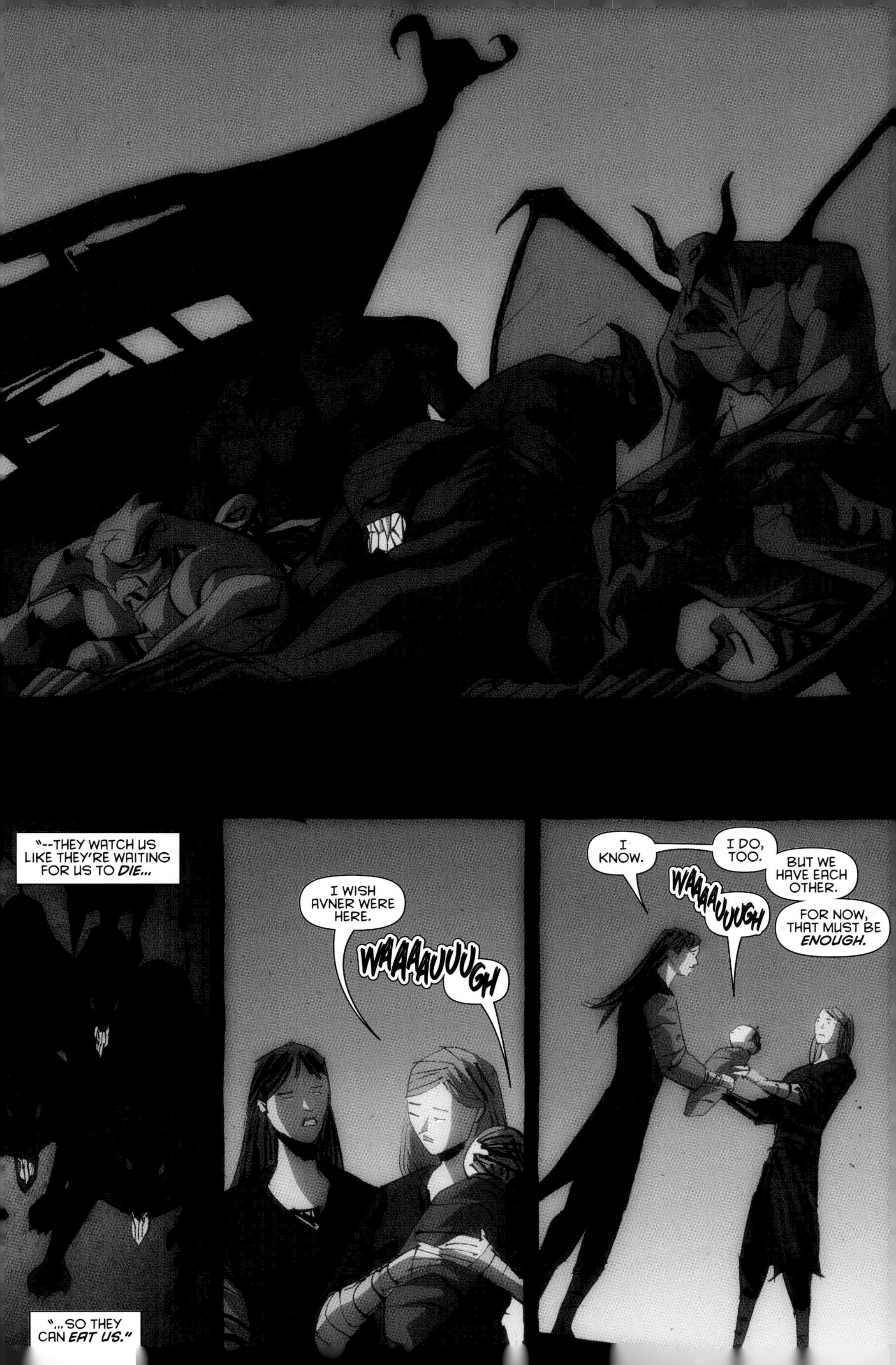
"--THEY WATCH US LIKE THEY'RE WAITING FOR US TO *DIE*...
"...SO THEY CAN *EAT US.*"
I WISH AVNER WERE HERE.
WAAAAUUUGH
I KNOW.
I DO, TOO.
WAAAAUUUGH
BUT WE HAVE EACH OTHER.
FOR NOW, THAT MUST BE *ENOUGH.*

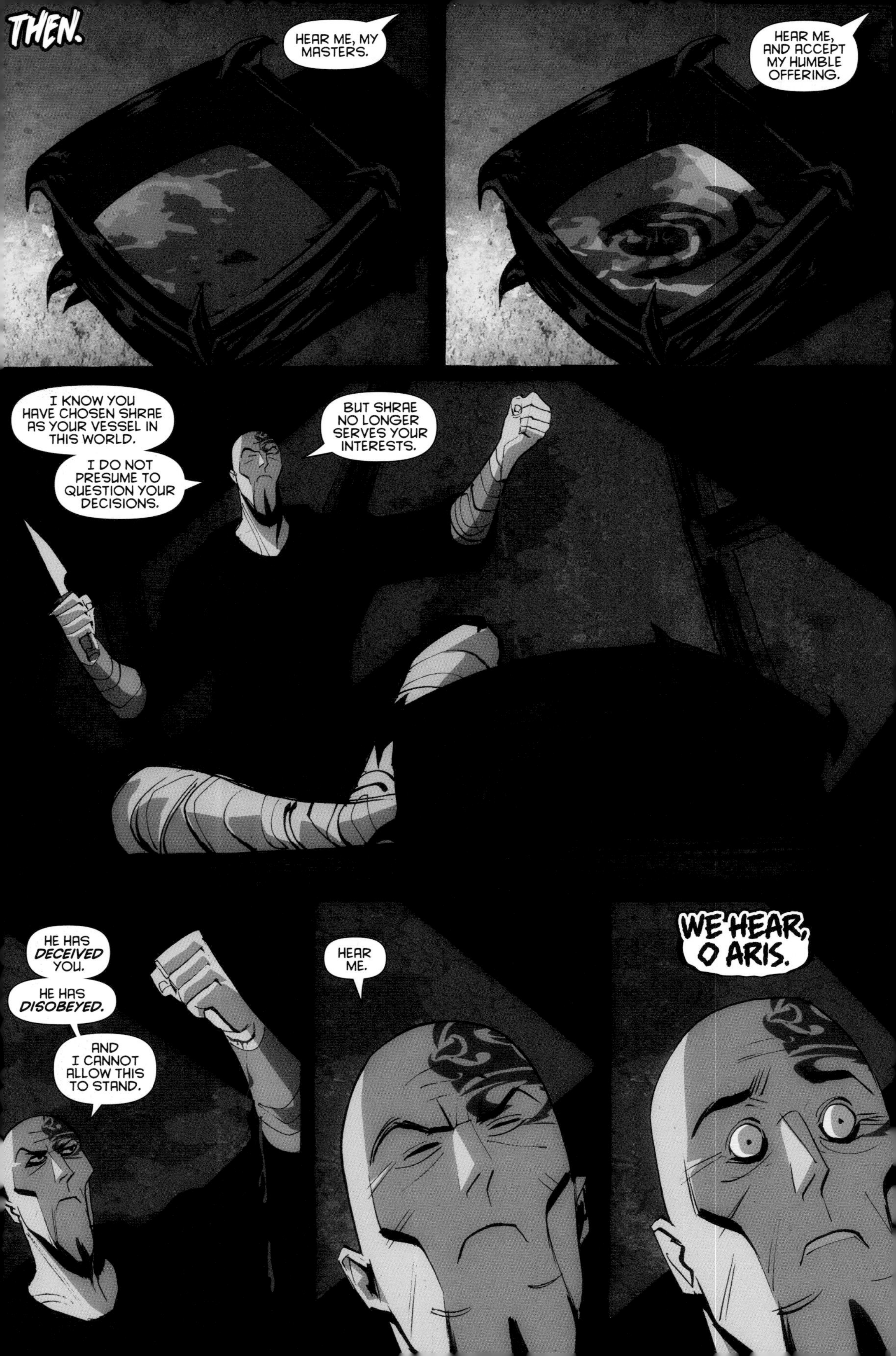
THEN.
HEAR ME, MY MASTERS.
HEAR ME, AND ACCEPT MY HUMBLE OFFERING.
I KNOW YOU HAVE CHOSEN SHRAE AS YOUR VESSEL IN THIS WORLD.
I DO NOT PRESUME TO QUESTION YOUR DECISIONS.
BUT SHRAE NO LONGER SERVES YOUR INTERESTS.
HE HAS *DECEIVED* YOU.
HE HAS *DISOBEYED.*
AND I CANNOT ALLOW THIS TO STAND.
HEAR ME.
WE HEAR, O ARIS.

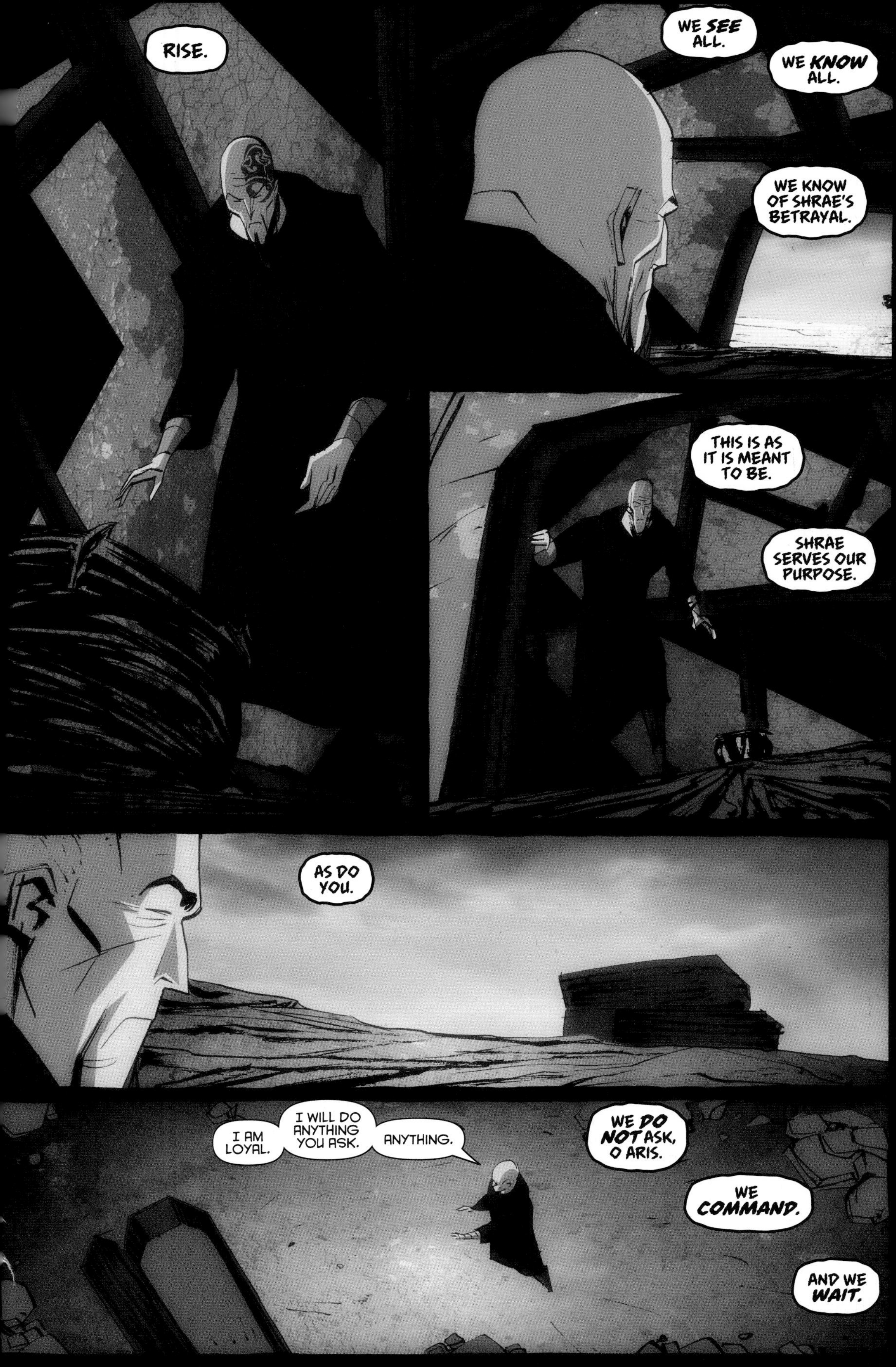
RISE.
WE SEE ALL.
WE KNOW ALL.
WE KNOW OF SHRAE'S BETRAYAL.
THIS IS AS IT IS MEANT TO BE.
SHRAE SERVES OUR PURPOSE.
AS DO YOU.
I AM LOYAL.
I WILL DO ANYTHING YOU ASK.
ANYTHING.
WE DO NOT ASK, O ARIS.
WE COMMAND.
AND WE WAIT.

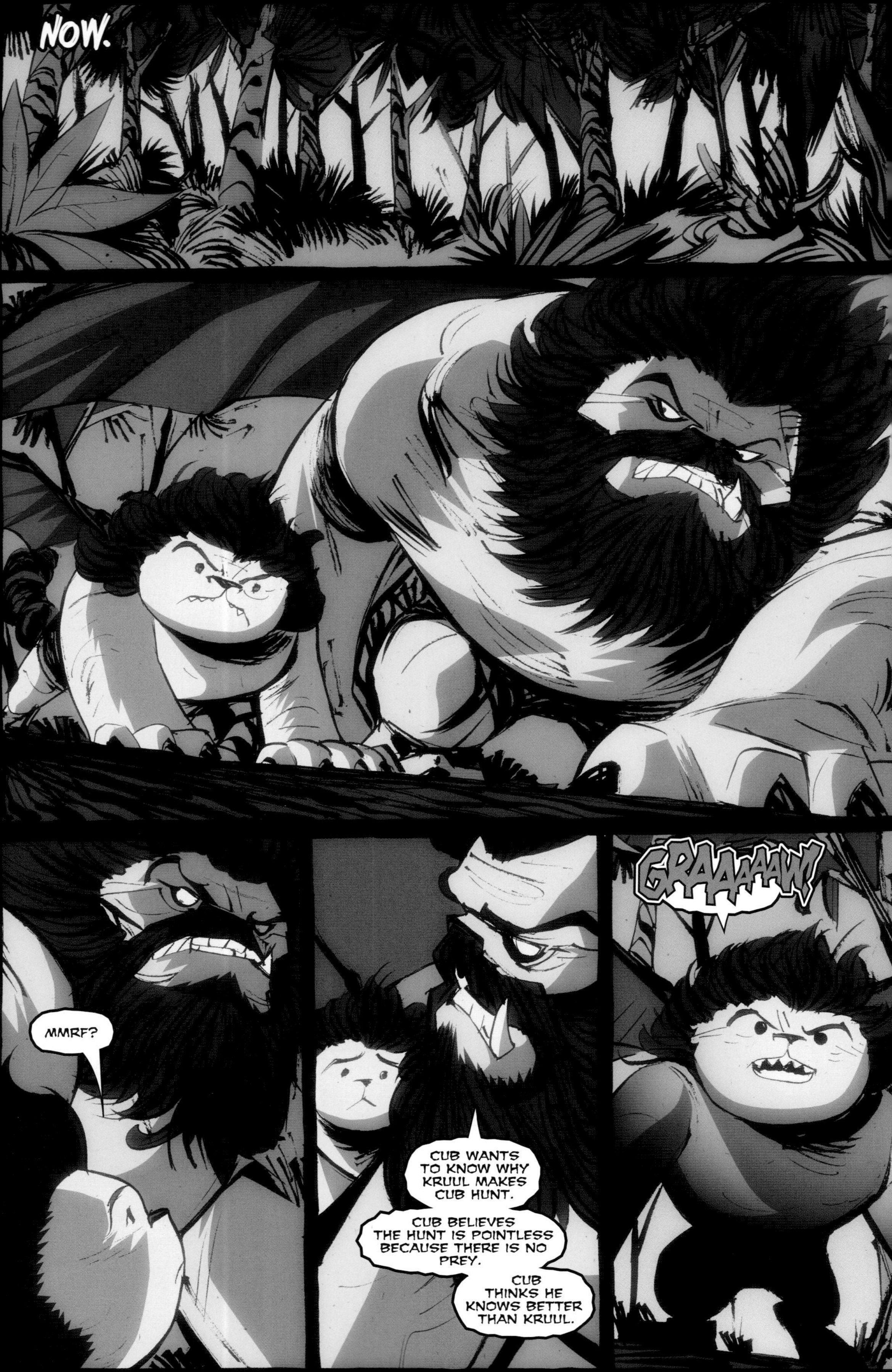
NOW.
MMRF?
CUB WANTS TO KNOW WHY KRUUL MAKES CUB HUNT.
CUB BELIEVES THE HUNT IS POINTLESS BECAUSE THERE IS NO PREY.
CUB THINKS HE KNOWS BETTER THAN KRUUL.
GRAAAAAW!

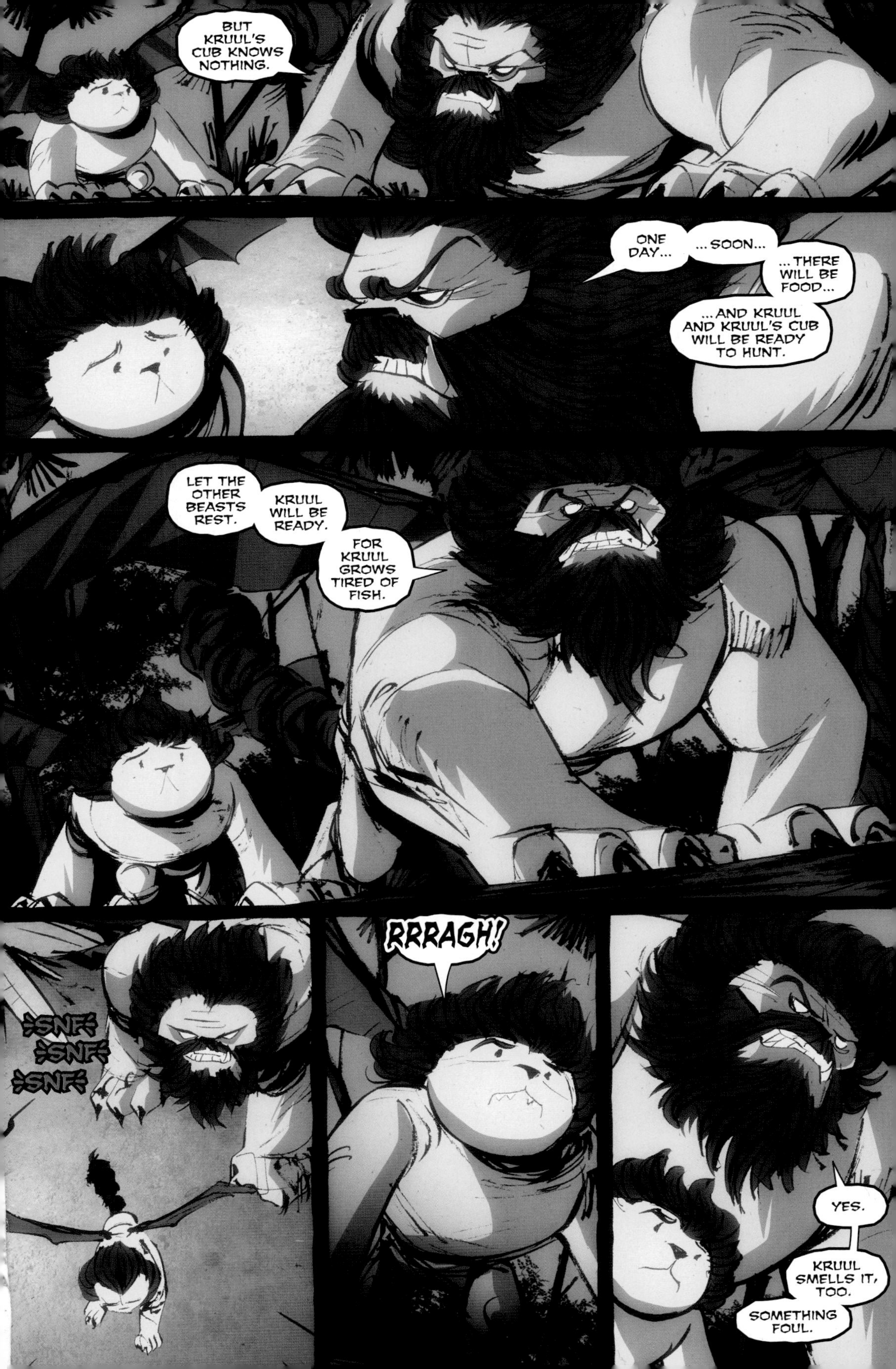
BUT KRUUL'S CUB KNOWS NOTHING.
ONE DAY...
...SOON...
...THERE WILL BE FOOD...
...AND KRUUL AND KRUUL'S CUB WILL BE READY TO HUNT.
LET THE OTHER BEASTS REST.
KRUUL WILL BE READY.
FOR KRUUL GROWS TIRED OF FISH.
SNF
SNF
SNF
RRRAGH!
YES.
KRUUL SMELLS IT, TOO.
SOMETHING FOUL.

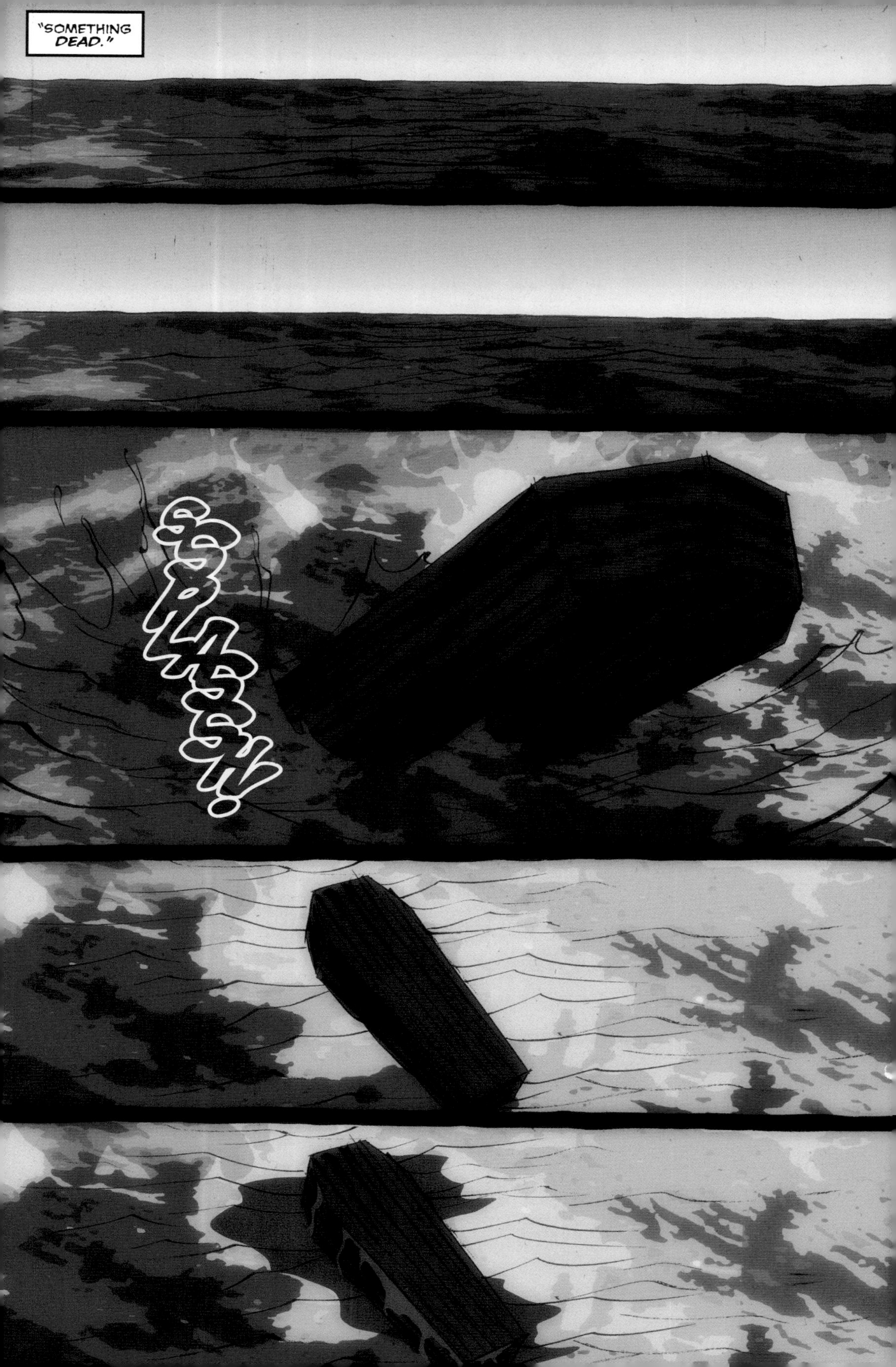
"SOMETHING DEAD."
SPLASH!

4

WONDERFUL THINGS

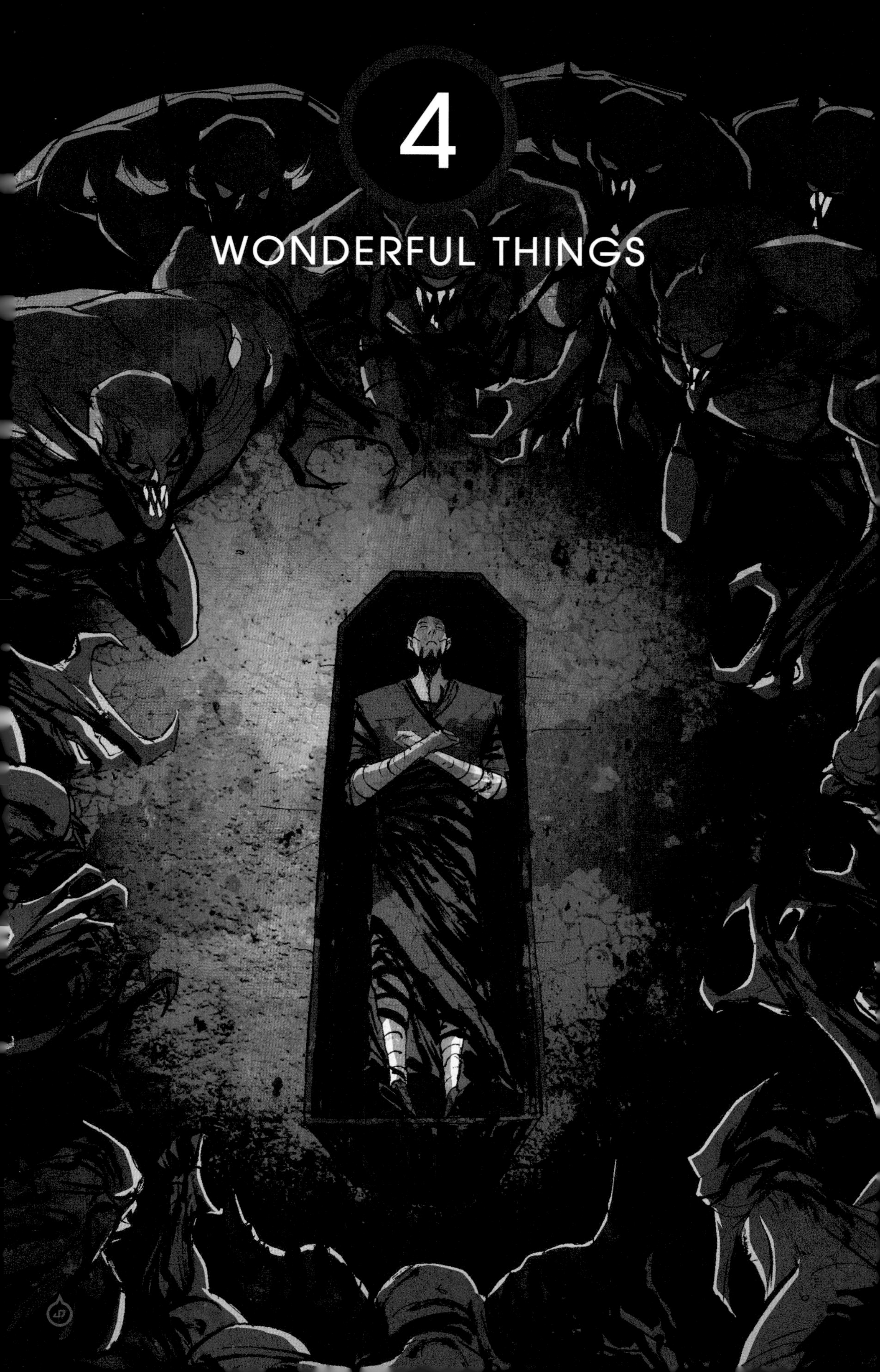

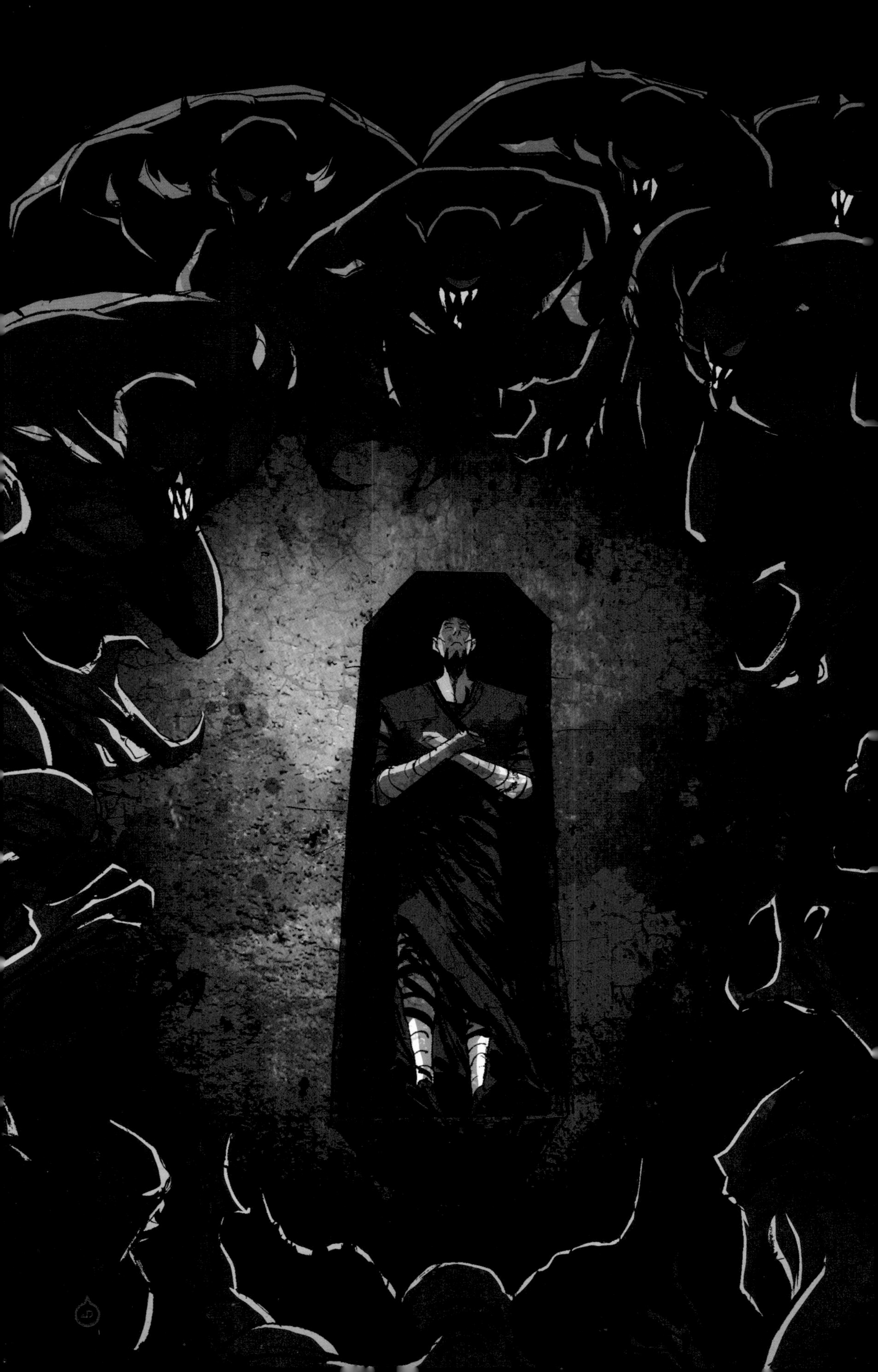

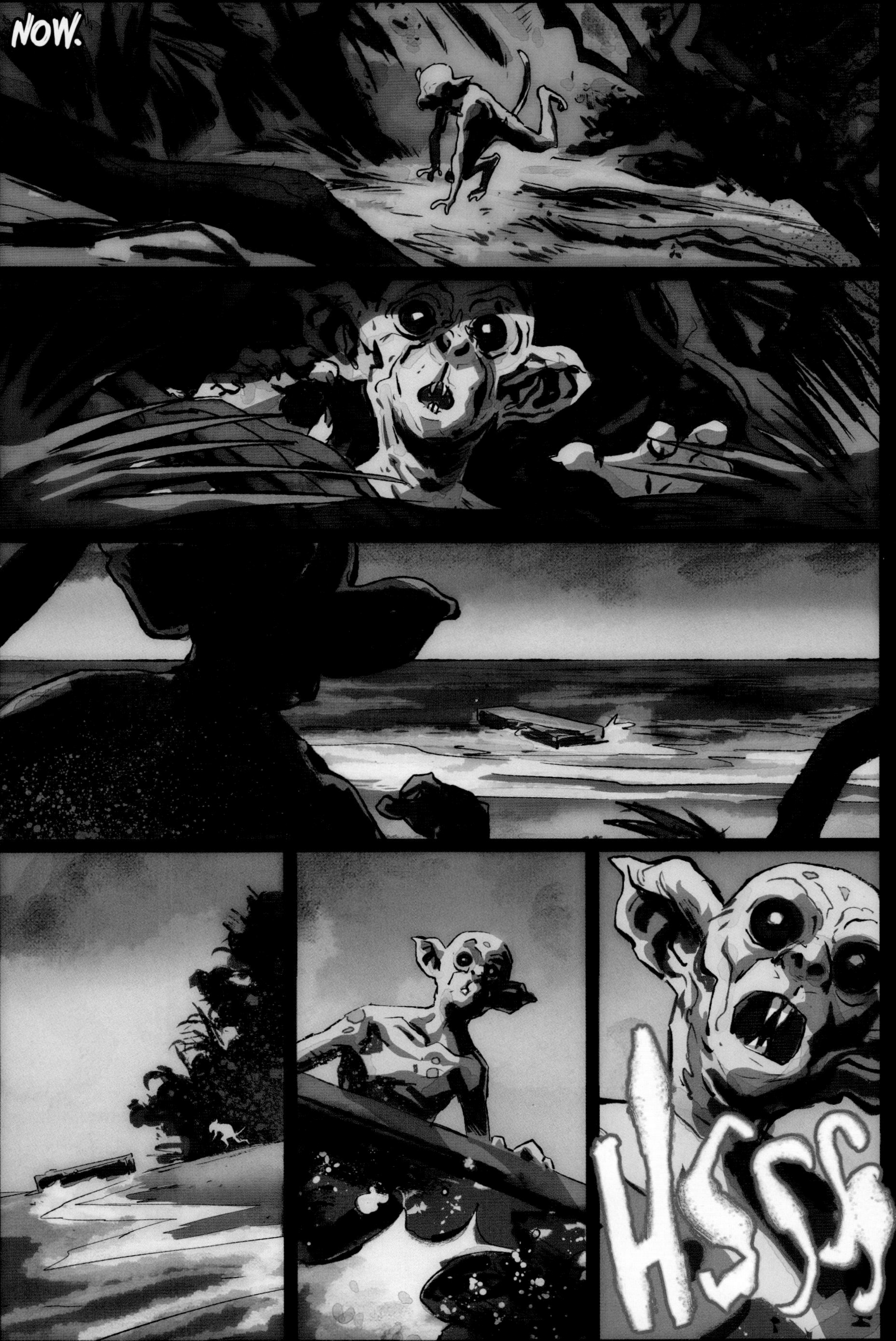
NOW.
HSSS

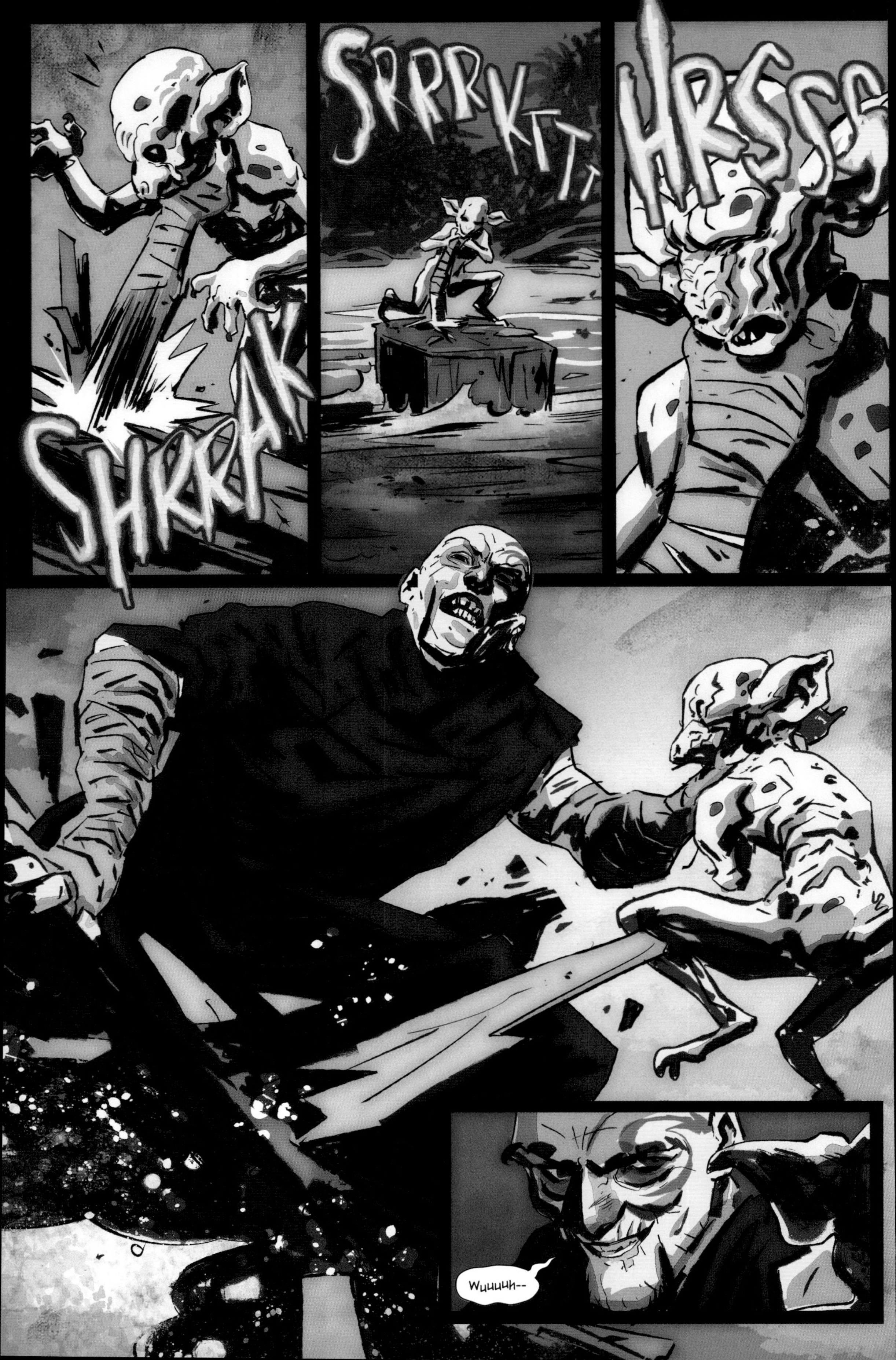
SHRRAK
SRRRKTTT
HRSSS
Wuuuuh--

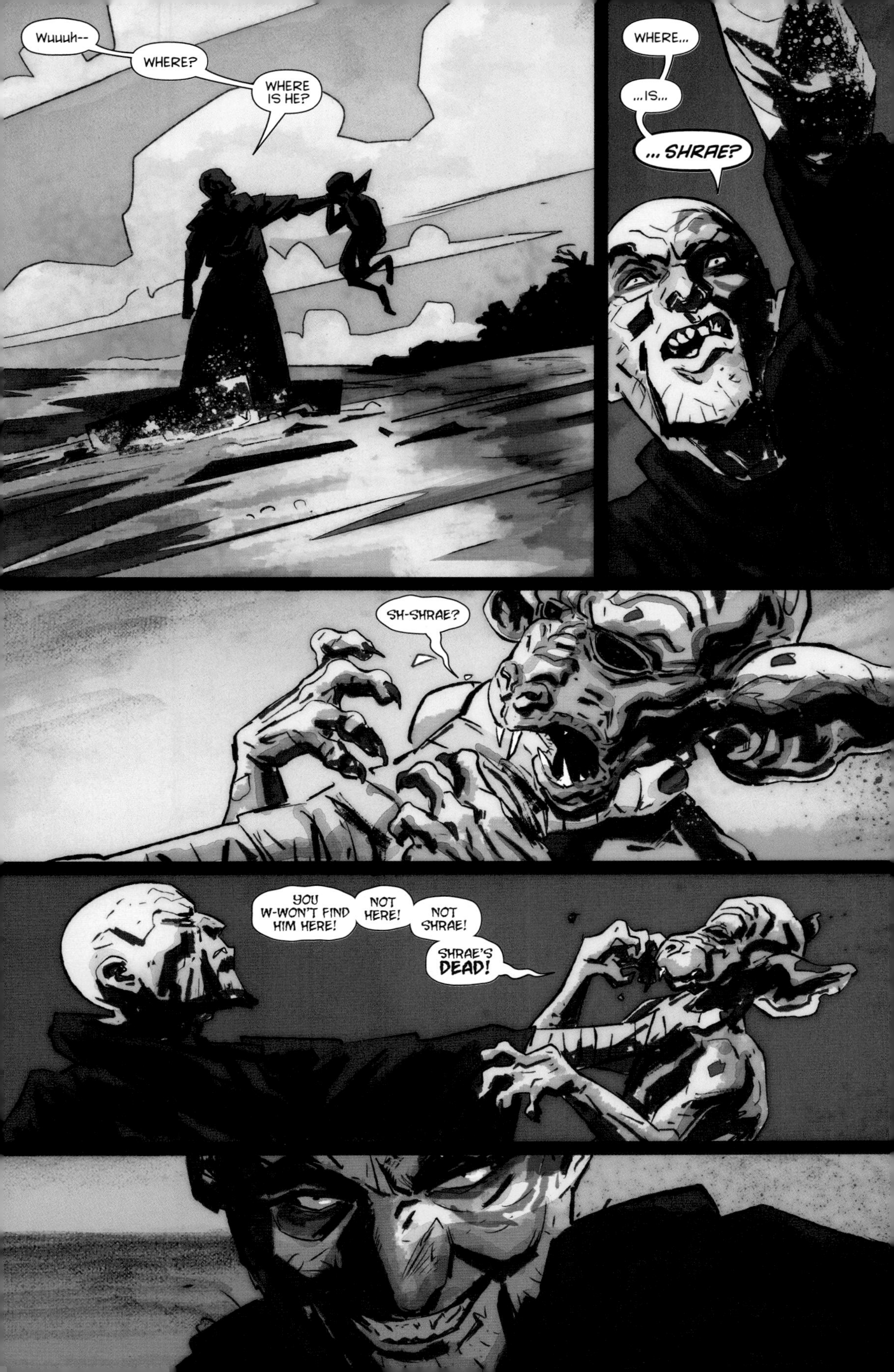
Wuuuh--
WHERE?
WHERE IS HE?
WHERE...
...IS...
... SHRAE?
SH-SHRAE?
YOU W-WON'T FIND HIM HERE!
NOT HERE!
NOT SHRAE!
SHRAE'S DEAD!

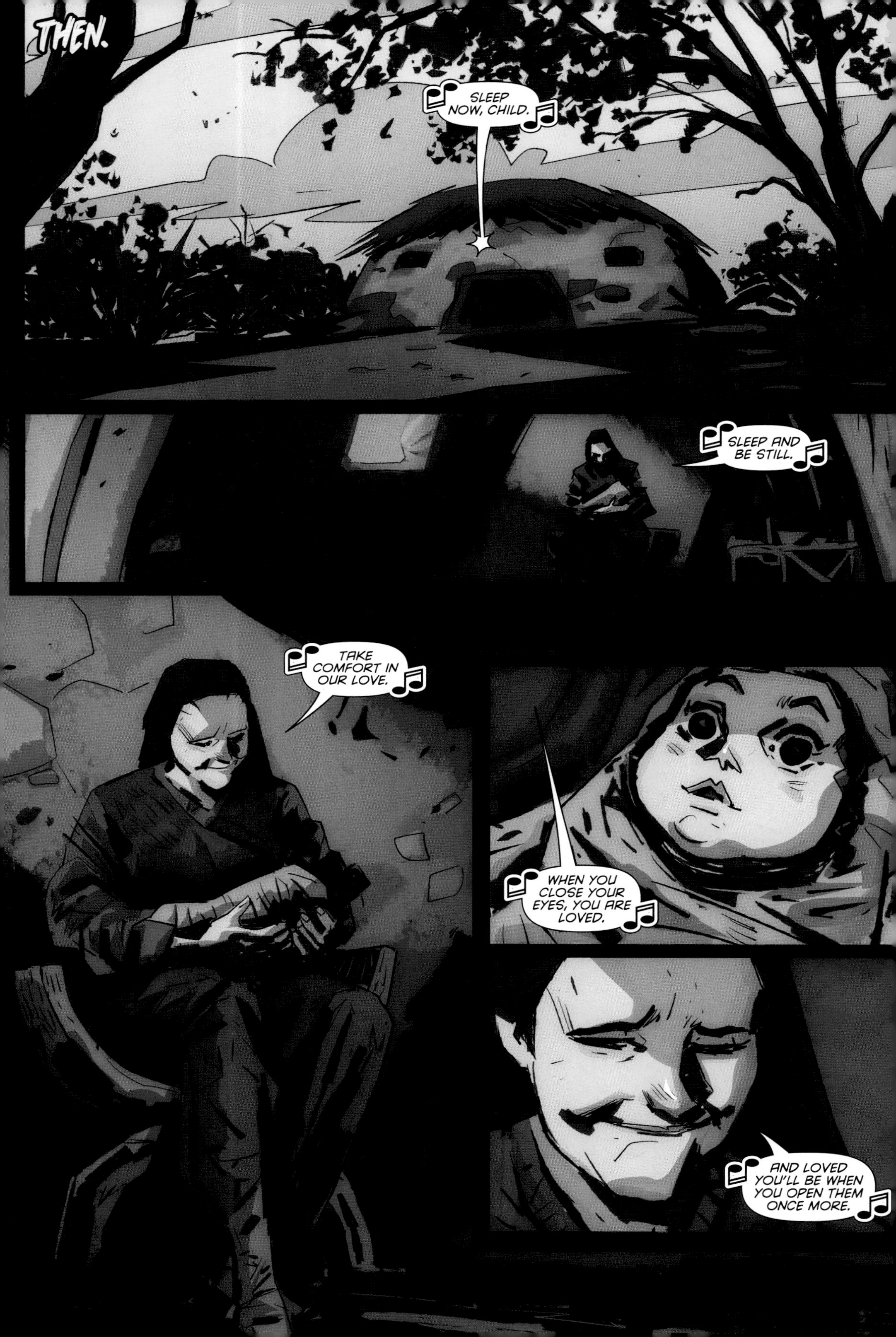
THEN.
SLEEP NOW, CHILD.
SLEEP AND BE STILL.
TAKE COMFORT IN OUR LOVE.
WHEN YOU CLOSE YOUR EYES, YOU ARE LOVED.
AND LOVED YOU'LL BE WHEN YOU OPEN THEM ONCE MORE.

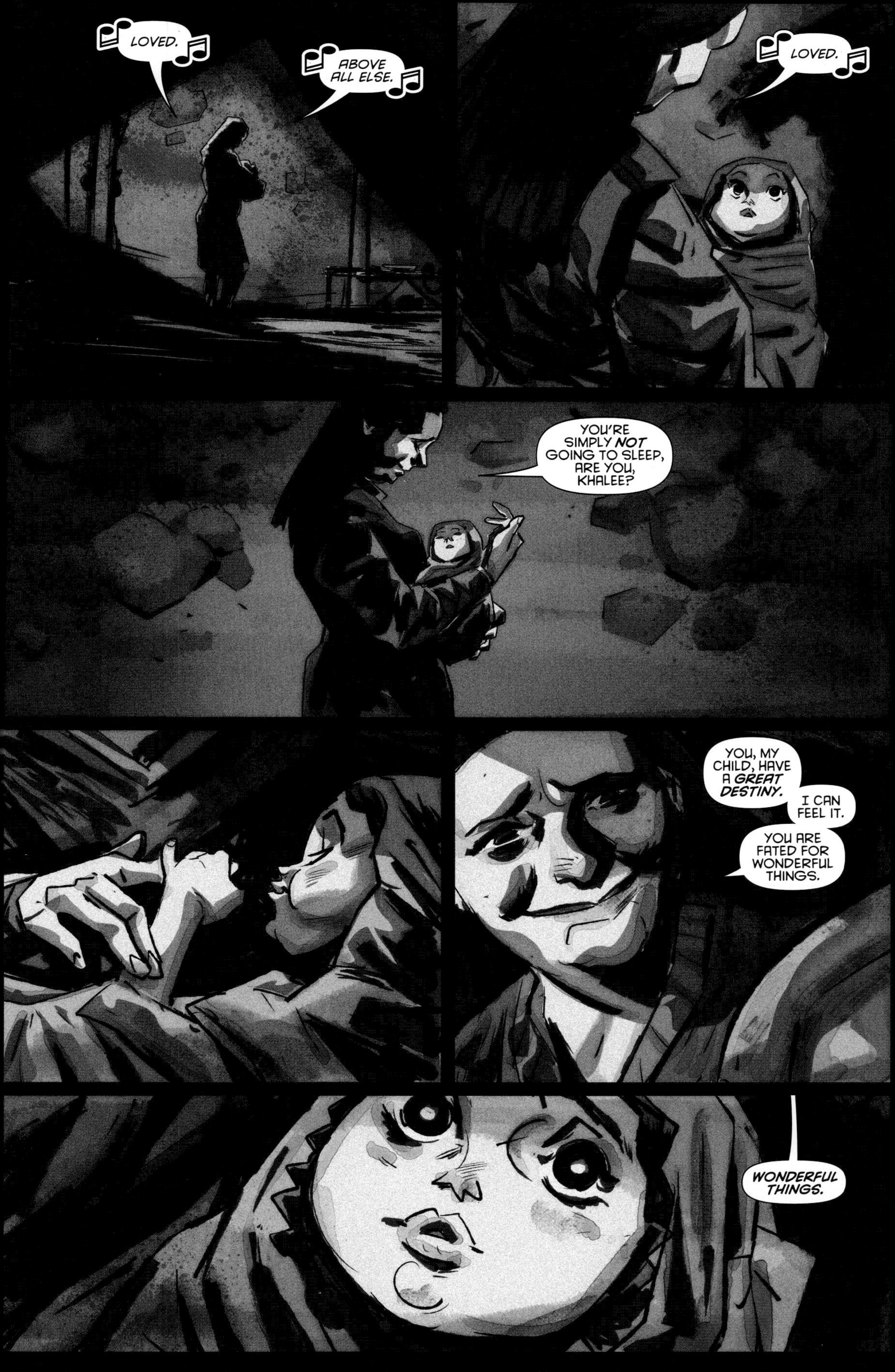
LOVED.
ABOVE ALL ELSE.
LOVED.
YOU'RE SIMPLY NOT GOING TO SLEEP, ARE YOU, KHALEE?
YOU, MY CHILD, HAVE A GREAT DESTINY.
I CAN FEEL IT.
YOU ARE FATED FOR WONDERFUL THINGS.
WONDERFUL THINGS.

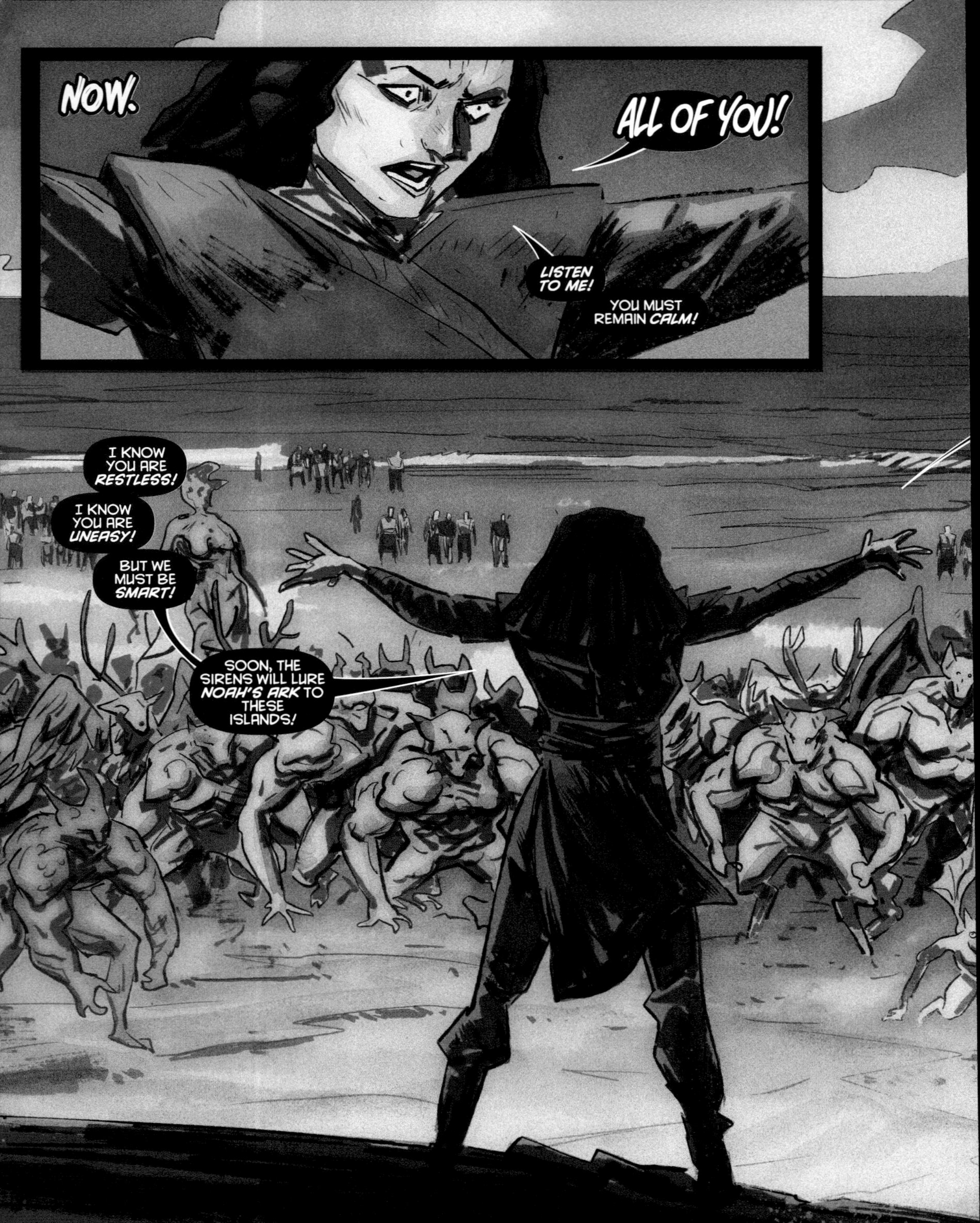
NOW.
ALL OF YOU!
LISTEN TO ME!
YOU MUST REMAIN CALM!
I KNOW YOU ARE RESTLESS!
I KNOW YOU ARE UNEASY!
BUT WE MUST BE SMART!
SOON, THE SIRENS WILL LURE NOAH'S ARK TO THESE ISLANDS!

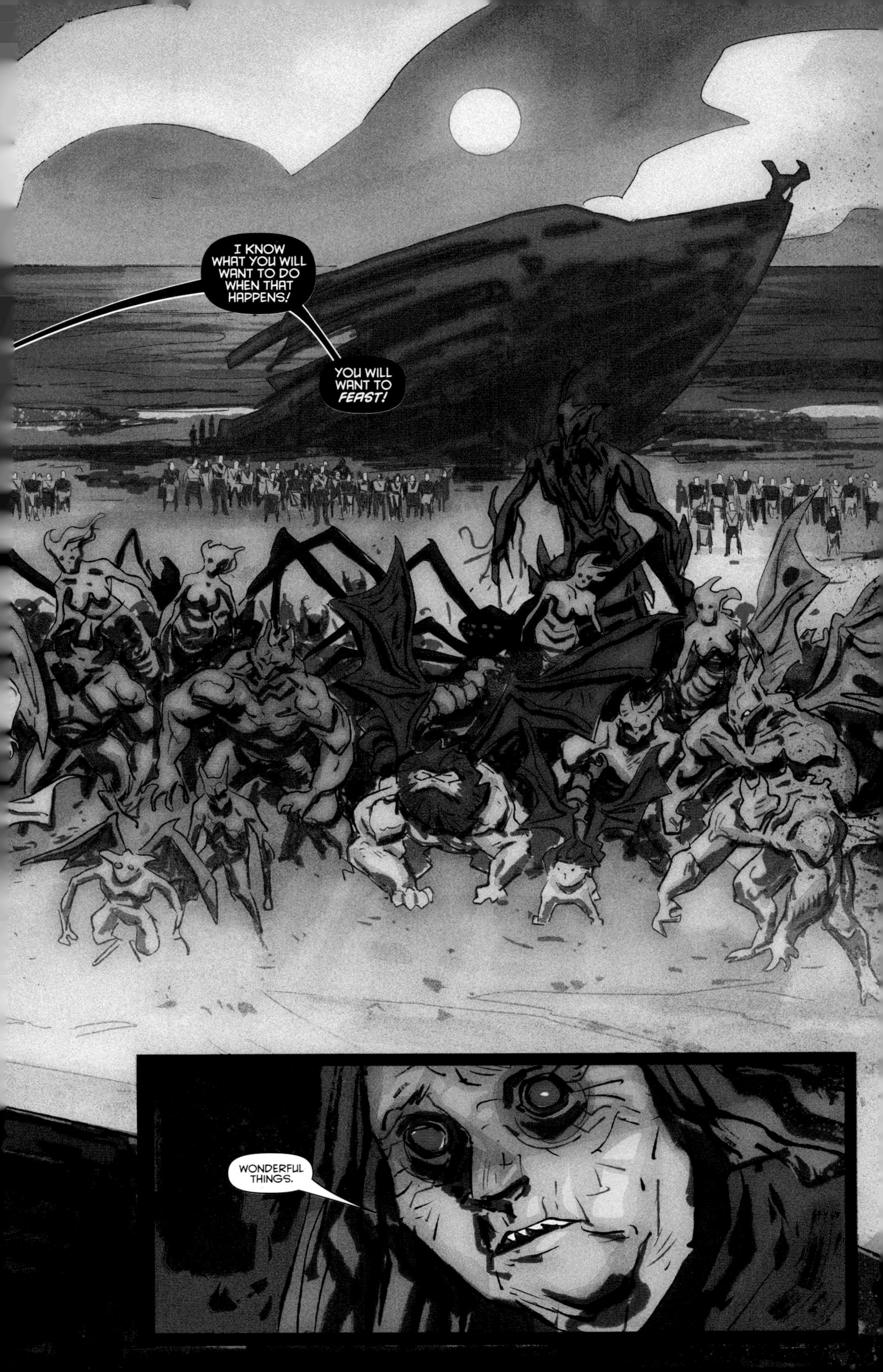
I KNOW WHAT YOU WILL WANT TO DO WHEN THAT HAPPENS!
YOU WILL WANT TO FEAST!
WONDERFUL THINGS.

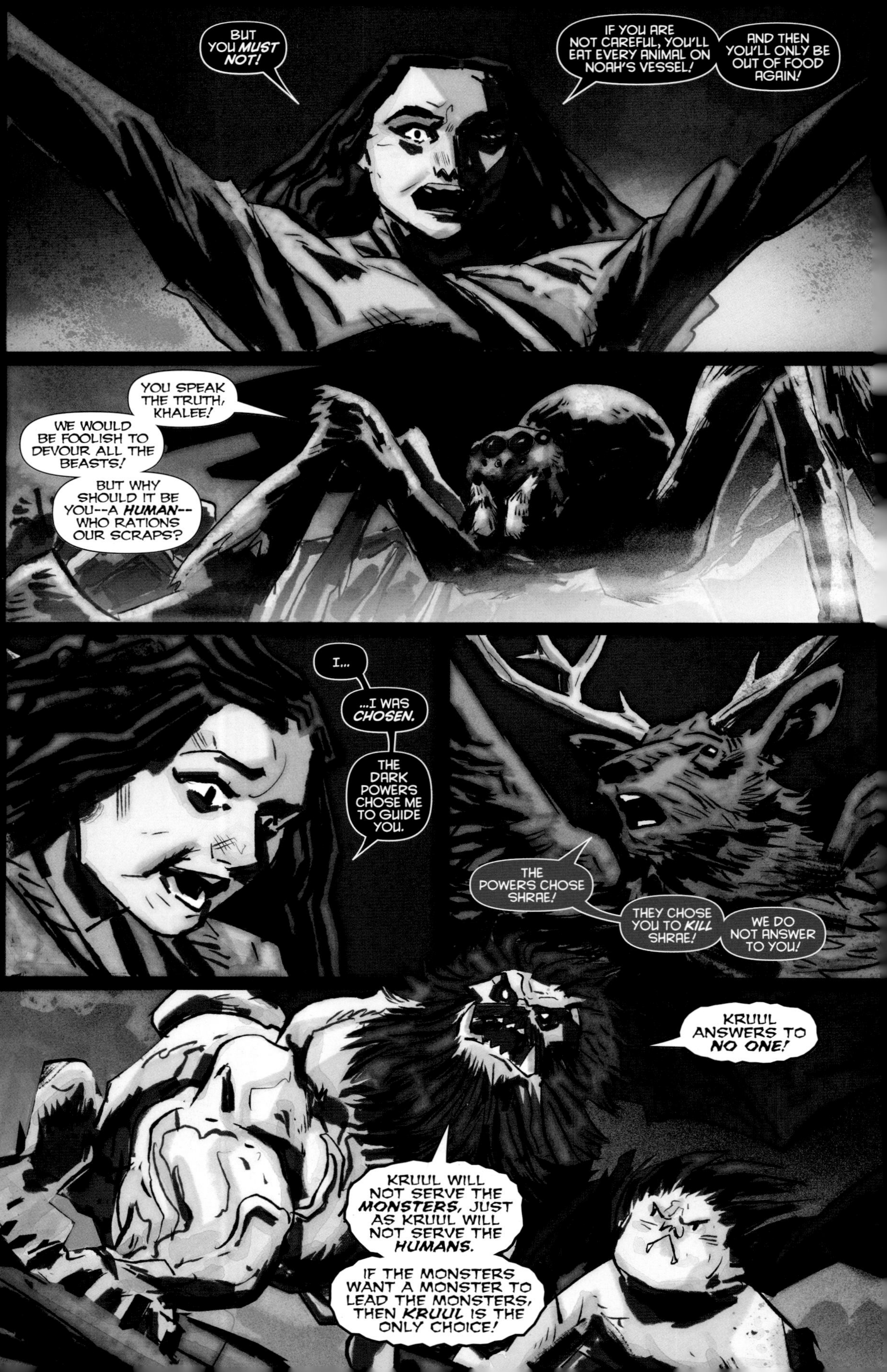
BUT YOU MUST NOT!
IF YOU ARE NOT CAREFUL, YOU'LL EAT EVERY ANIMAL ON NOAH'S VESSEL!
AND THEN YOU'LL ONLY BE OUT OF FOOD AGAIN!
YOU SPEAK THE TRUTH, KHALEE!
WE WOULD BE FOOLISH TO DEVOUR ALL THE BEASTS!
BUT WHY SHOULD IT BE YOU--A HUMAN--WHO RATIONS OUR SCRAPS?
I...
...I WAS CHOSEN.
THE DARK POWERS CHOSE ME TO GUIDE YOU.
THE POWERS CHOSE SHRAE!
THEY CHOSE YOU TO KILL SHRAE!
WE DO NOT ANSWER TO YOU!
KRUUL ANSWERS TO NO ONE!
KRUUL WILL NOT SERVE THE MONSTERS, JUST AS KRUUL WILL NOT SERVE THE HUMANS.
IF THE MONSTERS WANT A MONSTER TO LEAD THE MONSTERS, THEN KRUUL IS THE ONLY CHOICE!

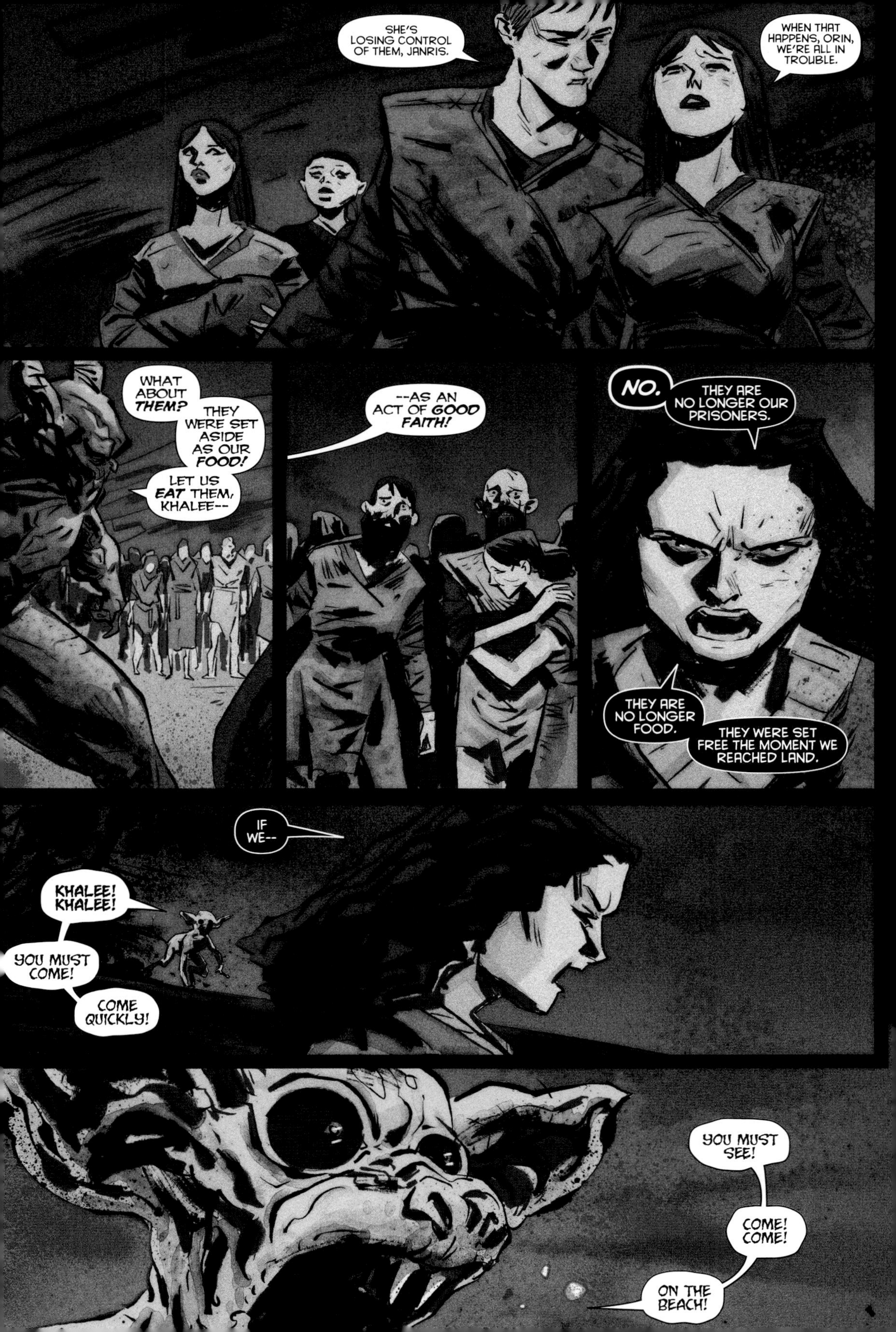
SHE'S LOSING CONTROL OF THEM, JANRIS.
WHEN THAT HAPPENS, ORIN, WE'RE ALL IN TROUBLE.
WHAT ABOUT THEM?
THEY WERE SET ASIDE AS OUR FOOD!
LET US EAT THEM, KHALEE--
--AS AN ACT OF GOOD FAITH!
NO.
THEY ARE NO LONGER OUR PRISONERS.
THEY ARE NO LONGER FOOD.
THEY WERE SET FREE THE MOMENT WE REACHED LAND.
IF WE--
KHALEE! KHALEE!
YOU MUST COME!
COME QUICKLY!
YOU MUST SEE!
COME! COME!
ON THE BEACH!

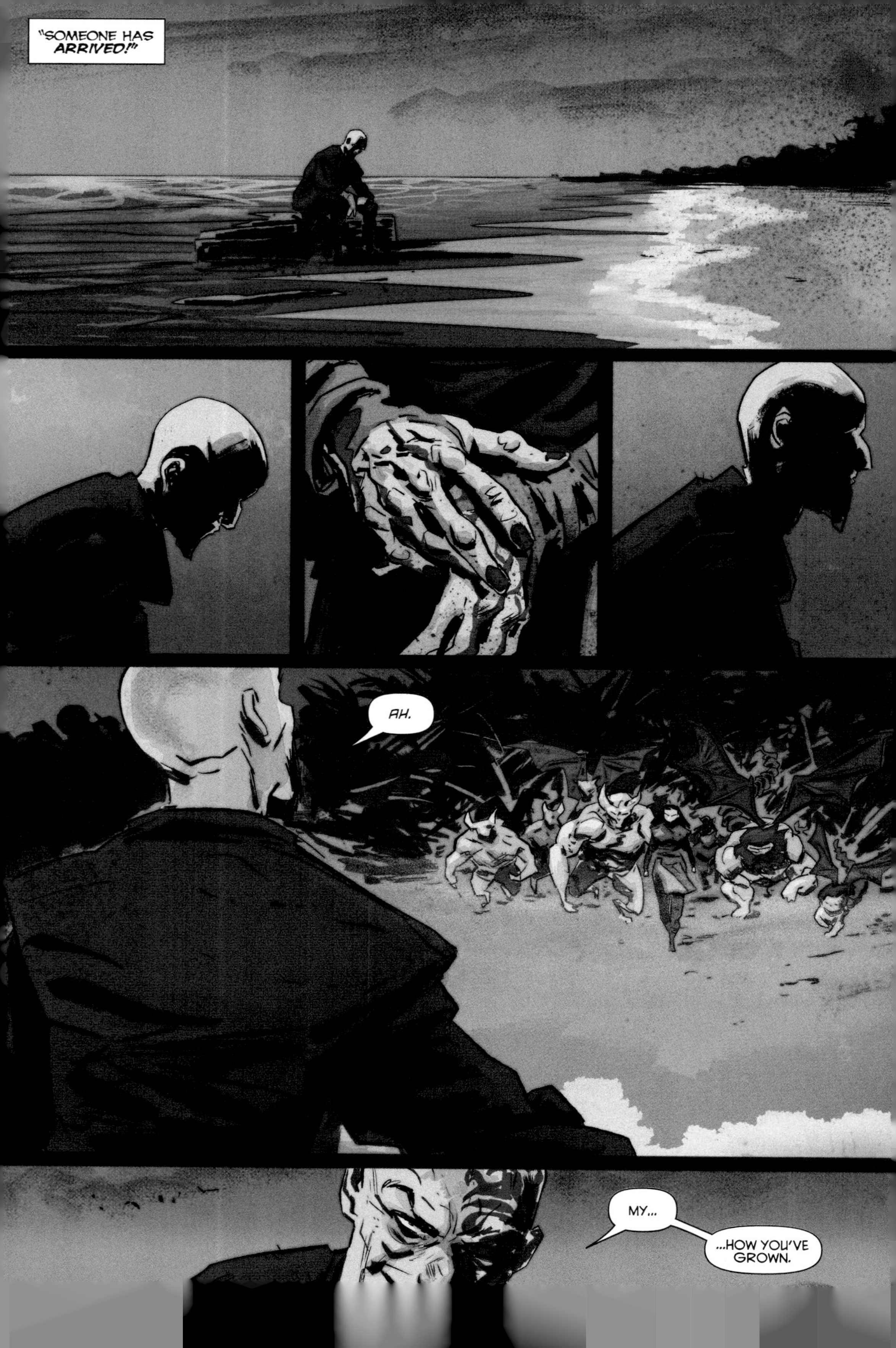
"SOMEONE HAS ARRIVED!"
AH.
MY...
...HOW YOU'VE GROWN.

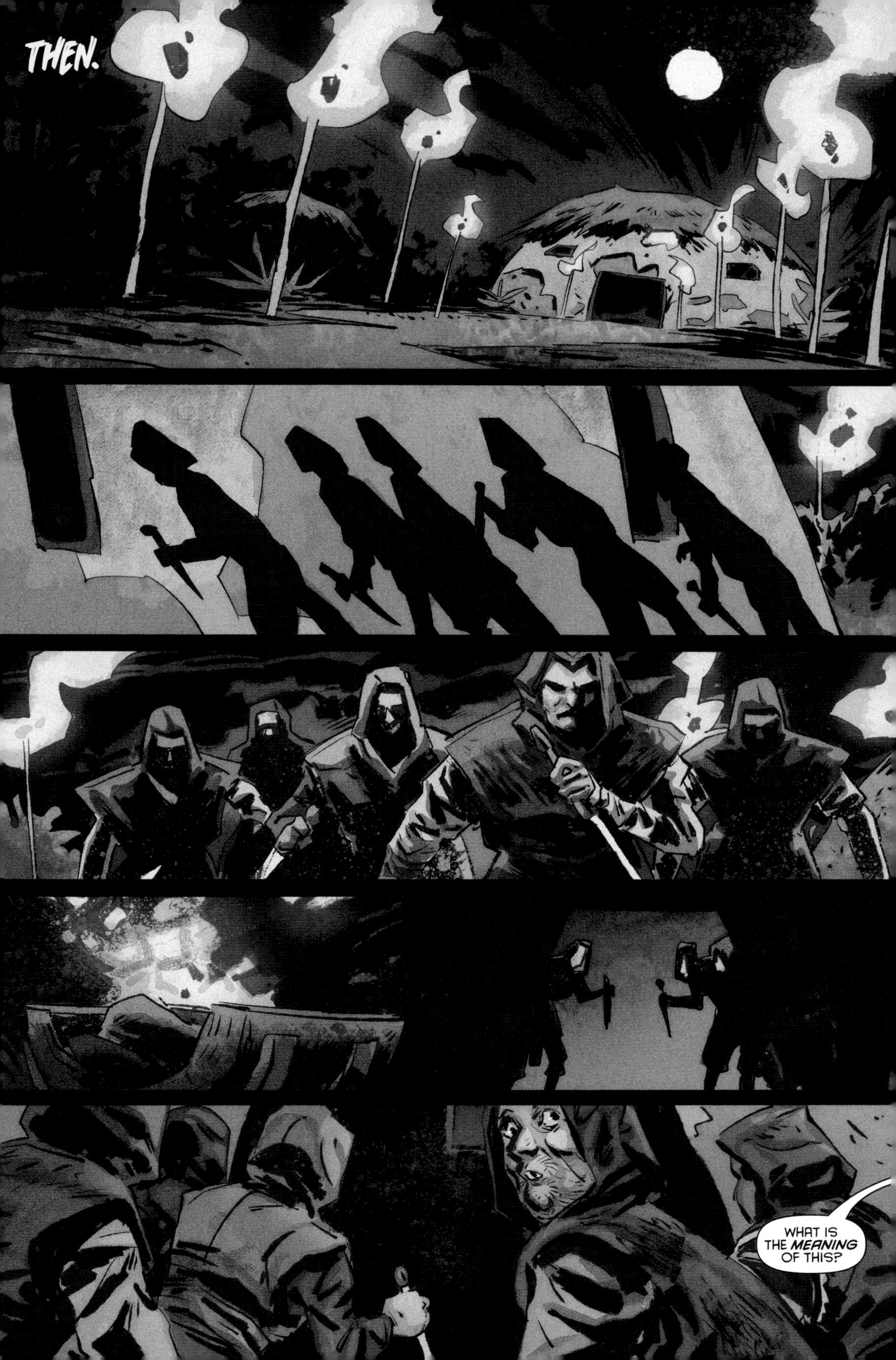
THEN.
WHAT IS THE MEANING OF THIS?

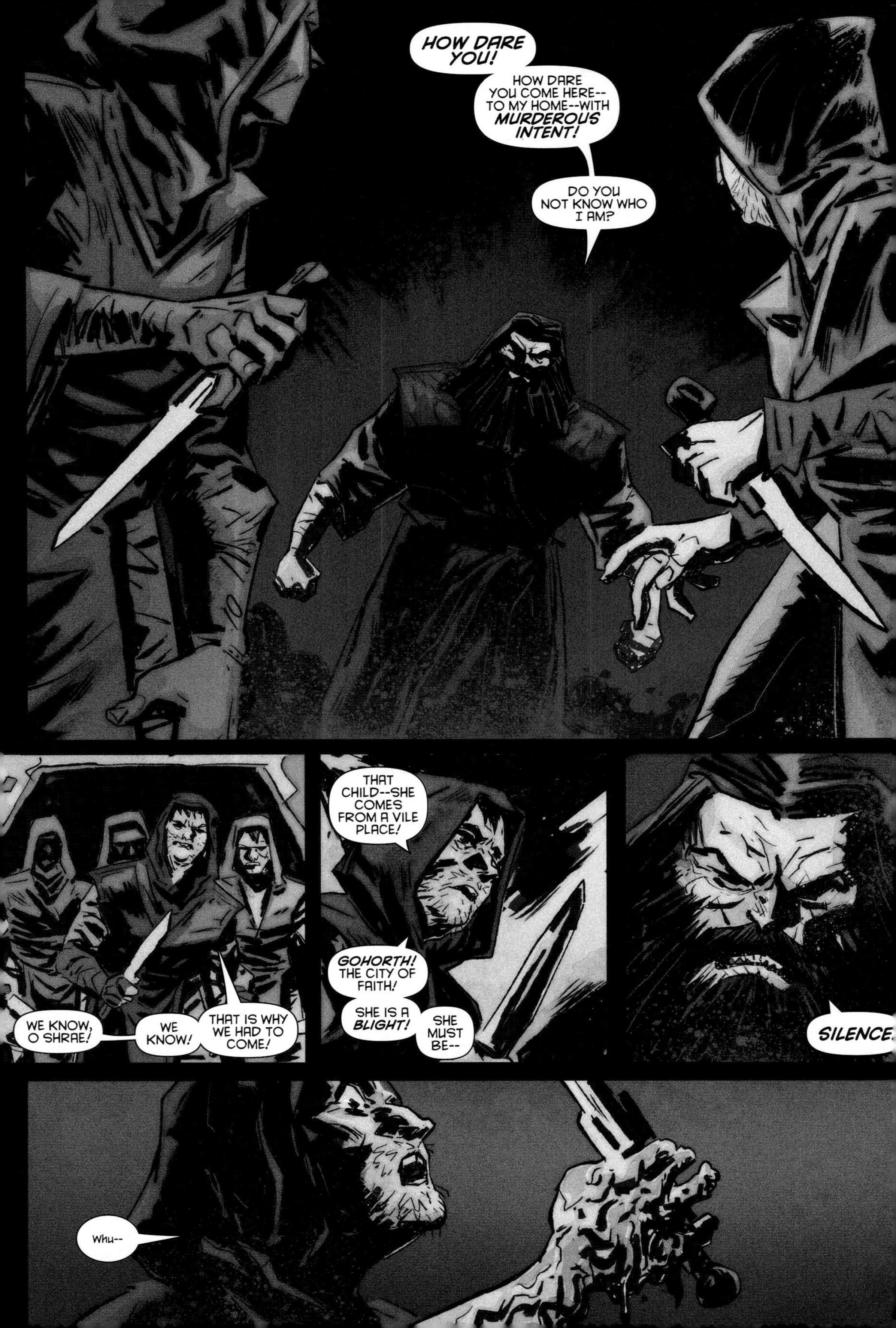
HOW DARE YOU!
HOW DARE YOU COME HERE-- TO MY HOME--WITH MURDEROUS INTENT!
DO YOU NOT KNOW WHO I AM?
WE KNOW, O SHRAE!
WE KNOW!
THAT IS WHY WE HAD TO COME!
THAT CHILD--SHE COMES FROM A VILE PLACE!
GOHORTH! THE CITY OF FAITH!
SHE IS A BLIGHT!
SHE MUST BE--
SILENCE.
Whu--

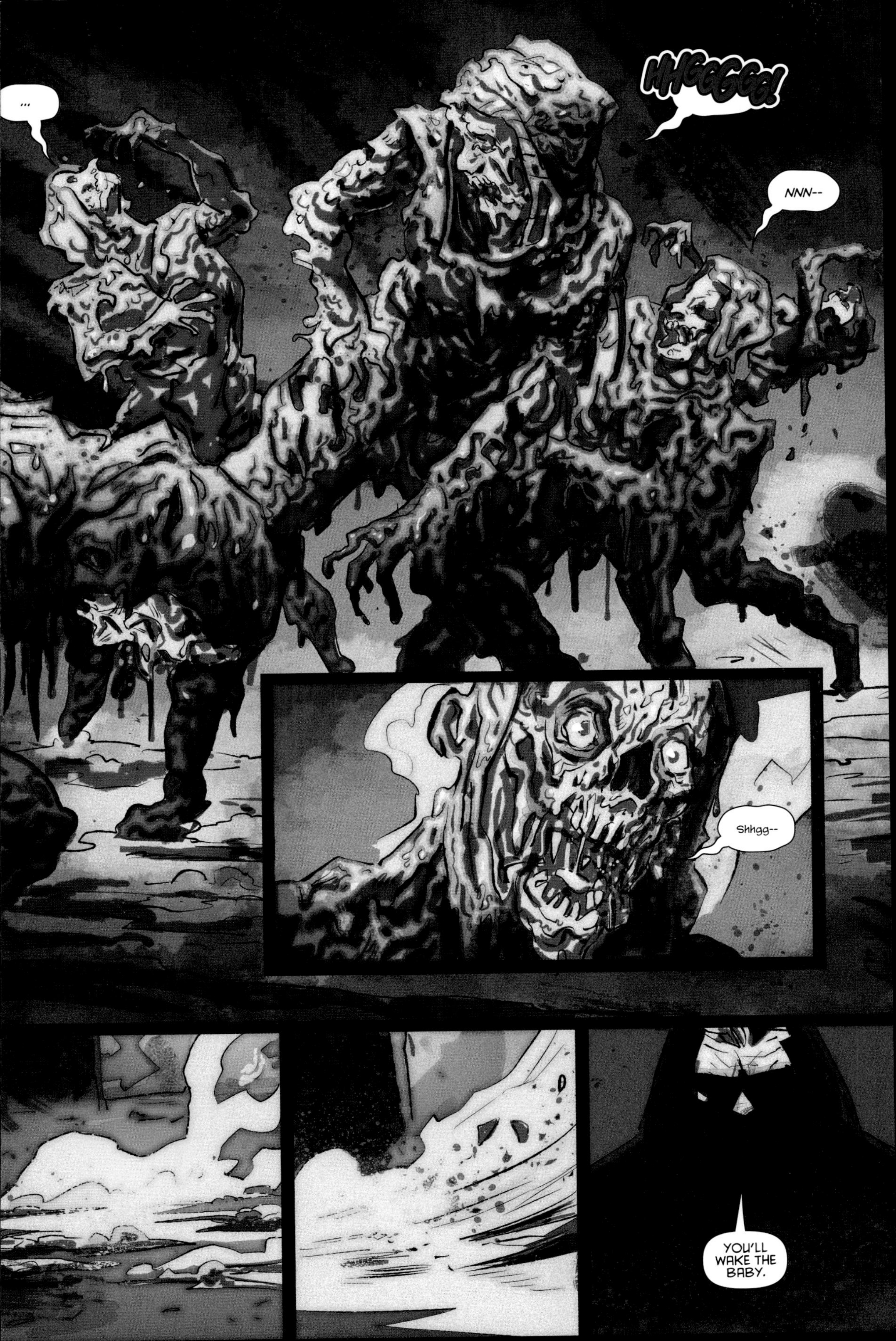
...
HHGGGGG!
NNN--
Shhgg--
YOU'LL WAKE THE BABY.

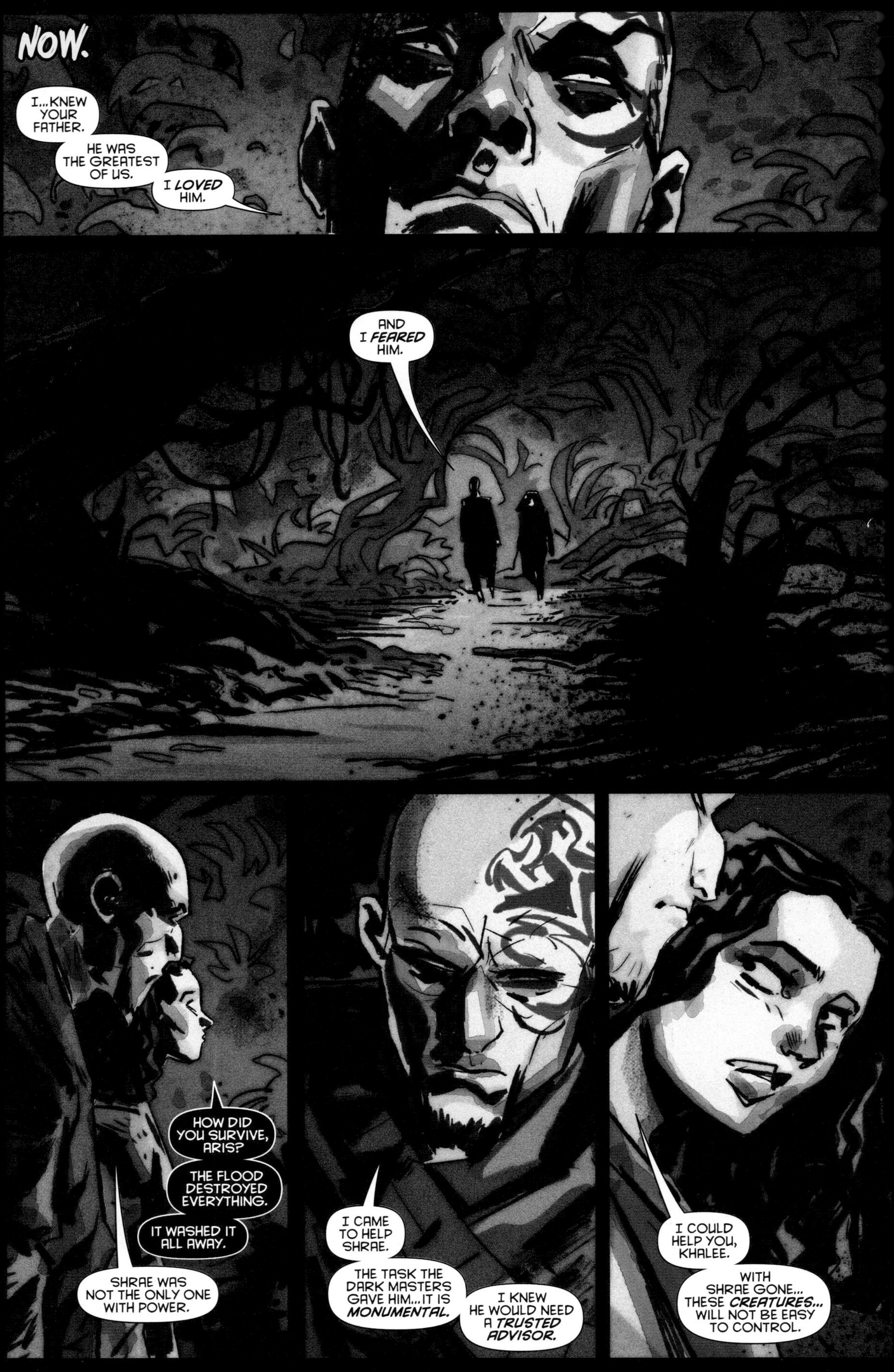
NOW.
I...KNEW YOUR FATHER.
HE WAS THE GREATEST OF US.
I LOVED HIM.
AND I FEARED HIM.
HOW DID YOU SURVIVE, ARIS?
THE FLOOD DESTROYED EVERYTHING.
IT WASHED IT ALL AWAY.
SHRAE WAS NOT THE ONLY ONE WITH POWER.
I CAME TO HELP SHRAE.
THE TASK THE DARK MASTERS GAVE HIM...IT IS MONUMENTAL.
I KNEW HE WOULD NEED A TRUSTED ADVISOR.
I COULD HELP YOU, KHALEE.
WITH SHRAE GONE... THESE CREATURES... WILL NOT BE EASY TO CONTROL.

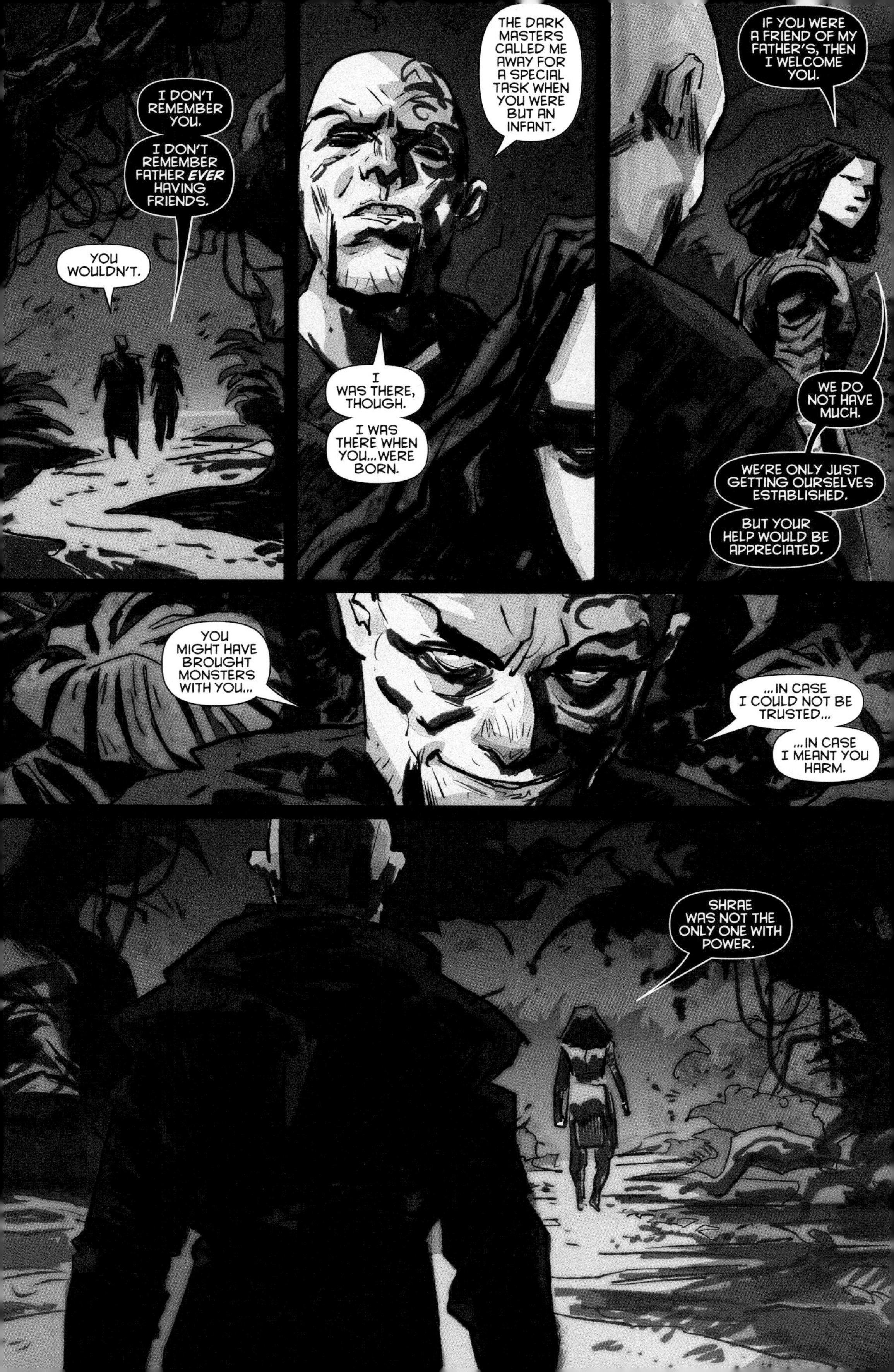
I DON'T REMEMBER YOU.
I DON'T REMEMBER FATHER EVER HAVING FRIENDS.
YOU WOULDN'T.
THE DARK MASTERS CALLED ME AWAY FOR A SPECIAL TASK WHEN YOU WERE BUT AN INFANT.
I WAS THERE, THOUGH.
I WAS THERE WHEN YOU...WERE BORN.
IF YOU WERE A FRIEND OF MY FATHER'S, THEN I WELCOME YOU.
WE DO NOT HAVE MUCH.
WE'RE ONLY JUST GETTING OURSELVES ESTABLISHED.
BUT YOUR HELP WOULD BE APPRECIATED.
YOU MIGHT HAVE BROUGHT MONSTERS WITH YOU...
...IN CASE I COULD NOT BE TRUSTED...
...IN CASE I MEANT YOU HARM.
SHRAE WAS NOT THE ONLY ONE WITH POWER.

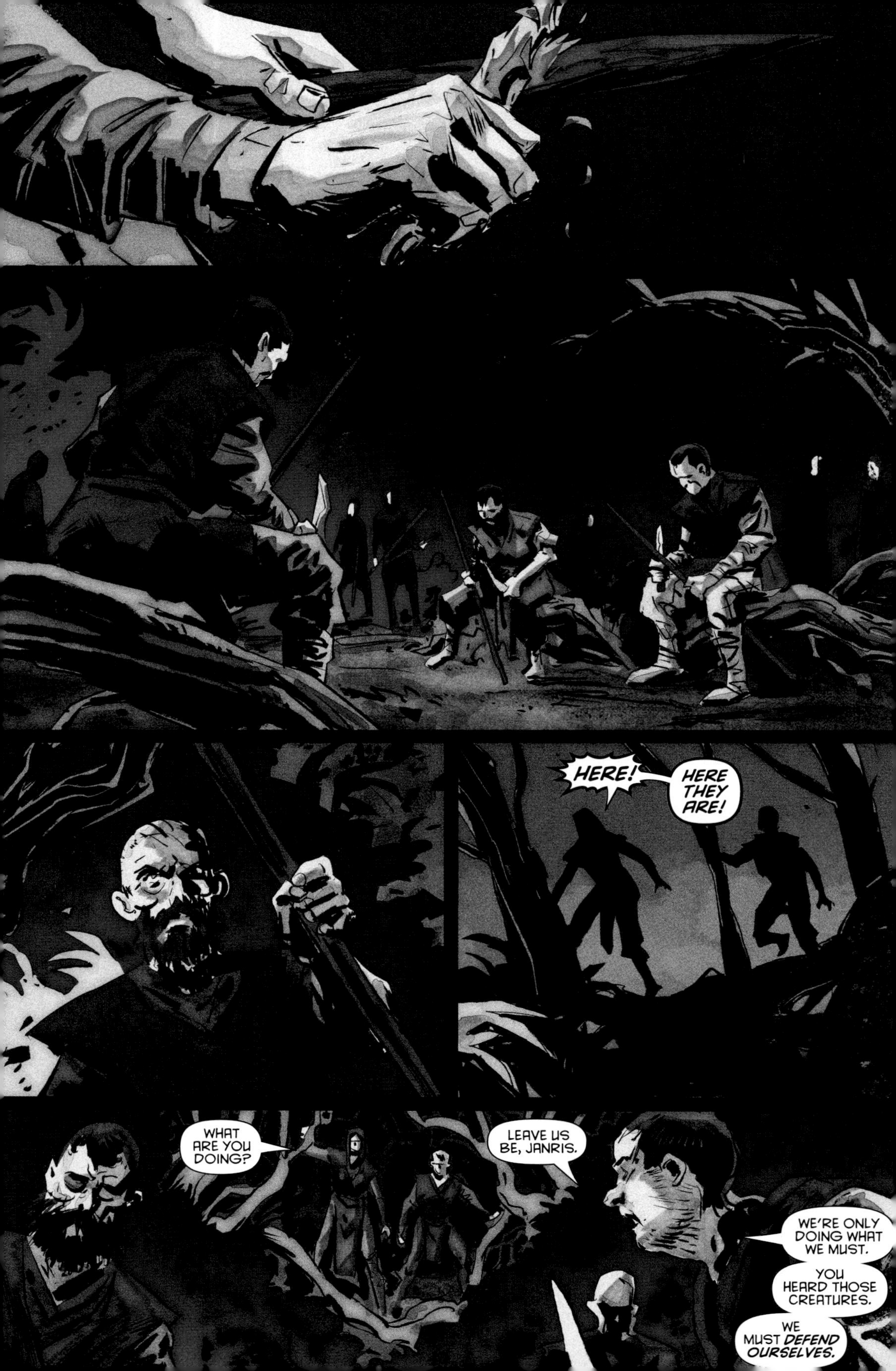
HERE!
HERE THEY ARE!
WHAT ARE YOU DOING?
LEAVE US BE, JANRIS.
WE'RE ONLY DOING WHAT WE MUST.
YOU HEARD THOSE CREATURES.
WE MUST DEFEND OURSELVES.

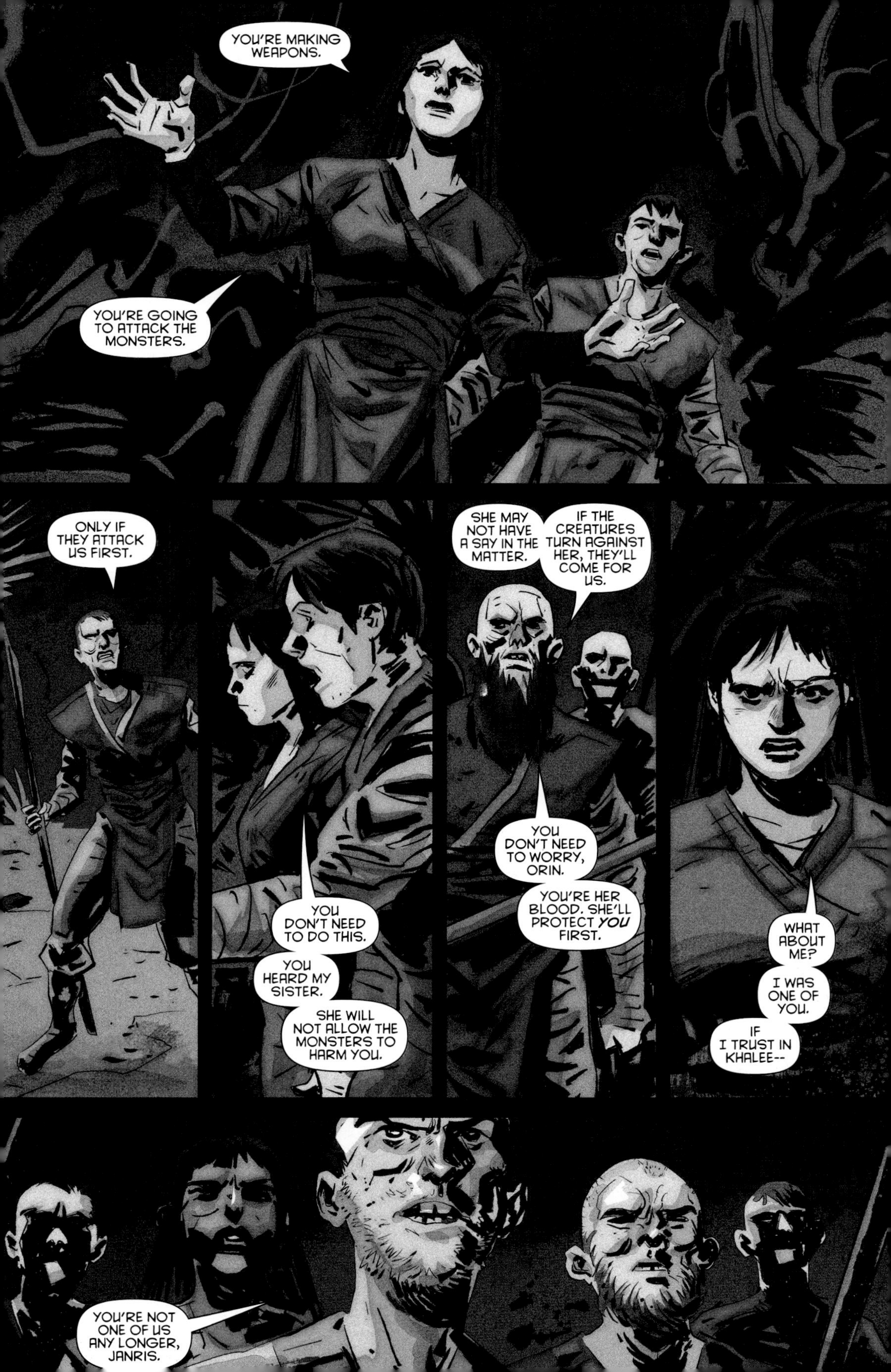
YOU'RE MAKING WEAPONS.
YOU'RE GOING TO ATTACK THE MONSTERS.
ONLY IF THEY ATTACK US FIRST.
YOU DON'T NEED TO DO THIS.
YOU HEARD MY SISTER.
SHE WILL NOT ALLOW THE MONSTERS TO HARM YOU.
SHE MAY NOT HAVE A SAY IN THE MATTER.
IF THE CREATURES TURN AGAINST HER, THEY'LL COME FOR US.
YOU DON'T NEED TO WORRY, ORIN.
YOU'RE HER BLOOD. SHE'LL PROTECT YOU FIRST.
WHAT ABOUT ME?
I WAS ONE OF YOU.
IF I TRUST IN KHALEE--
YOU'RE NOT ONE OF US ANY LONGER, JANRIS.

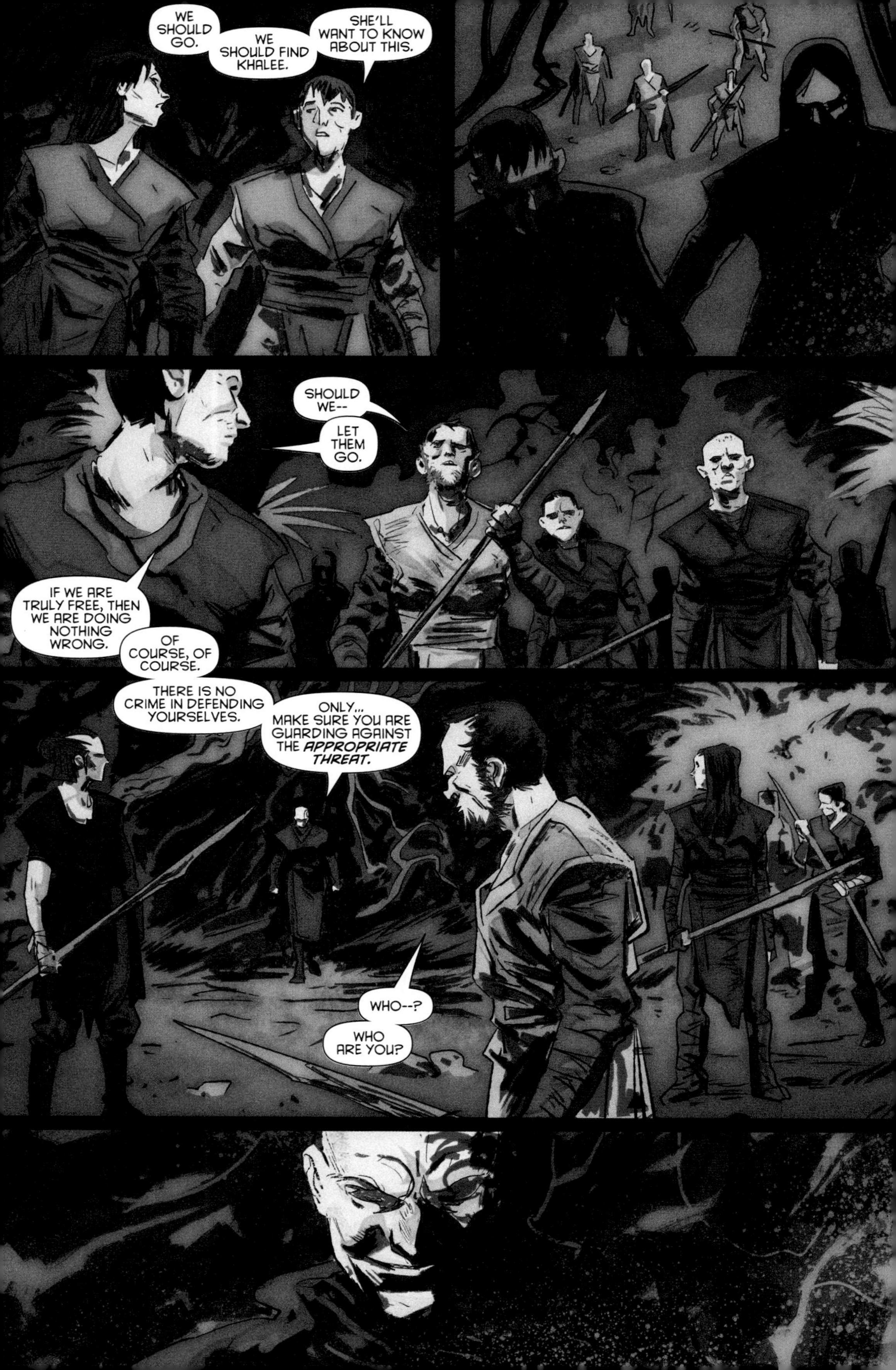
WE SHOULD GO.
WE SHOULD FIND KHALEE.
SHE'LL WANT TO KNOW ABOUT THIS.
SHOULD WE--
LET THEM GO.
IF WE ARE TRULY FREE, THEN WE ARE DOING NOTHING WRONG.
OF COURSE, OF COURSE.
THERE IS NO CRIME IN DEFENDING YOURSELVES.
ONLY... MAKE SURE YOU ARE GUARDING AGAINST THE *APPROPRIATE THREAT.*
WHO--?
WHO ARE YOU?

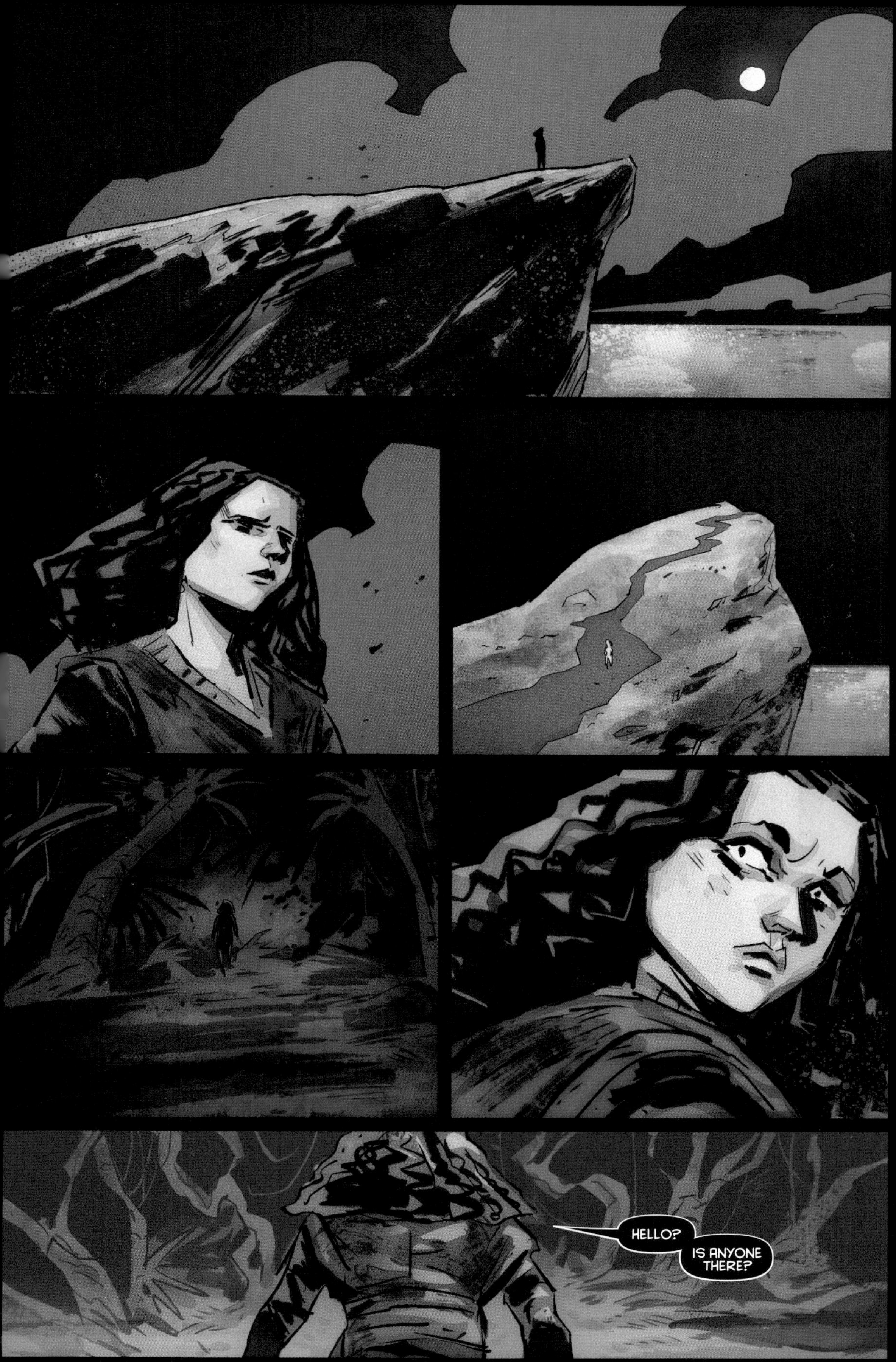
HELLO?
IS ANYONE THERE?

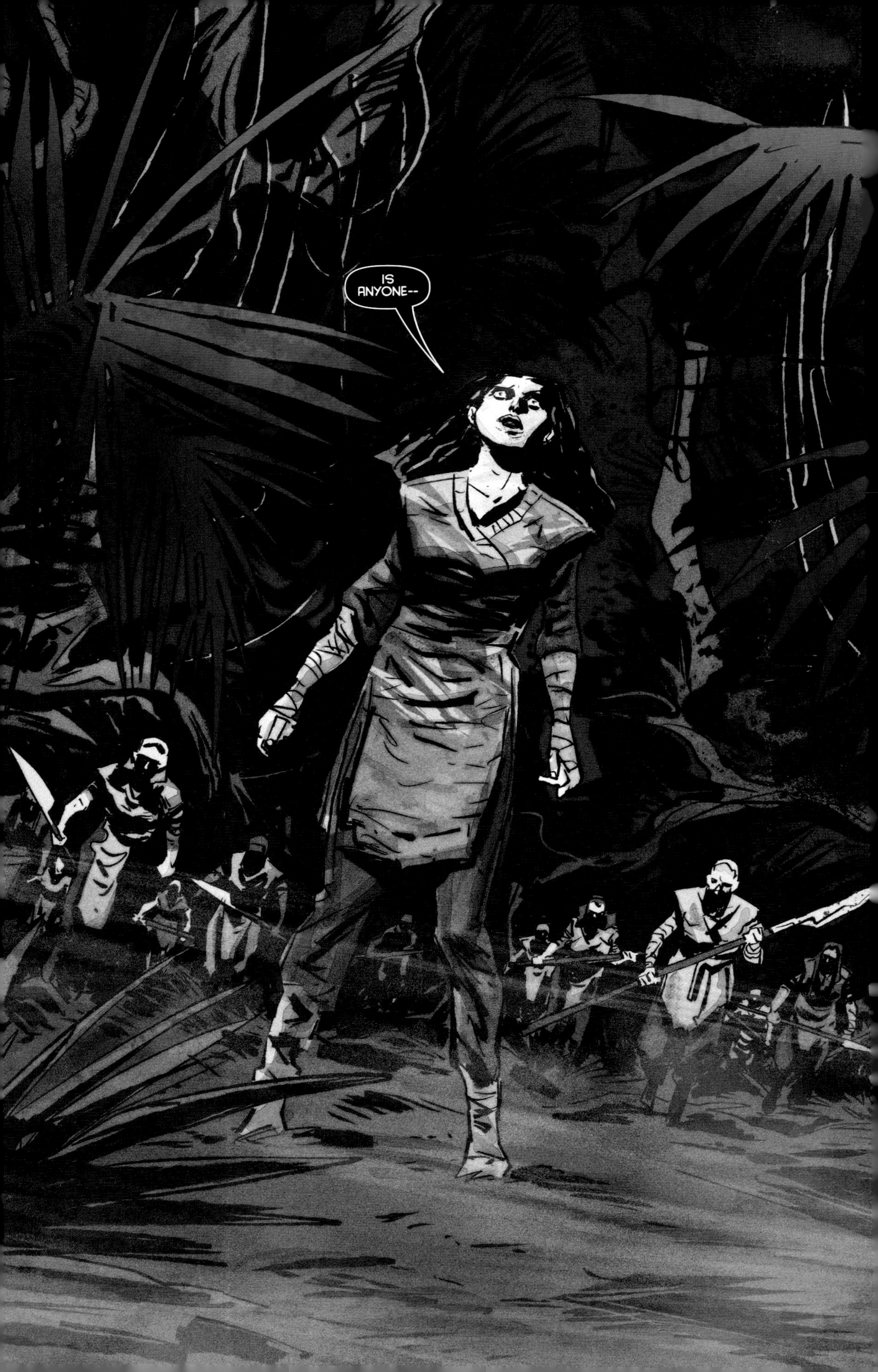
IS ANYONE--

5

FLOWERS LIKE PRAYERS

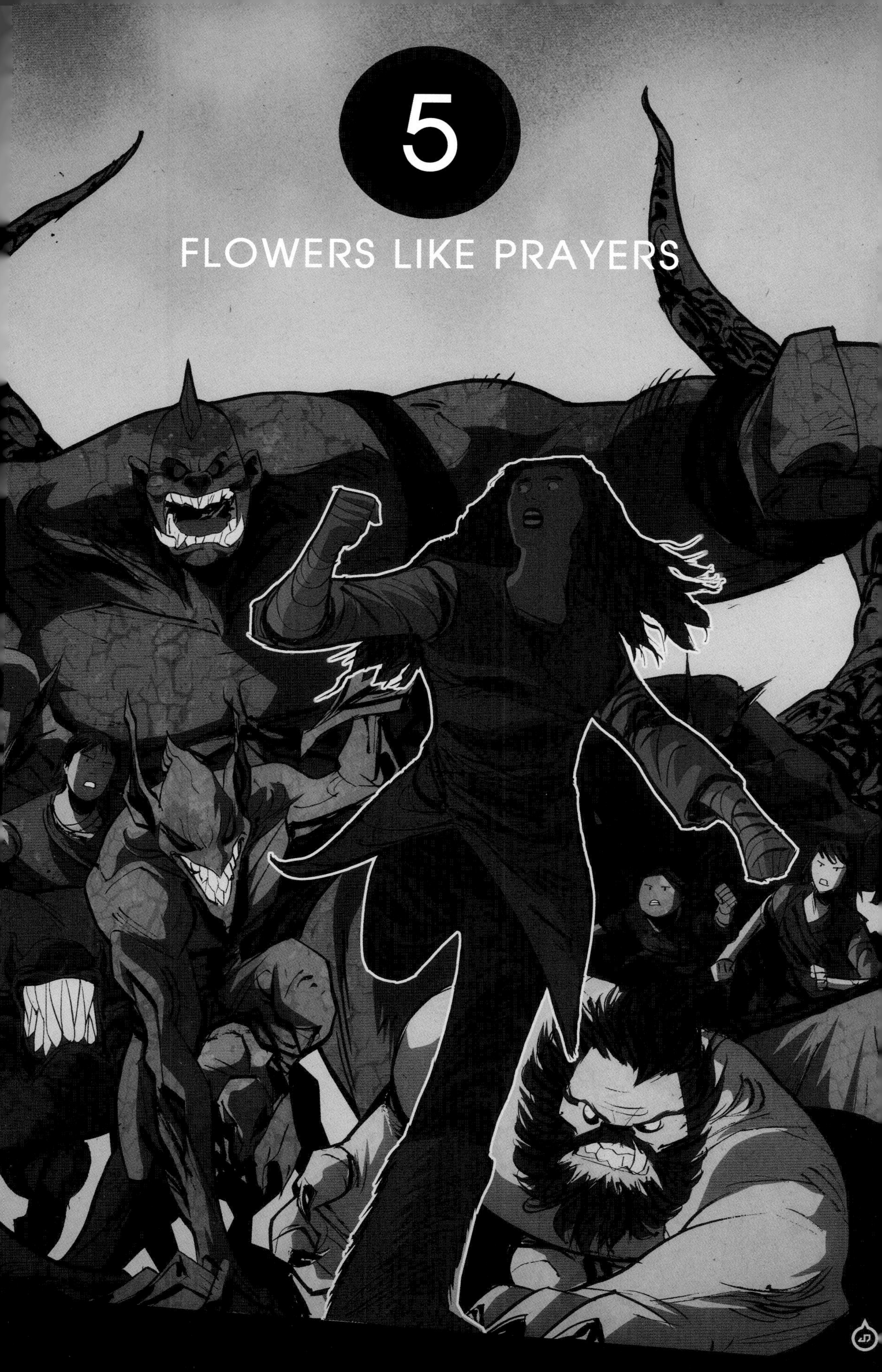

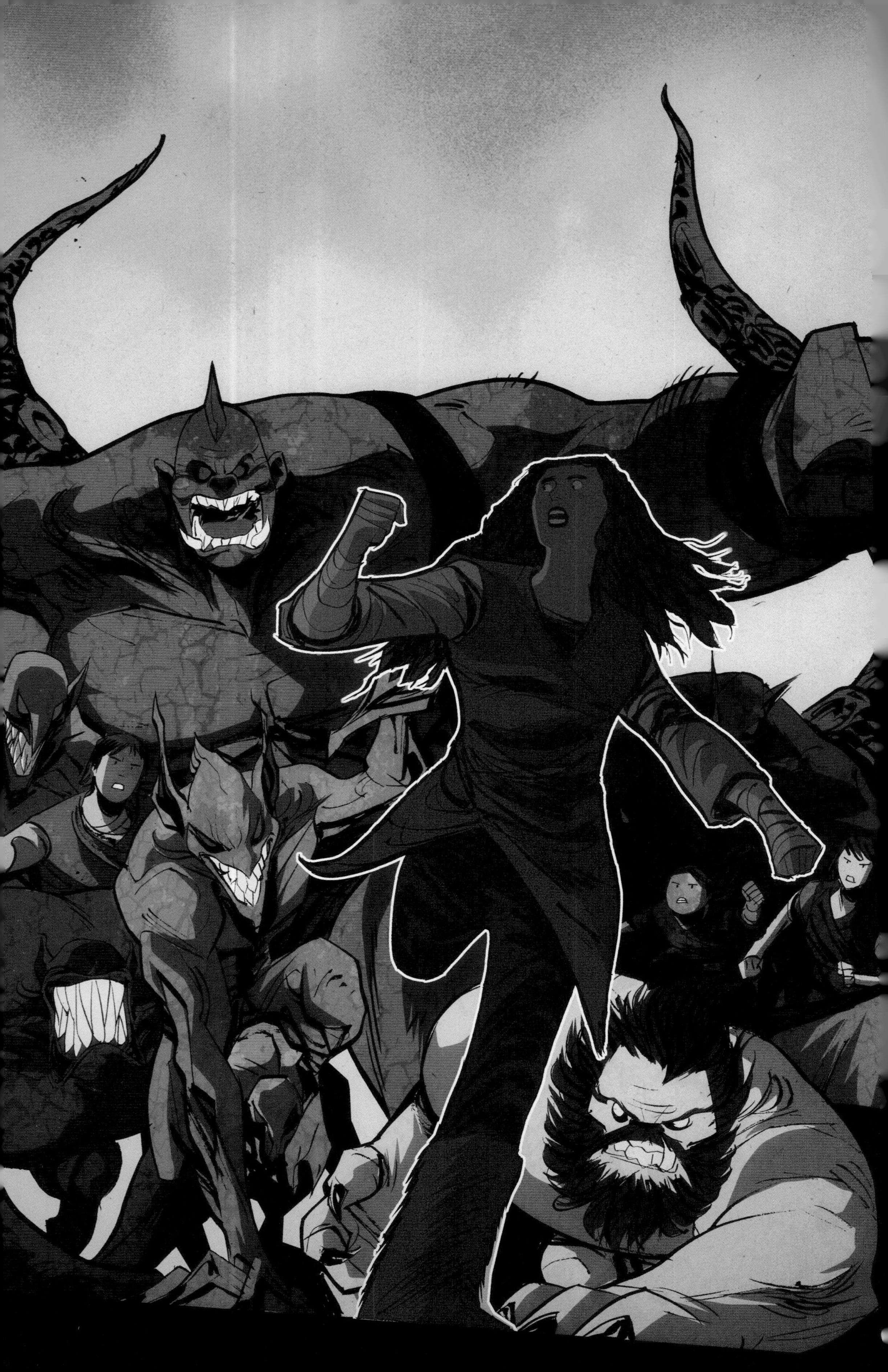

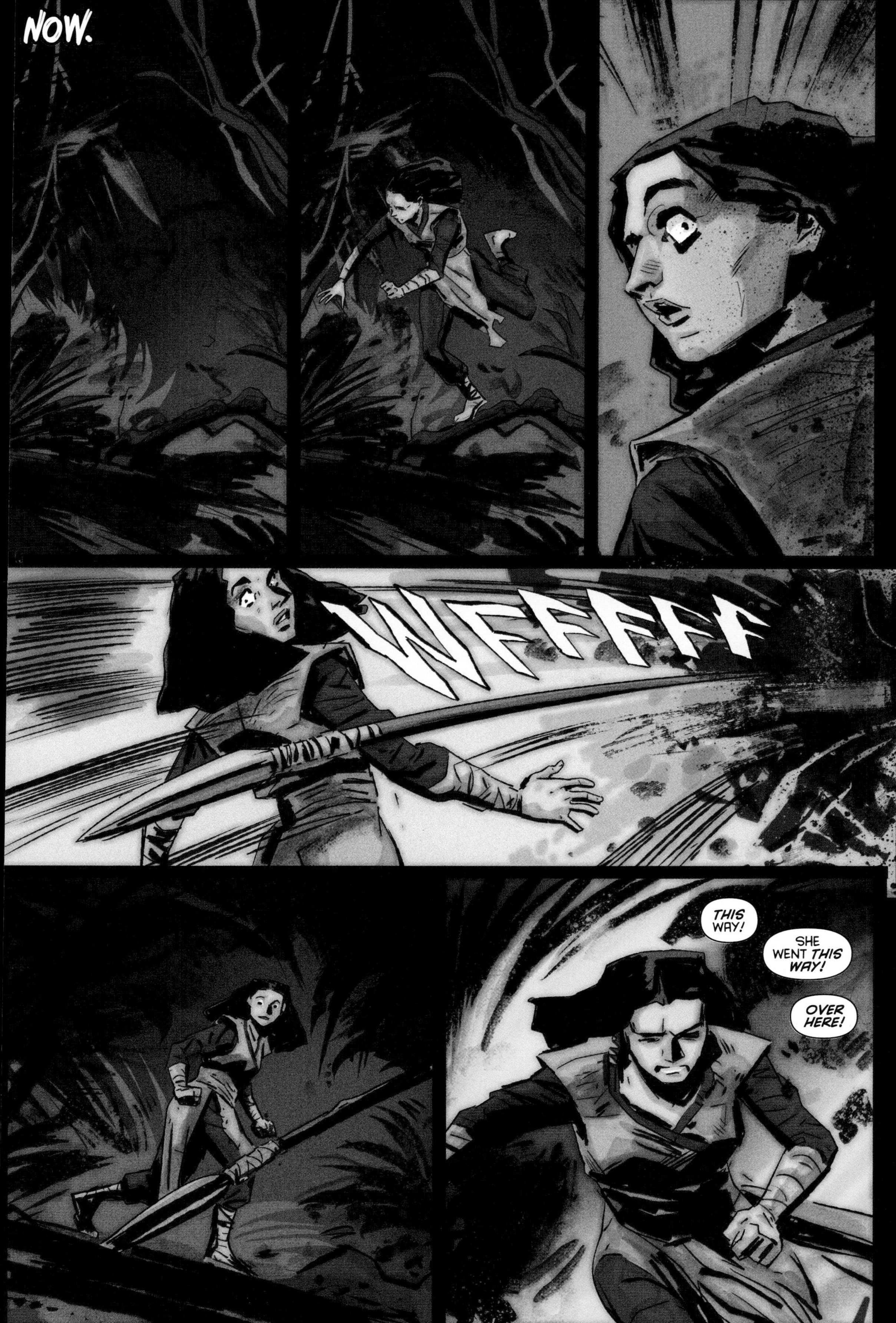
NOW.
WFFFFF
THIS WAY!
SHE WENT THIS WAY!
OVER HERE!

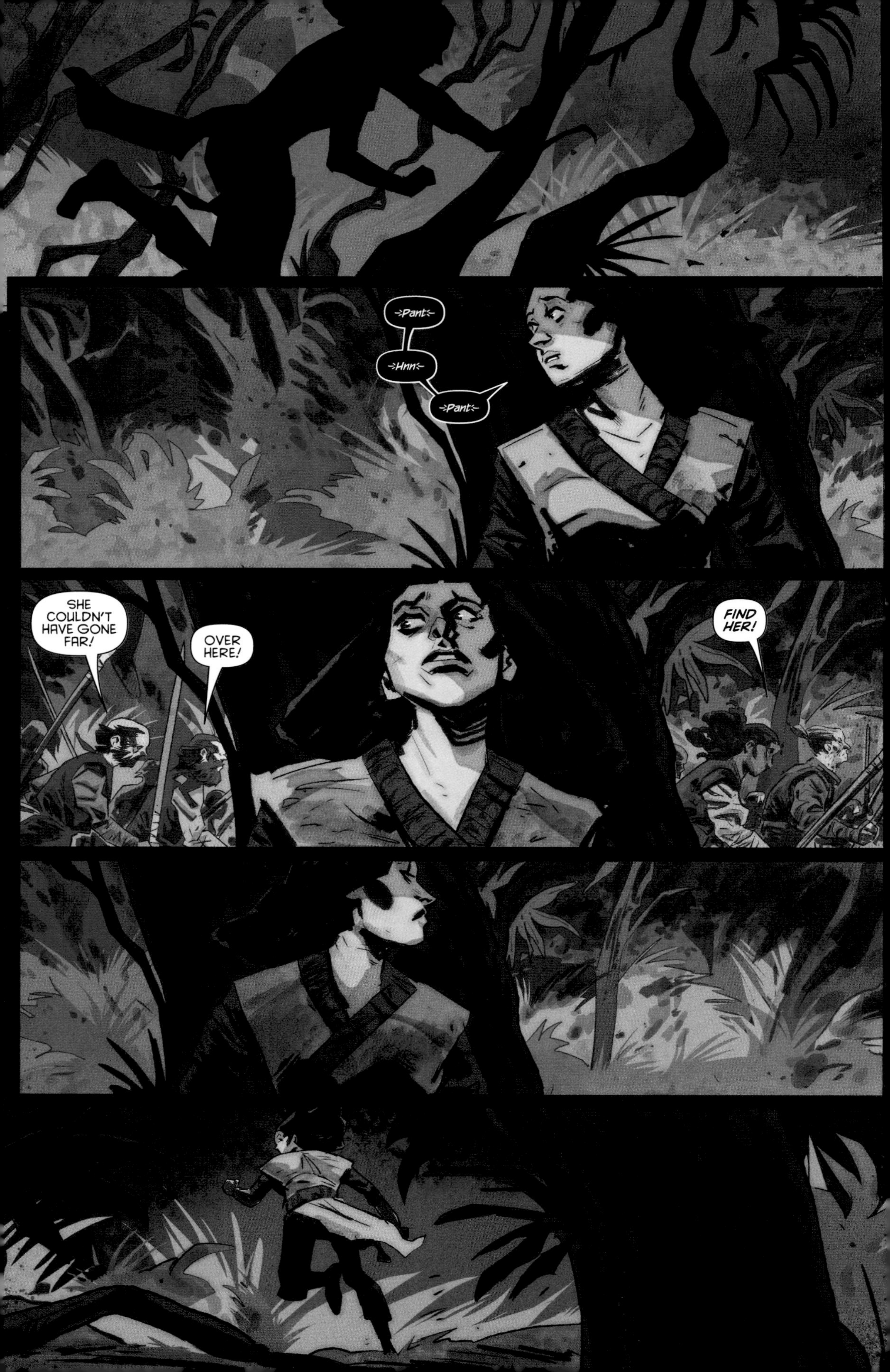

Pant
Hnn
Pant
SHE COULDN'T HAVE GONE FAR!
OVER HERE!
FIND HER!

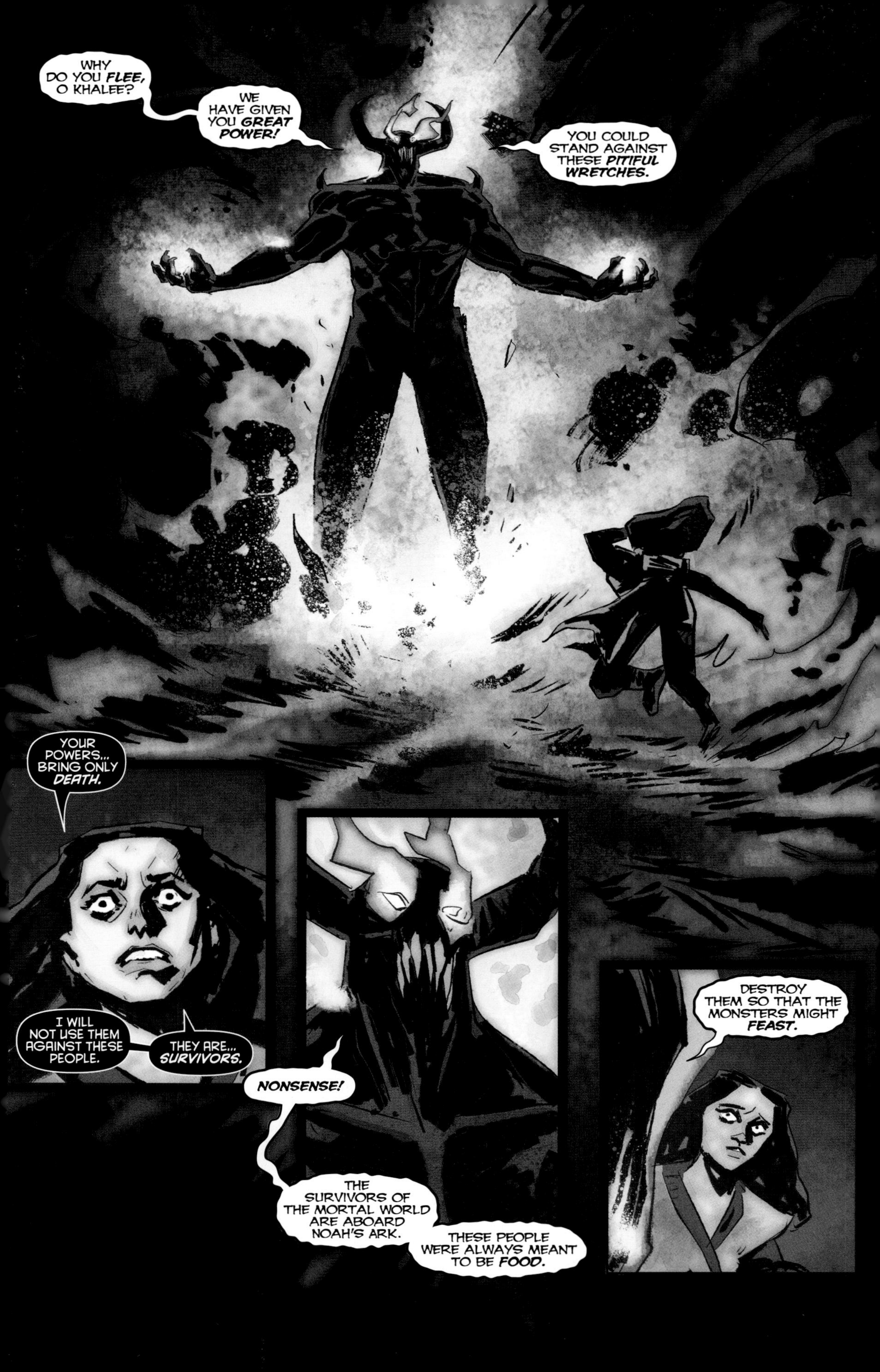
WHY DO YOU FLEE, O KHALEE?
WE HAVE GIVEN YOU GREAT POWER!
YOU COULD STAND AGAINST THESE PITIFUL WRETCHES.
YOUR POWERS... BRING ONLY DEATH.
I WILL NOT USE THEM AGAINST THESE PEOPLE.
THEY ARE... SURVIVORS.
NONSENSE!
THE SURVIVORS OF THE MORTAL WORLD ARE ABOARD NOAH'S ARK.
THESE PEOPLE WERE ALWAYS MEANT TO BE FOOD.
DESTROY THEM SO THAT THE MONSTERS MIGHT FEAST.

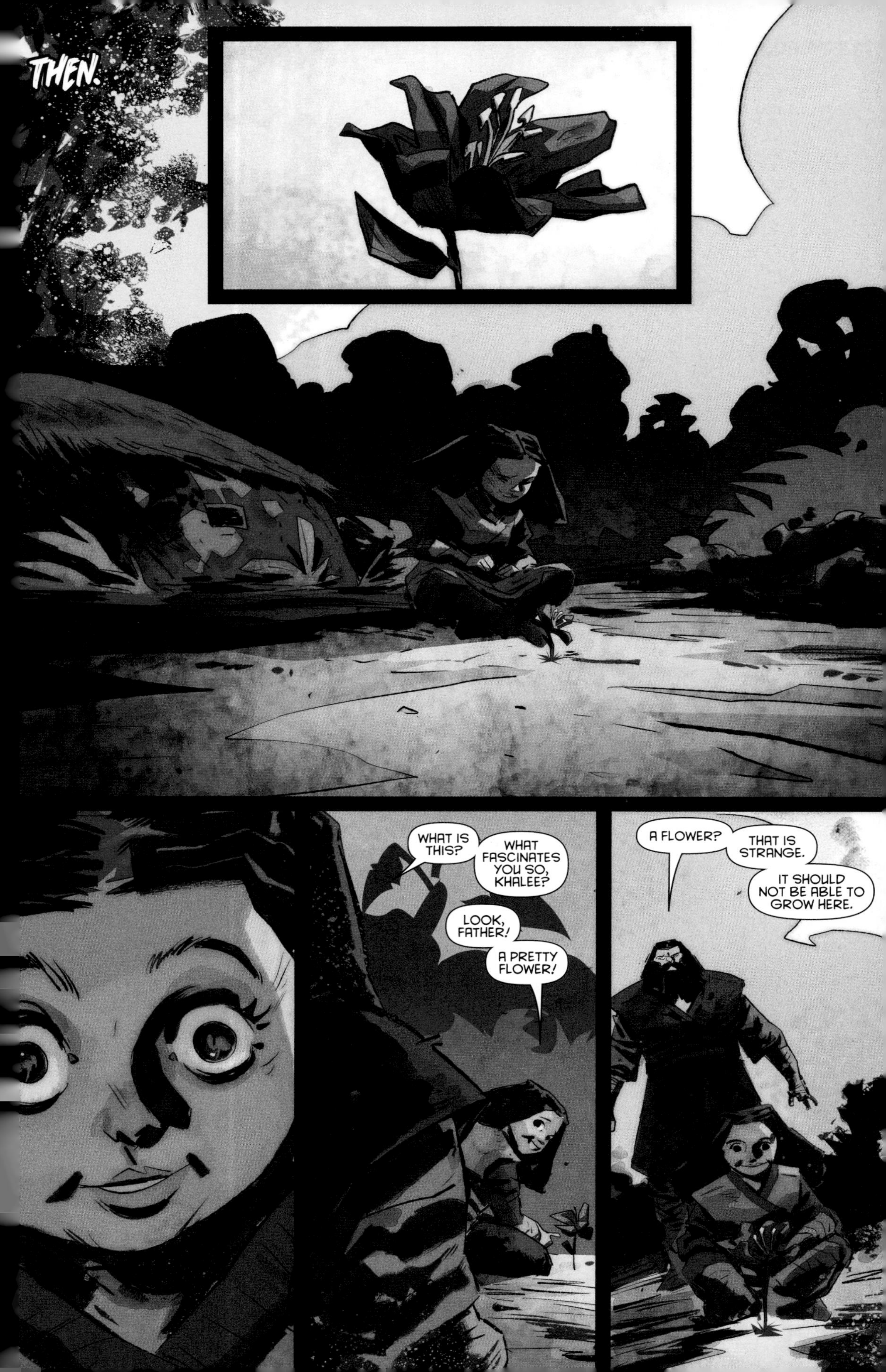
THEN.
WHAT IS THIS?
WHAT FASCINATES YOU SO, KHALEE?
LOOK, FATHER!
A PRETTY FLOWER!
A FLOWER?
THAT IS STRANGE.
IT SHOULD NOT BE ABLE TO GROW HERE.

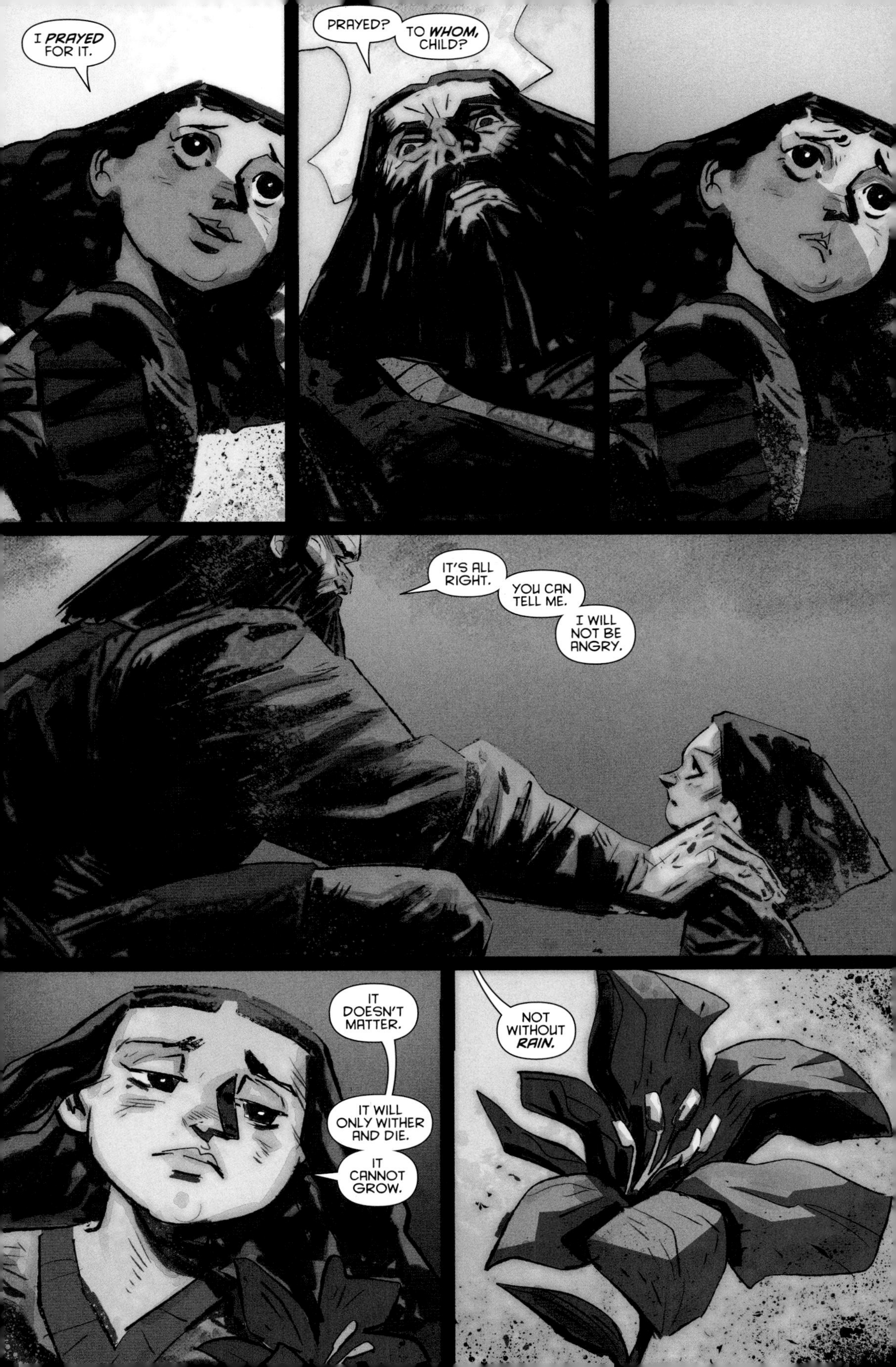
I PRAYED FOR IT.
PRAYED?
TO WHOM, CHILD?
IT'S ALL RIGHT.
YOU CAN TELL ME.
I WILL NOT BE ANGRY.
IT DOESN'T MATTER.
IT WILL ONLY WITHER AND DIE.
IT CANNOT GROW.
NOT WITHOUT RAIN.

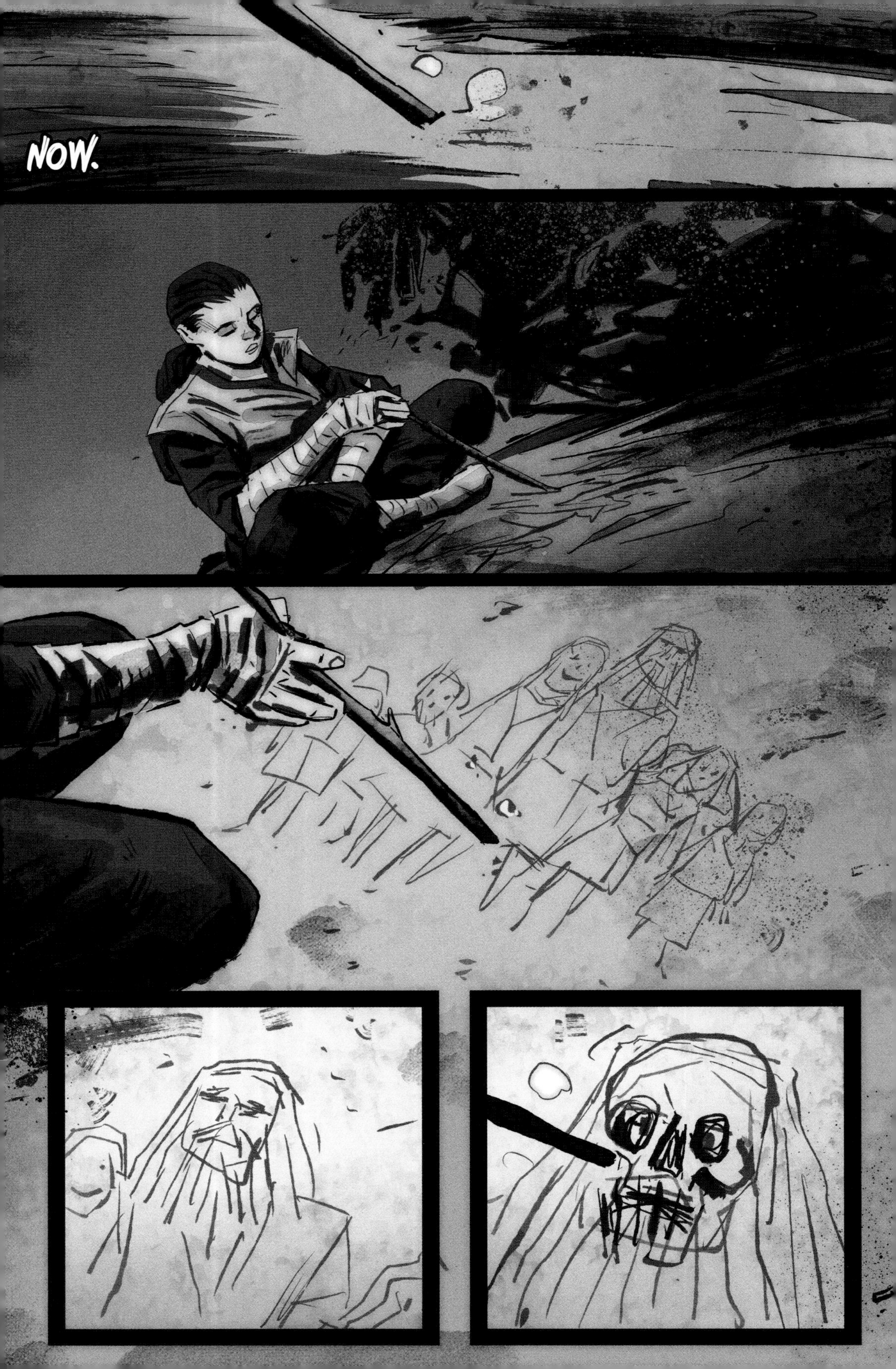
NOW.

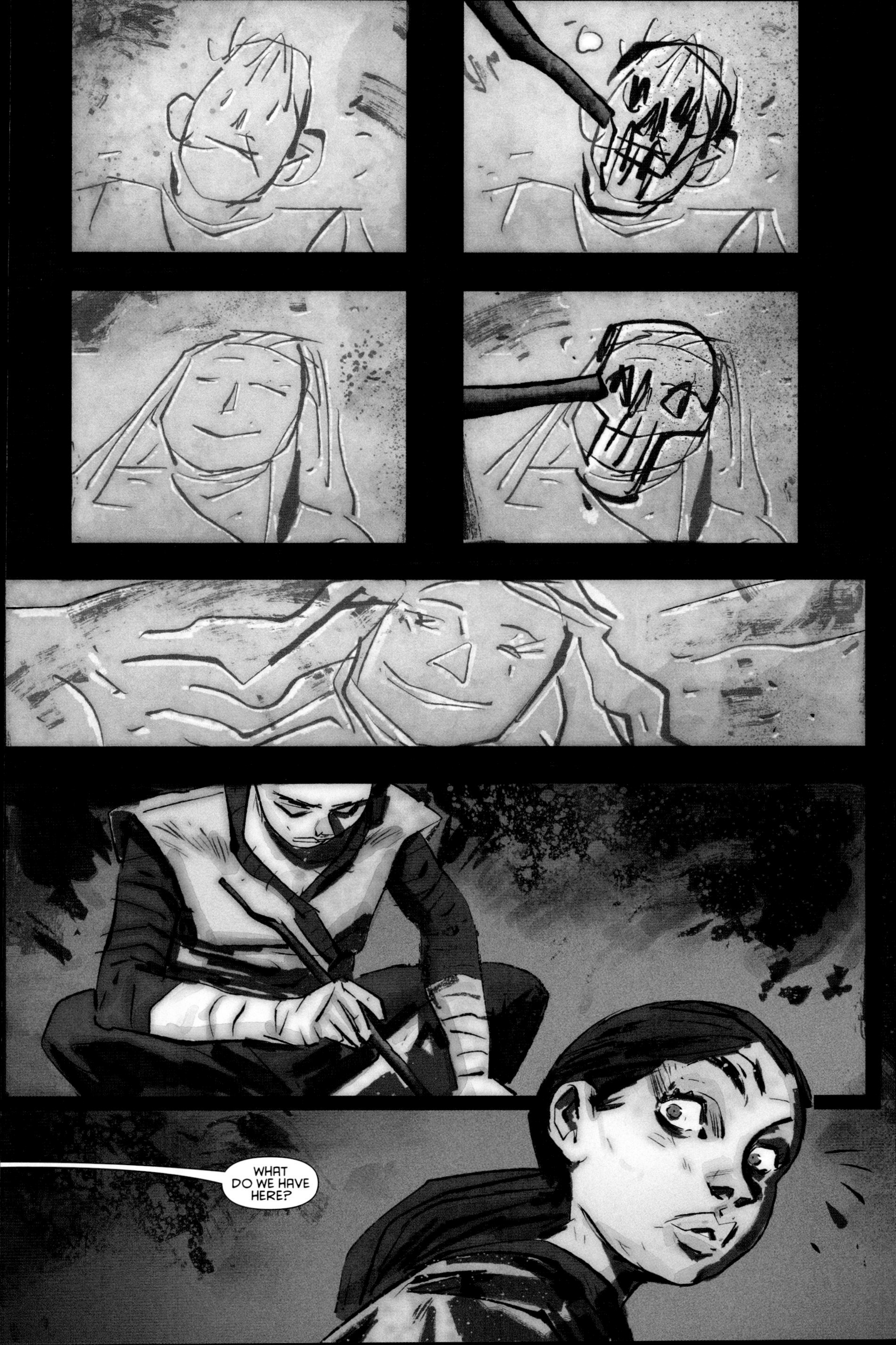
WHAT DO WE HAVE HERE?

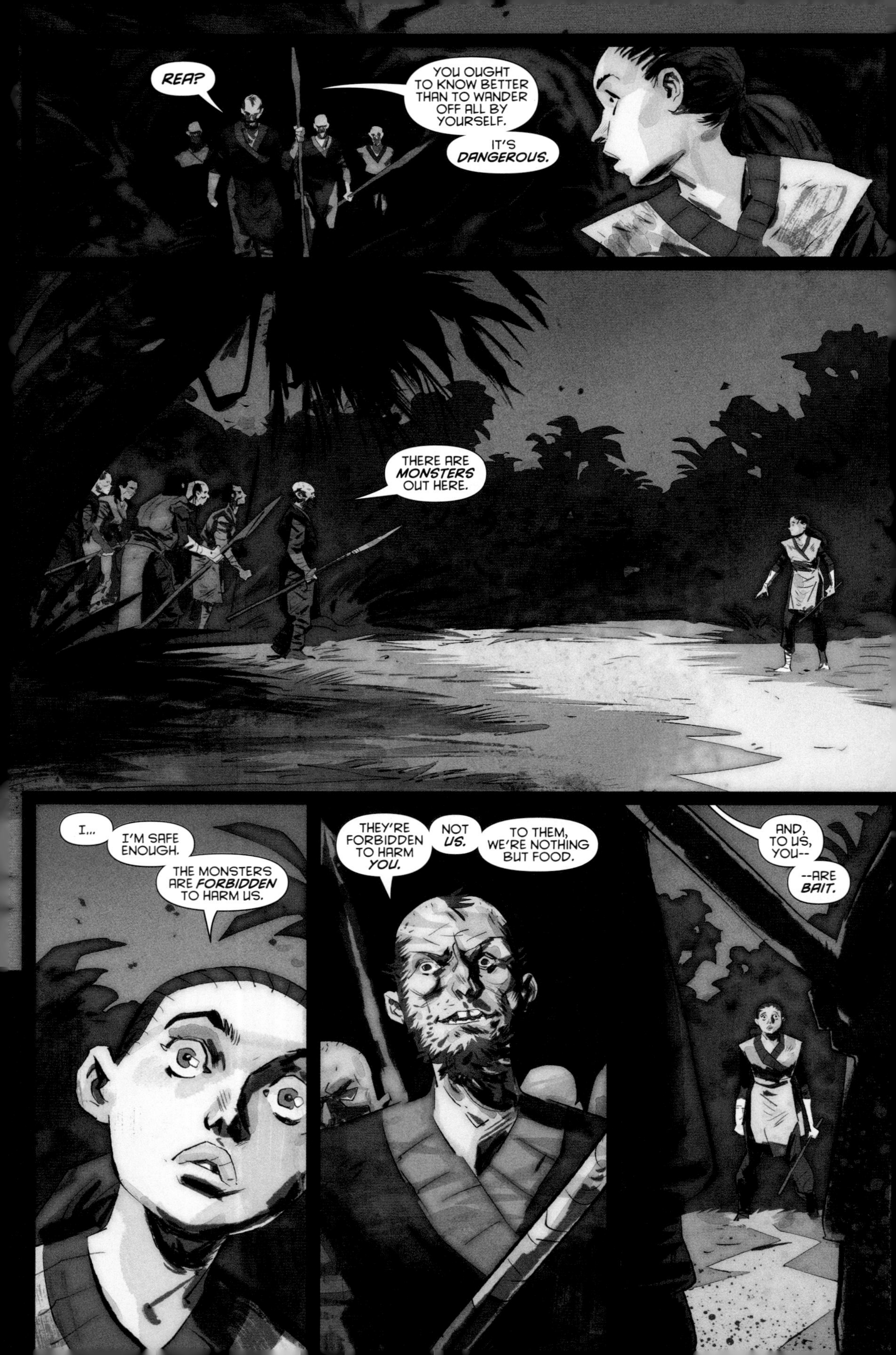
REA?
YOU OUGHT TO KNOW BETTER THAN TO WANDER OFF ALL BY YOURSELF.
IT'S DANGEROUS.
THERE ARE MONSTERS OUT HERE.
I...
I'M SAFE ENOUGH.
THE MONSTERS ARE FORBIDDEN TO HARM US.
THEY'RE FORBIDDEN TO HARM YOU.
NOT US.
TO THEM, WE'RE NOTHING BUT FOOD.
AND, TO US, YOU--
--ARE BAIT.

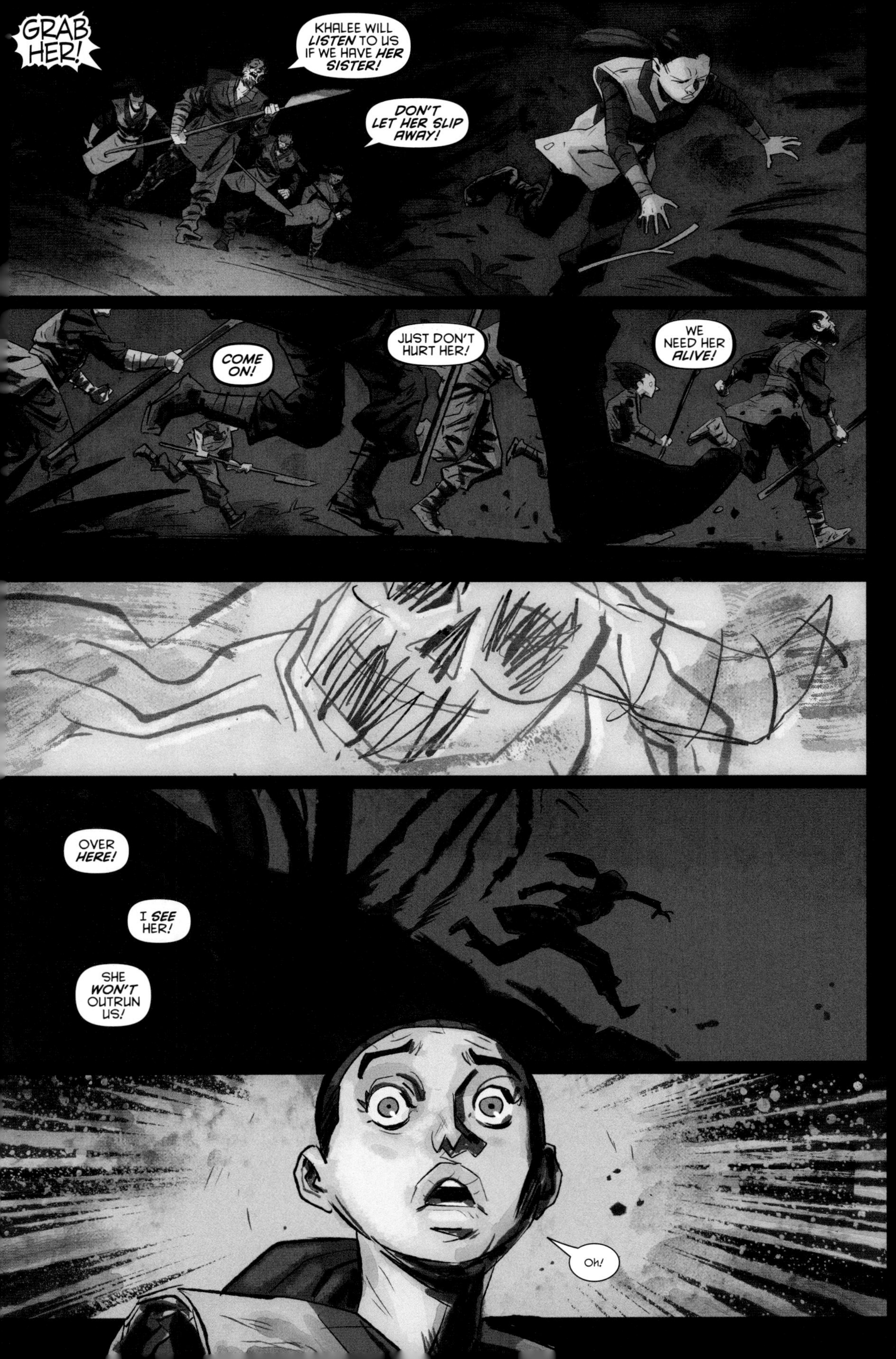
GRAB HER!
KHALEE WILL LISTEN TO US IF WE HAVE HER SISTER!
DON'T LET HER SLIP AWAY!
COME ON!
JUST DON'T HURT HER!
WE NEED HER ALIVE!
OVER HERE!
I SEE HER!
SHE WON'T OUTRUN US!
Oh!

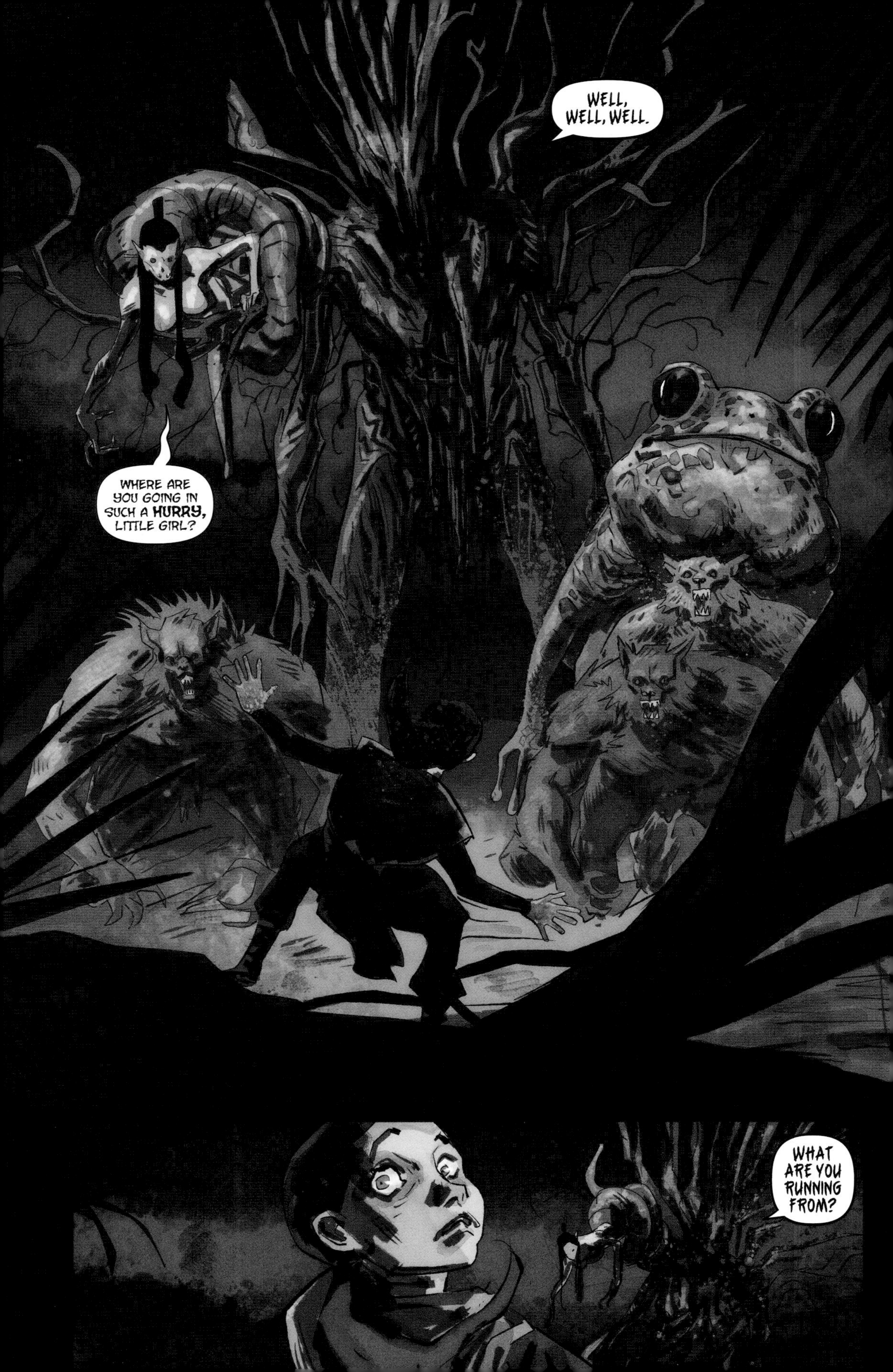
WELL, WELL, WELL.
WHERE ARE YOU GOING IN SUCH A **HURRY,** LITTLE GIRL?
WHAT ARE YOU RUNNING FROM?

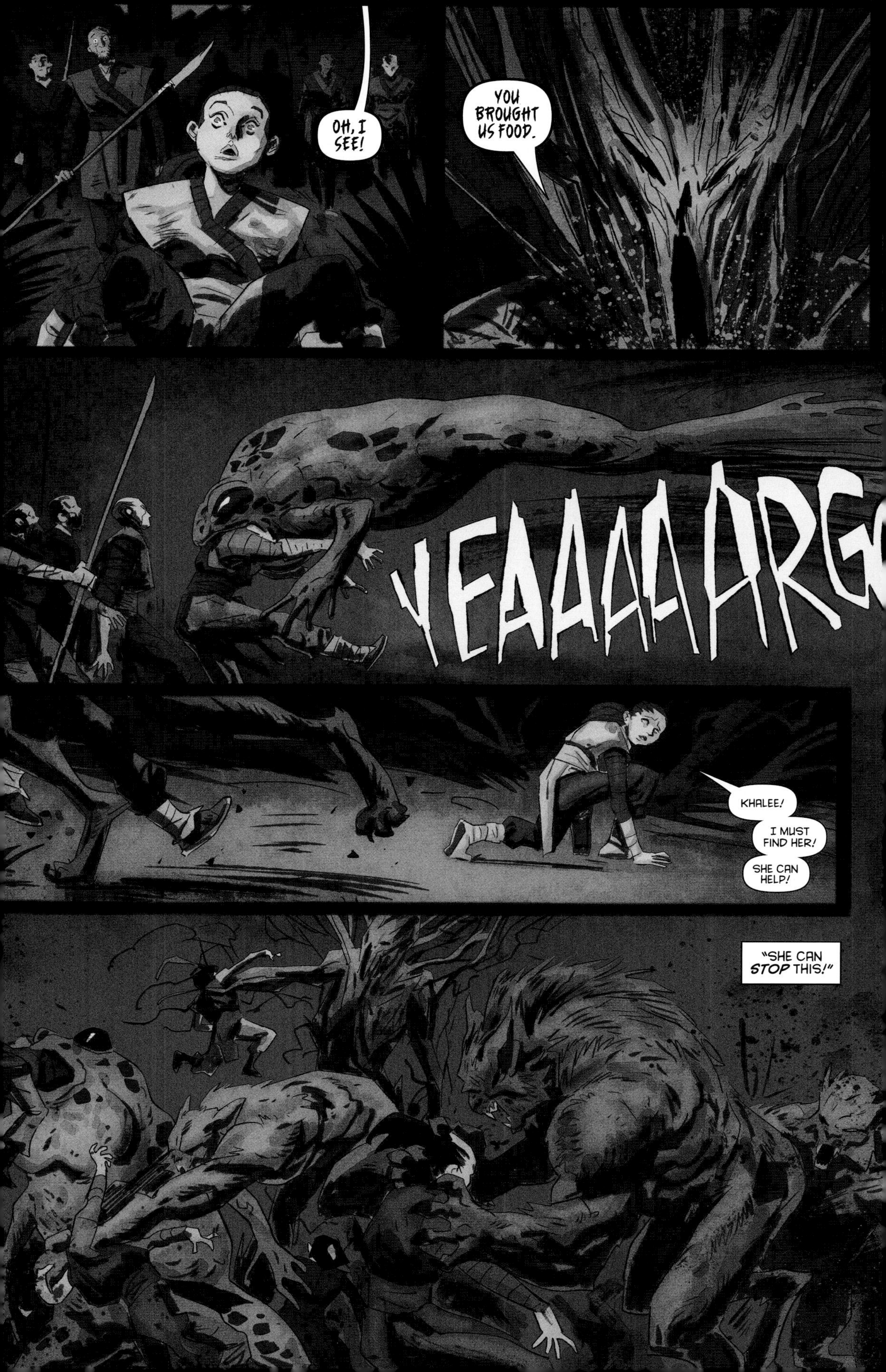
OH, I SEE!
YOU BROUGHT US FOOD.
YEAAAAARG
KHALEE!
I MUST FIND HER!
SHE CAN HELP!
"SHE CAN STOP THIS!"

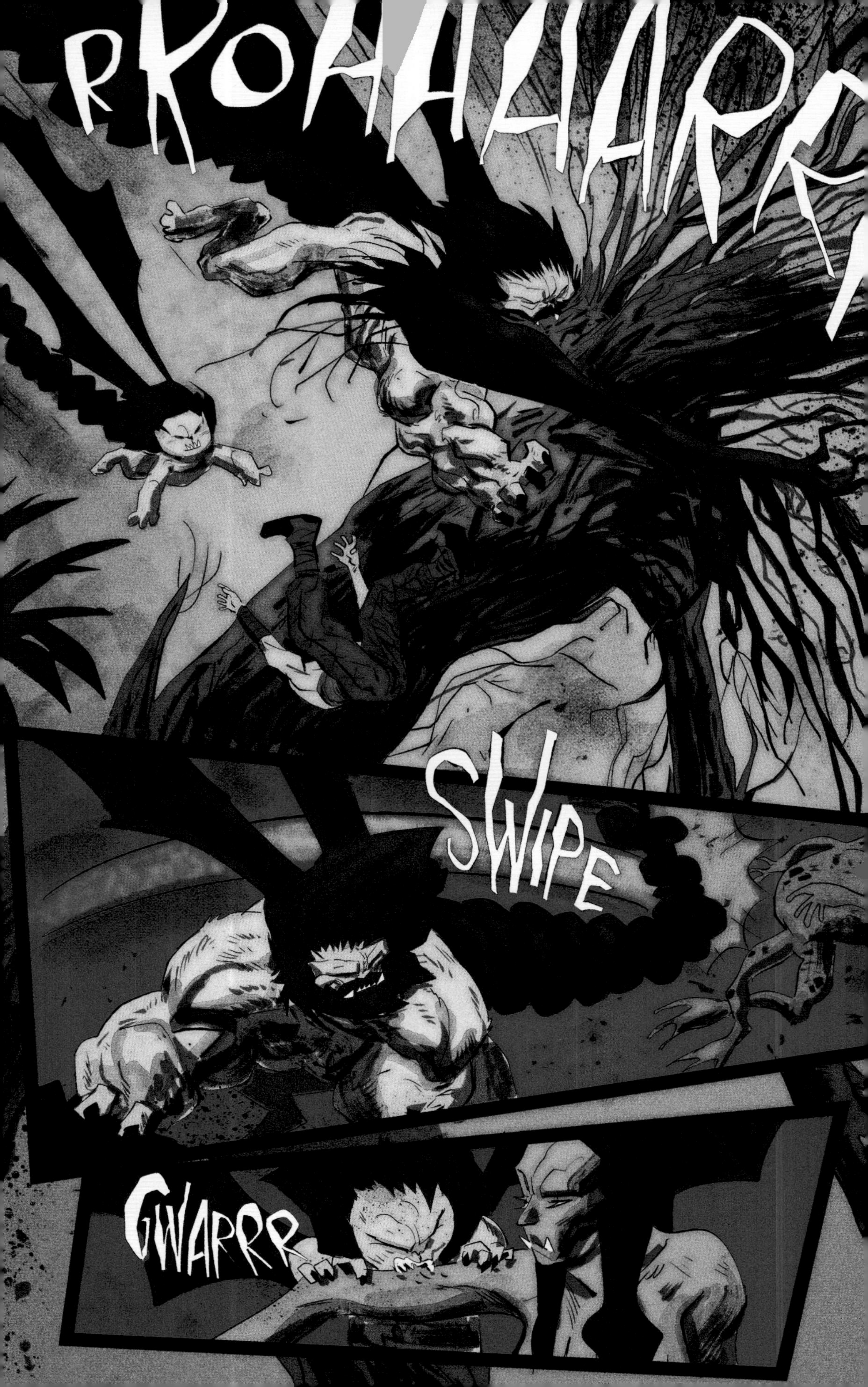
RROAHHARR
SWIPE
GWARRR

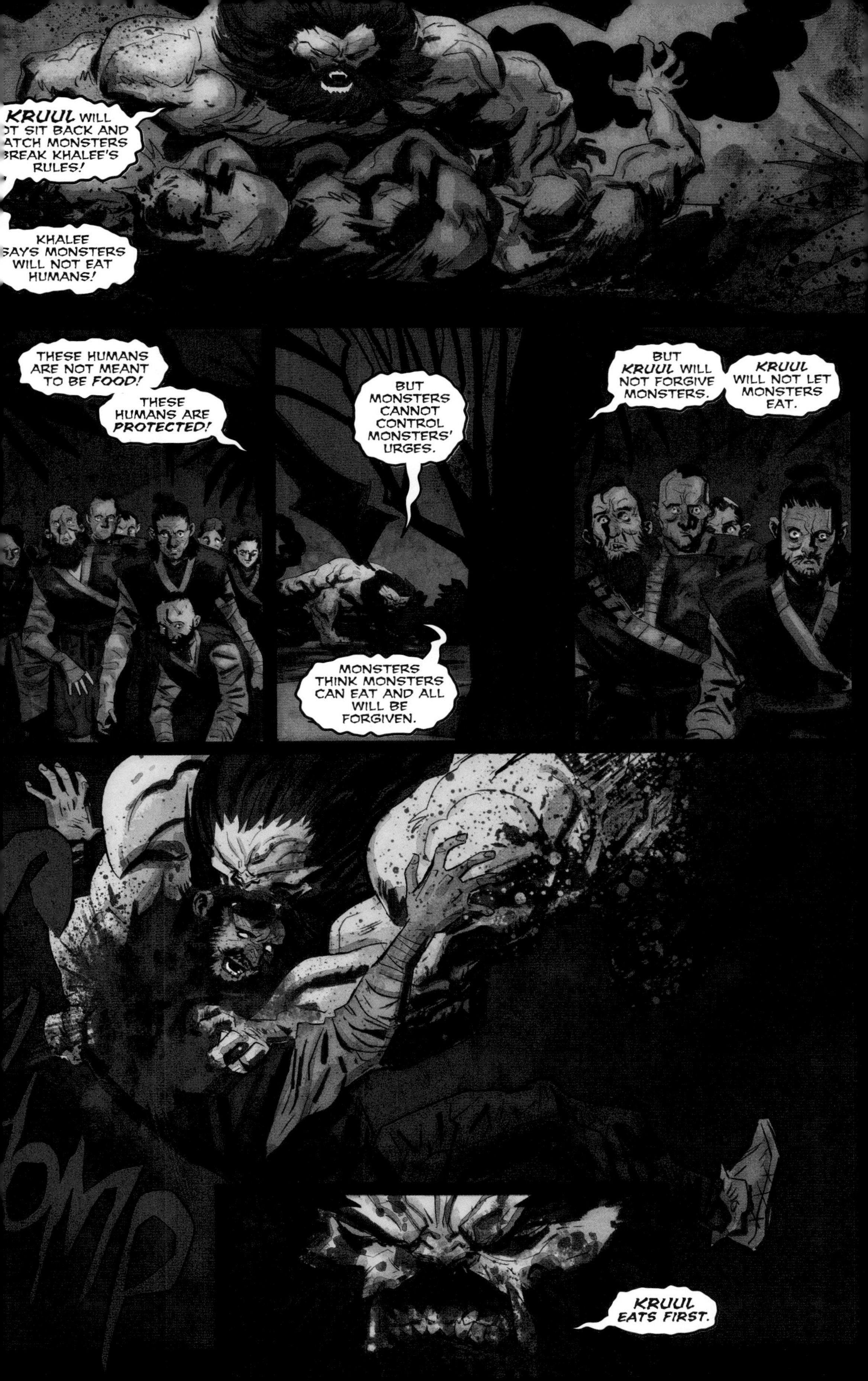
KRUUL WILL OT SIT BACK AND ATCH MONSTERS REAK KHALEE'S RULES!
KHALEE AYS MONSTERS WILL NOT EAT HUMANS!
THESE HUMANS ARE NOT MEANT TO BE FOOD!
THESE HUMANS ARE PROTECTED!
BUT MONSTERS CANNOT CONTROL MONSTERS' URGES.
MONSTERS THINK MONSTERS CAN EAT AND ALL WILL BE FORGIVEN.
BUT KRUUL WILL NOT FORGIVE MONSTERS.
KRUUL WILL NOT LET MONSTERS EAT.
KRUUL EATS FIRST.

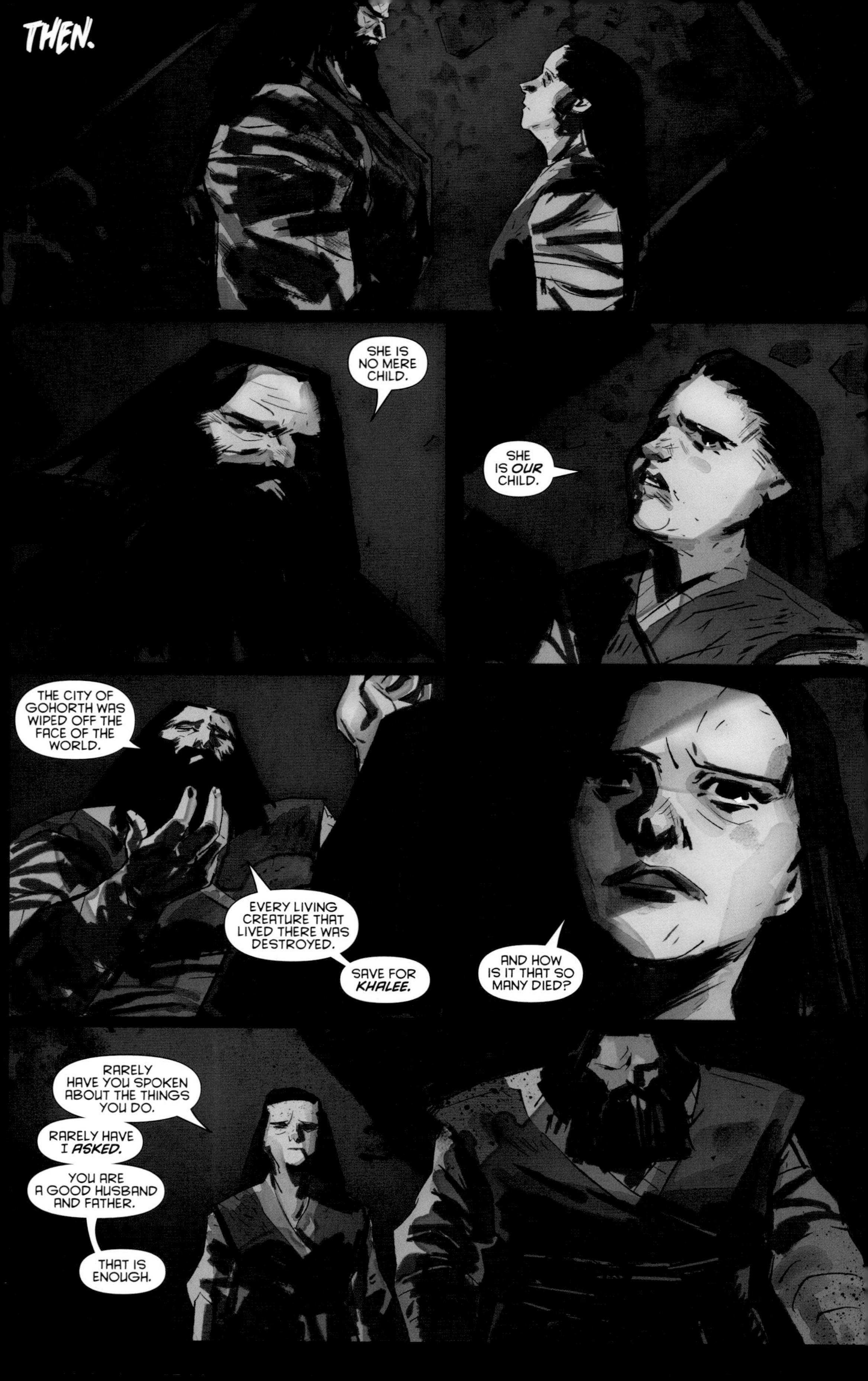
THEN.
SHE IS NO MERE CHILD.
SHE IS *OUR* CHILD.
THE CITY OF GOHORTH WAS WIPED OFF THE FACE OF THE WORLD.
EVERY LIVING CREATURE THAT LIVED THERE WAS DESTROYED.
SAVE FOR *KHALEE.*
AND HOW IS IT THAT SO MANY DIED?
RARELY HAVE YOU SPOKEN ABOUT THE THINGS YOU DO.
RARELY HAVE I *ASKED.*
YOU ARE A GOOD HUSBAND AND FATHER.
THAT IS ENOUGH.

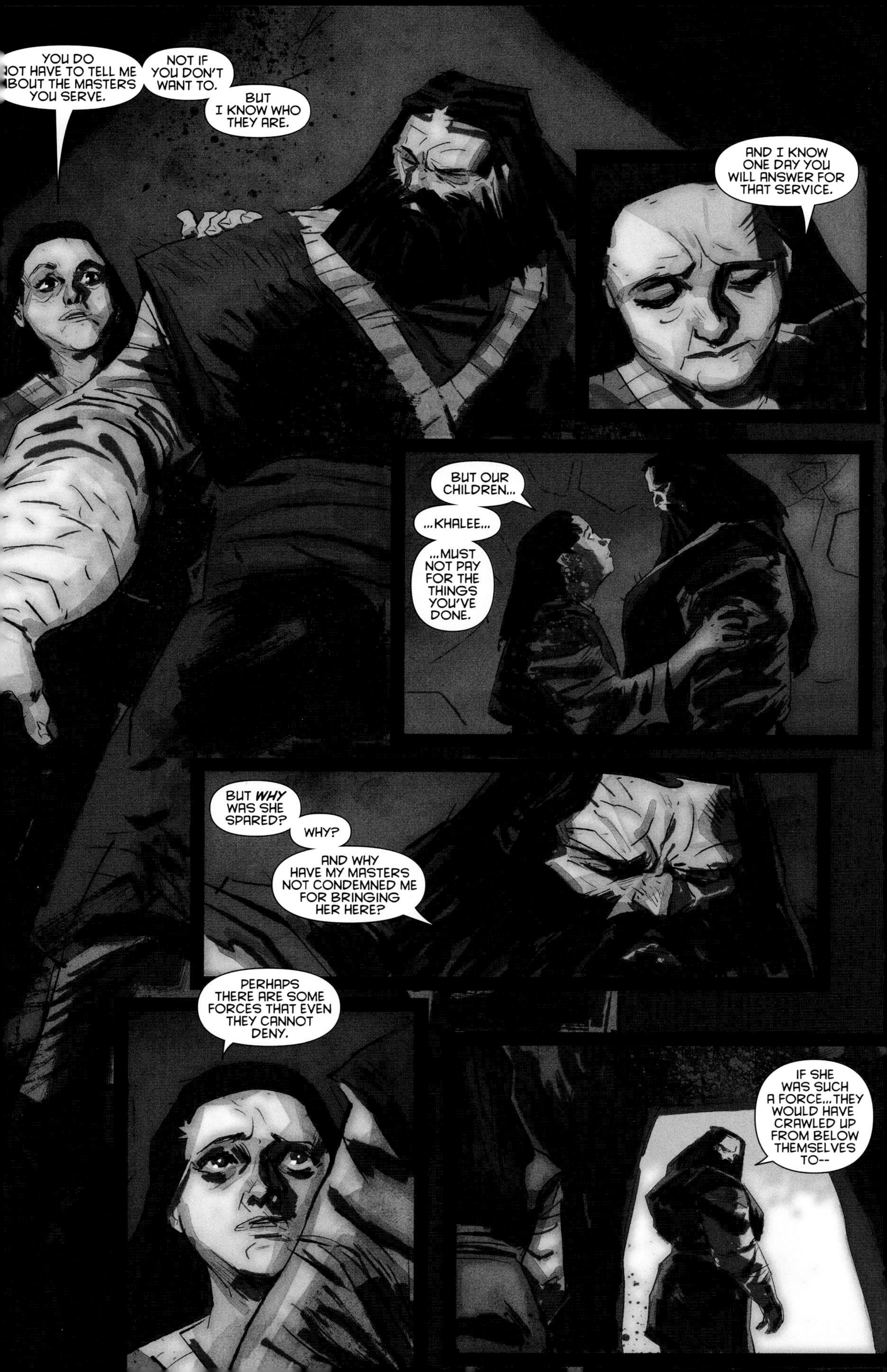
YOU DO NOT HAVE TO TELL ME ABOUT THE MASTERS YOU SERVE.
NOT IF YOU DON'T WANT TO.
BUT I KNOW WHO THEY ARE.
AND I KNOW ONE DAY YOU WILL ANSWER FOR THAT SERVICE.
BUT OUR CHILDREN...
...KHALEE...
...MUST NOT PAY FOR THE THINGS YOU'VE DONE.
BUT ***WHY*** WAS SHE SPARED?
WHY?
AND WHY HAVE MY MASTERS NOT CONDEMNED ME FOR BRINGING HER HERE?
PERHAPS THERE ARE SOME FORCES THAT EVEN THEY CANNOT DENY.
IF SHE WAS SUCH A FORCE...THEY WOULD HAVE CRAWLED UP FROM BELOW THEMSELVES TO--

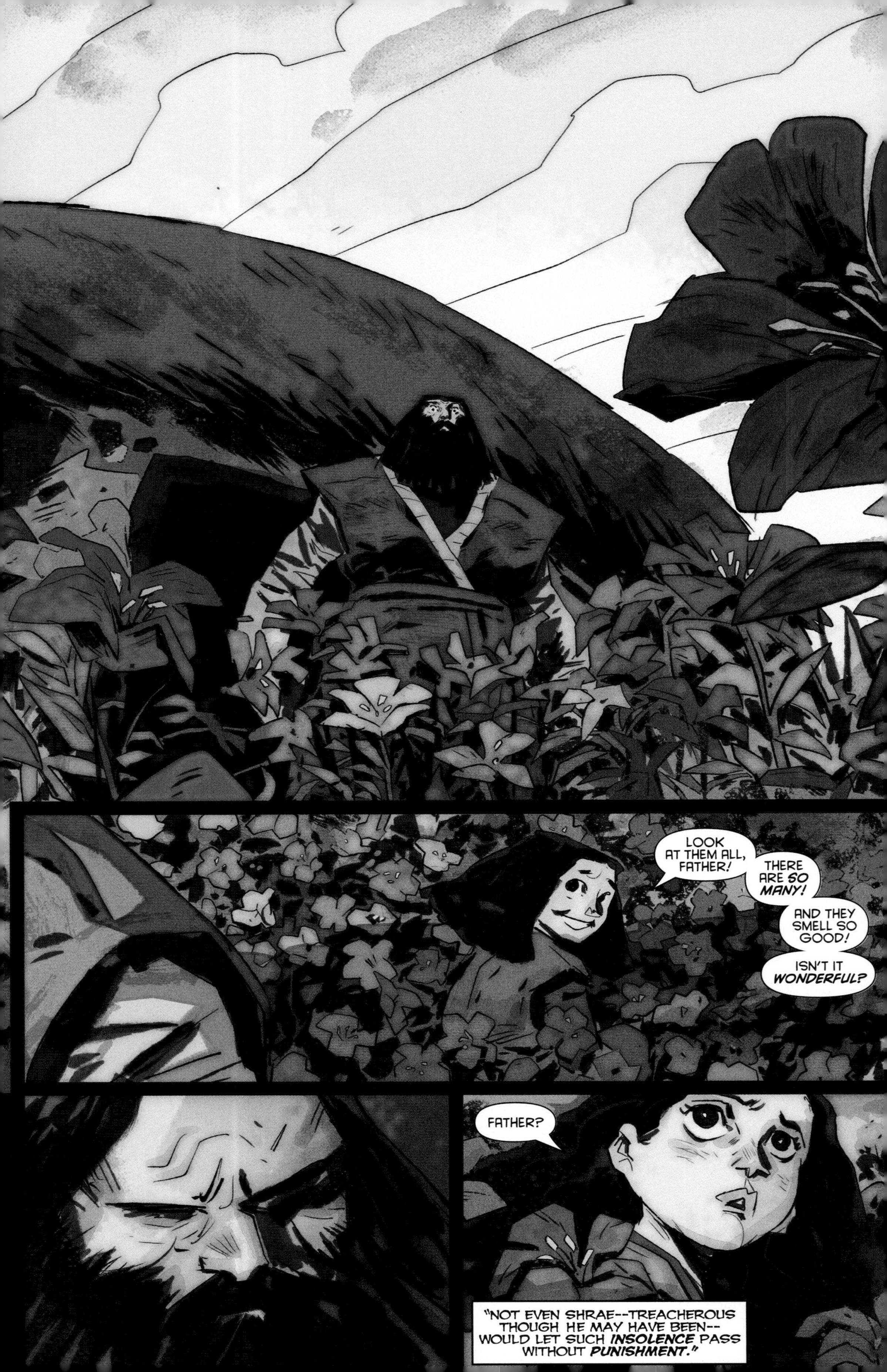
LOOK AT THEM ALL, FATHER!
THERE ARE SO MANY!
AND THEY SMELL SO GOOD!
ISN'T IT WONDERFUL?
FATHER?
"NOT EVEN SHRAE--TREACHEROUS THOUGH HE MAY HAVE BEEN--WOULD LET SUCH INSOLENCE PASS WITHOUT PUNISHMENT."

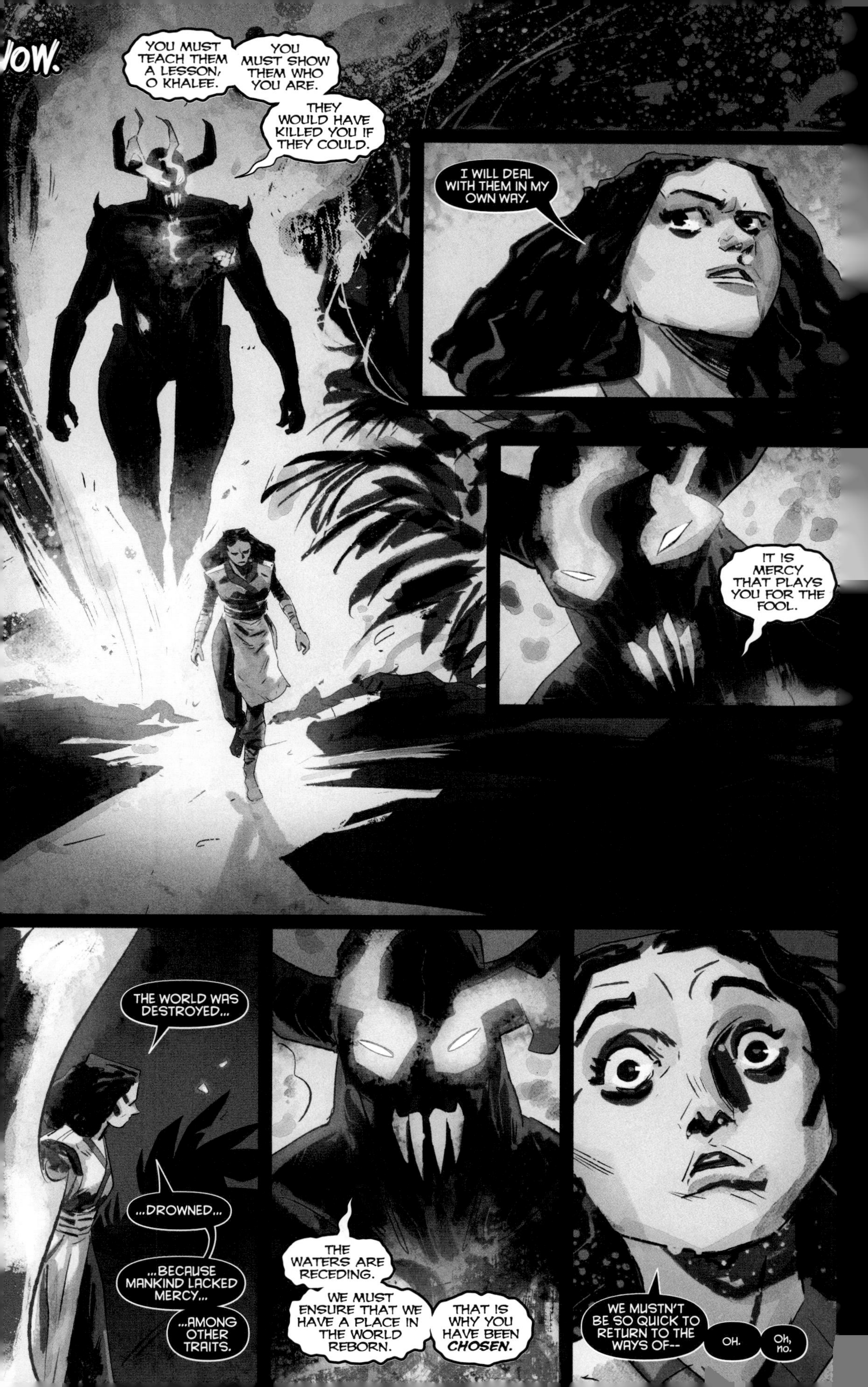

OW.
YOU MUST TEACH THEM A LESSON, O KHALEE.
YOU MUST SHOW THEM WHO YOU ARE.
THEY WOULD HAVE KILLED YOU IF THEY COULD.
I WILL DEAL WITH THEM IN MY OWN WAY.
IT IS MERCY THAT PLAYS YOU FOR THE FOOL.
THE WORLD WAS DESTROYED...
...DROWNED...
...BECAUSE MANKIND LACKED MERCY...
...AMONG OTHER TRAITS.
THE WATERS ARE RECEDING.
WE MUST ENSURE THAT WE HAVE A PLACE IN THE WORLD REBORN.
THAT IS WHY YOU HAVE BEEN *CHOSEN.*
WE MUSTN'T BE SO QUICK TO RETURN TO THE WAYS OF--
OH.
Oh, no.

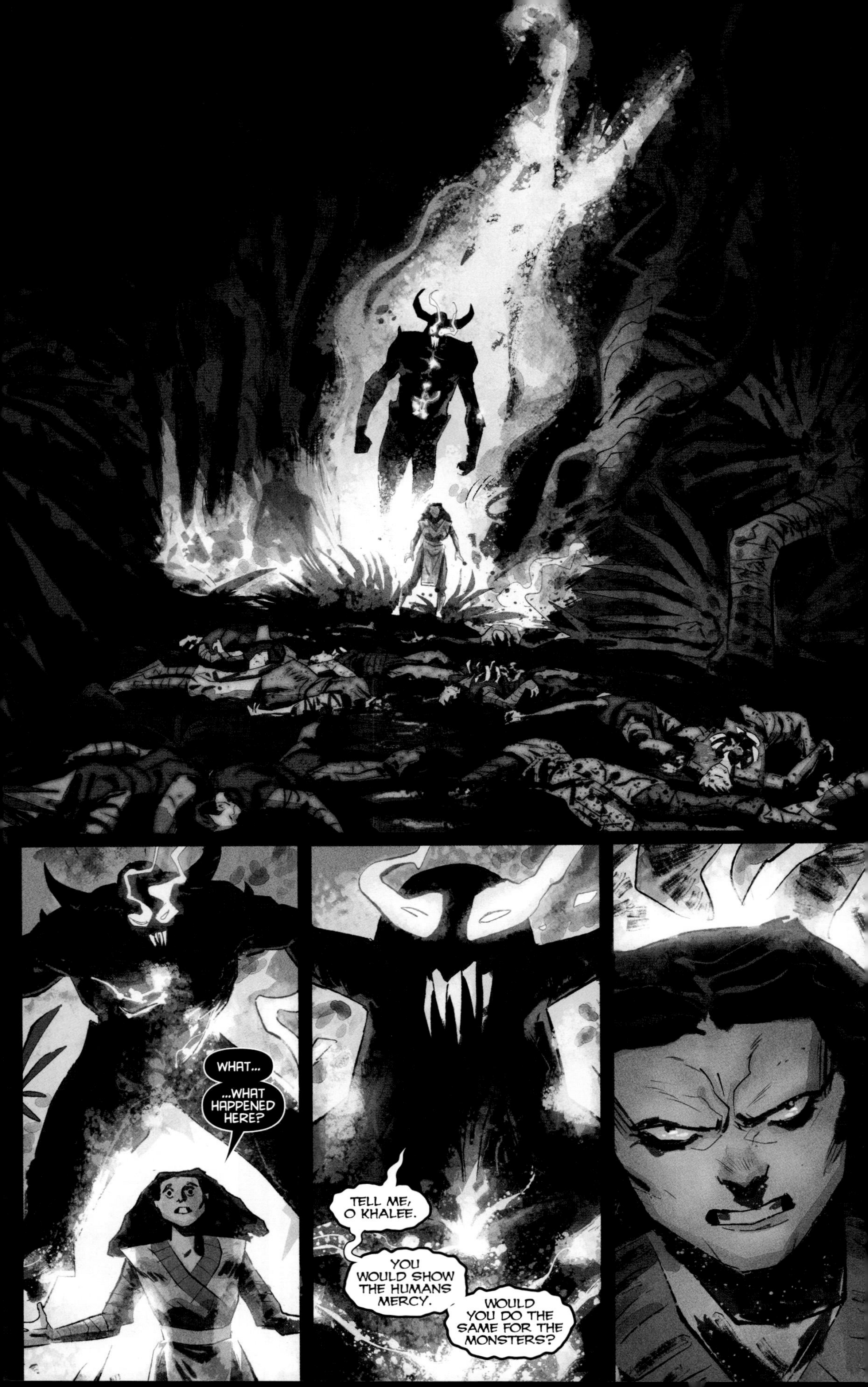
WHAT...
...WHAT HAPPENED HERE?
TELL ME, O KHALEE.
YOU WOULD SHOW THE HUMANS MERCY.
WOULD YOU DO THE SAME FOR THE MONSTERS?

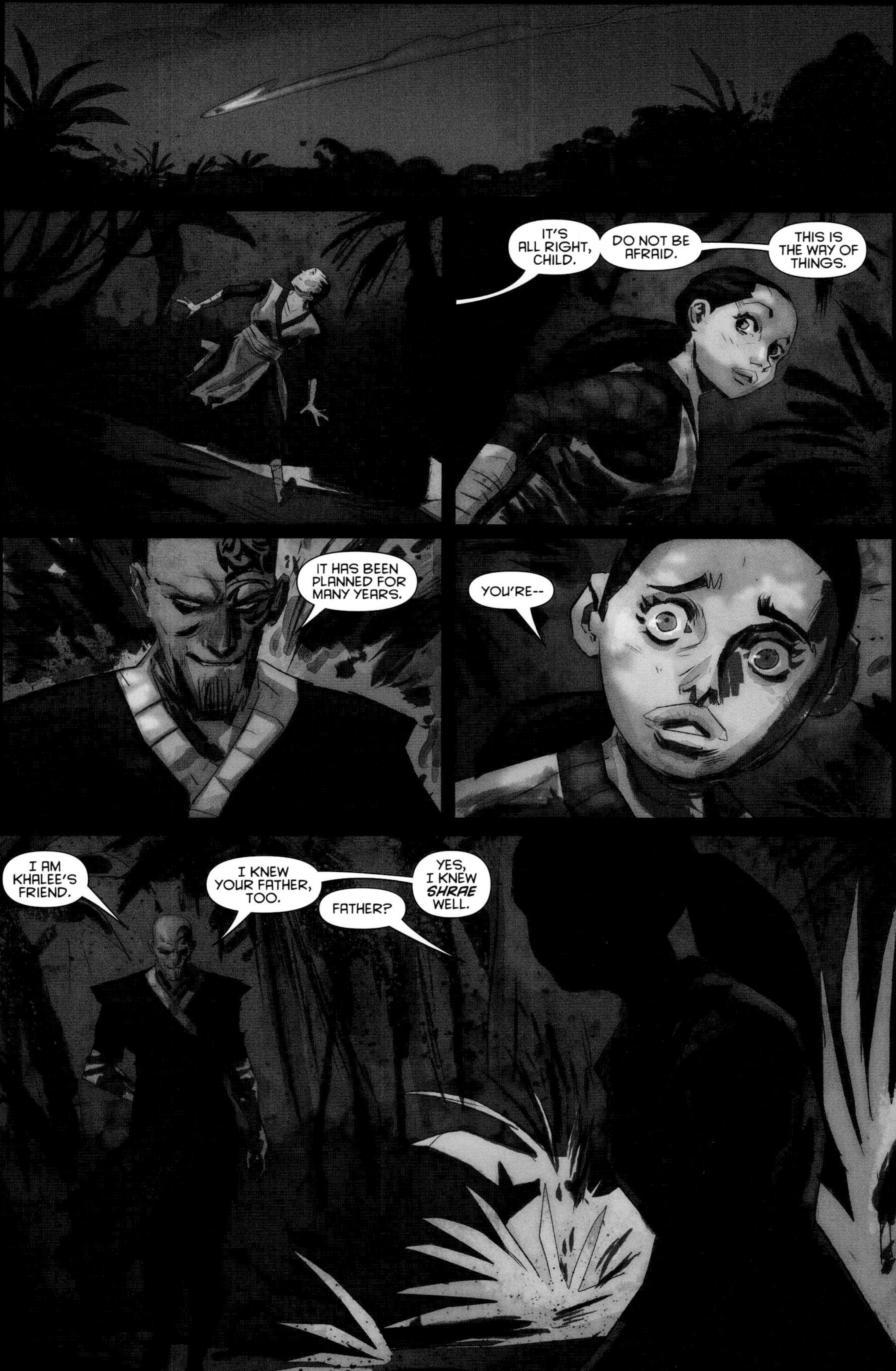
IT'S ALL RIGHT, CHILD.
DO NOT BE AFRAID.
THIS IS THE WAY OF THINGS.
IT HAS BEEN PLANNED FOR MANY YEARS.
YOU'RE--
I AM KHALEE'S FRIEND.
I KNEW YOUR FATHER, TOO.
FATHER?
YES, I KNEW SHRAE WELL.

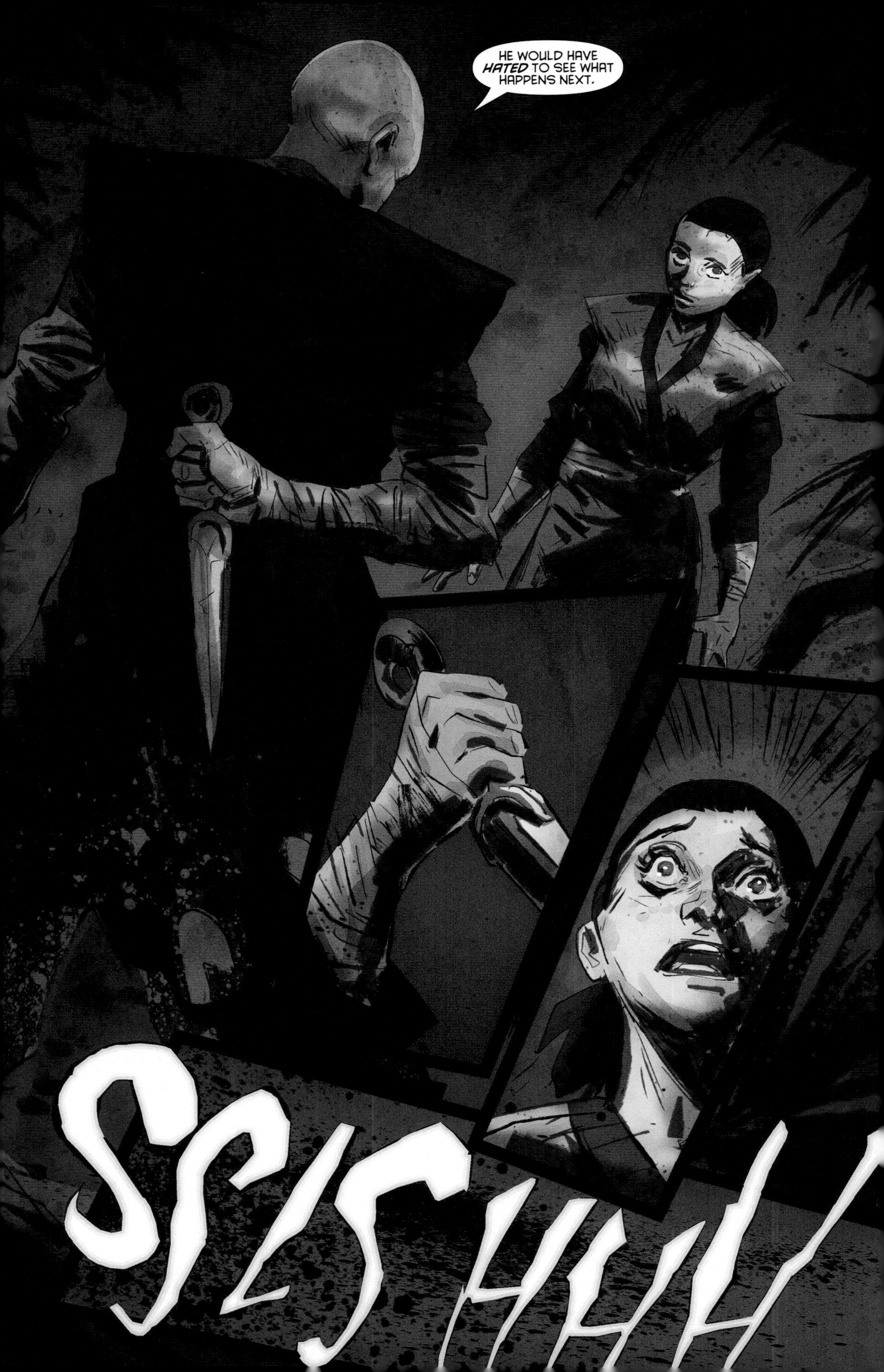
HE WOULD HAVE *HATED* TO SEE WHAT HAPPENS NEXT.
SSCSHHH!

6

THE LORD TAKES NOTICE

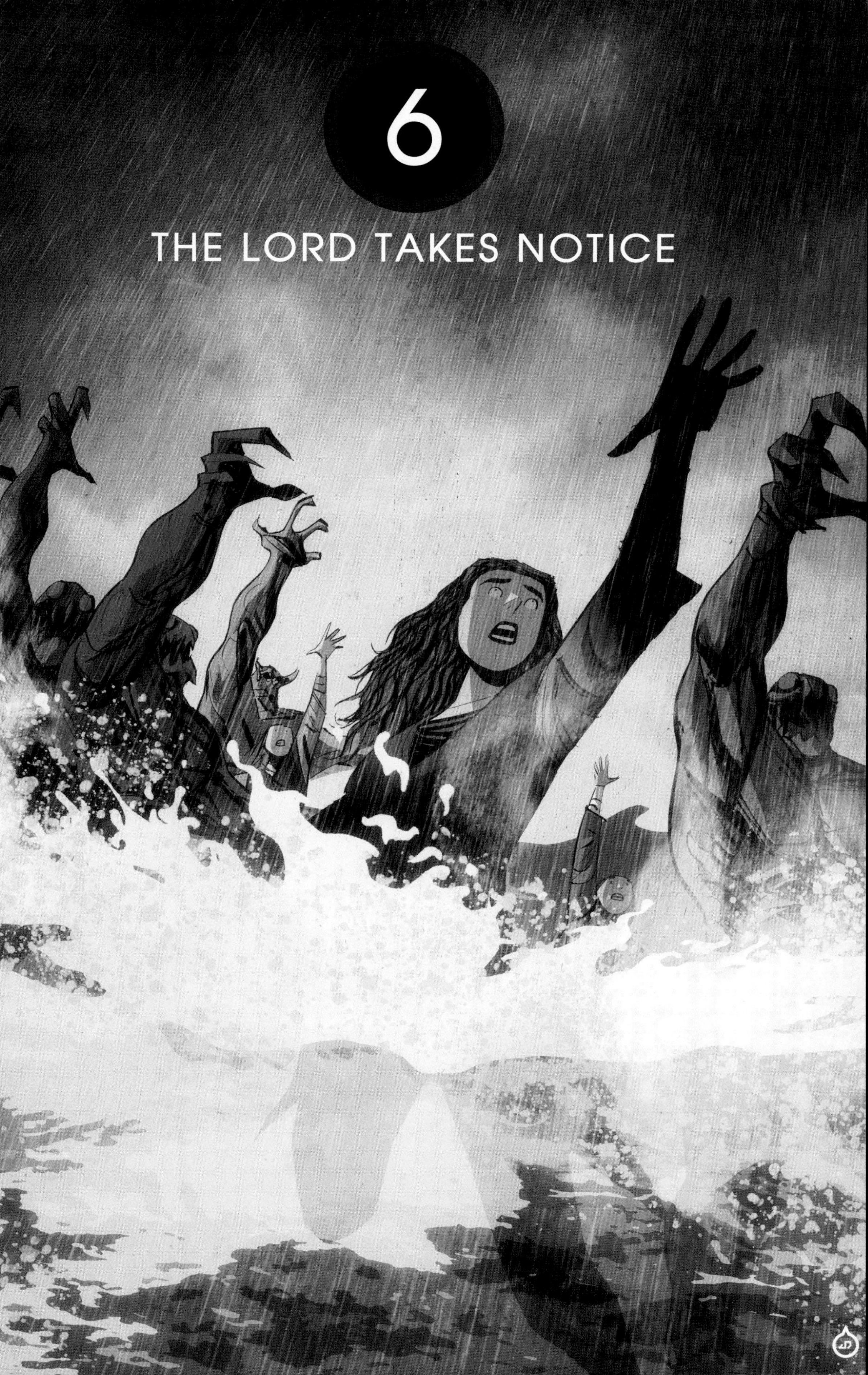

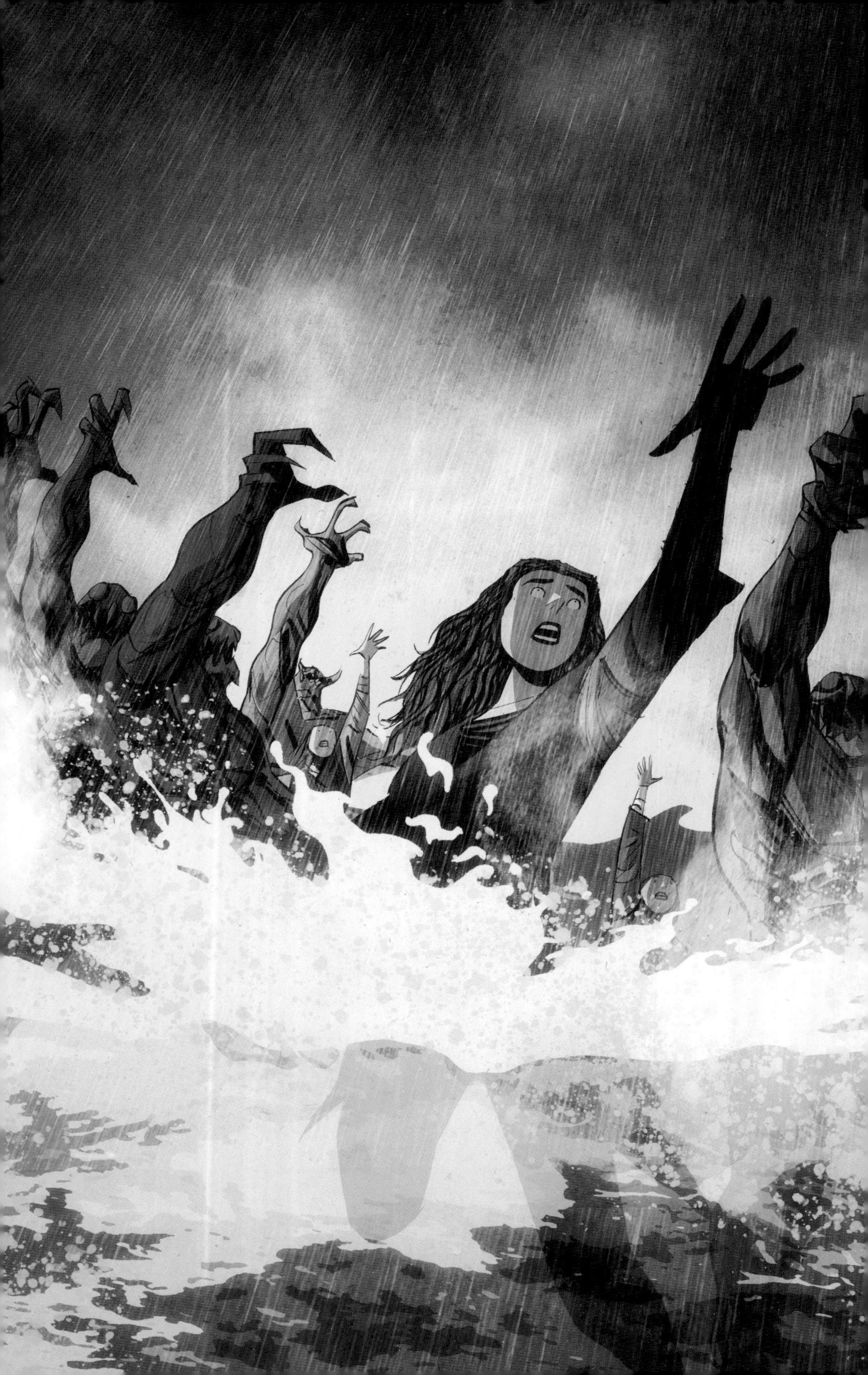

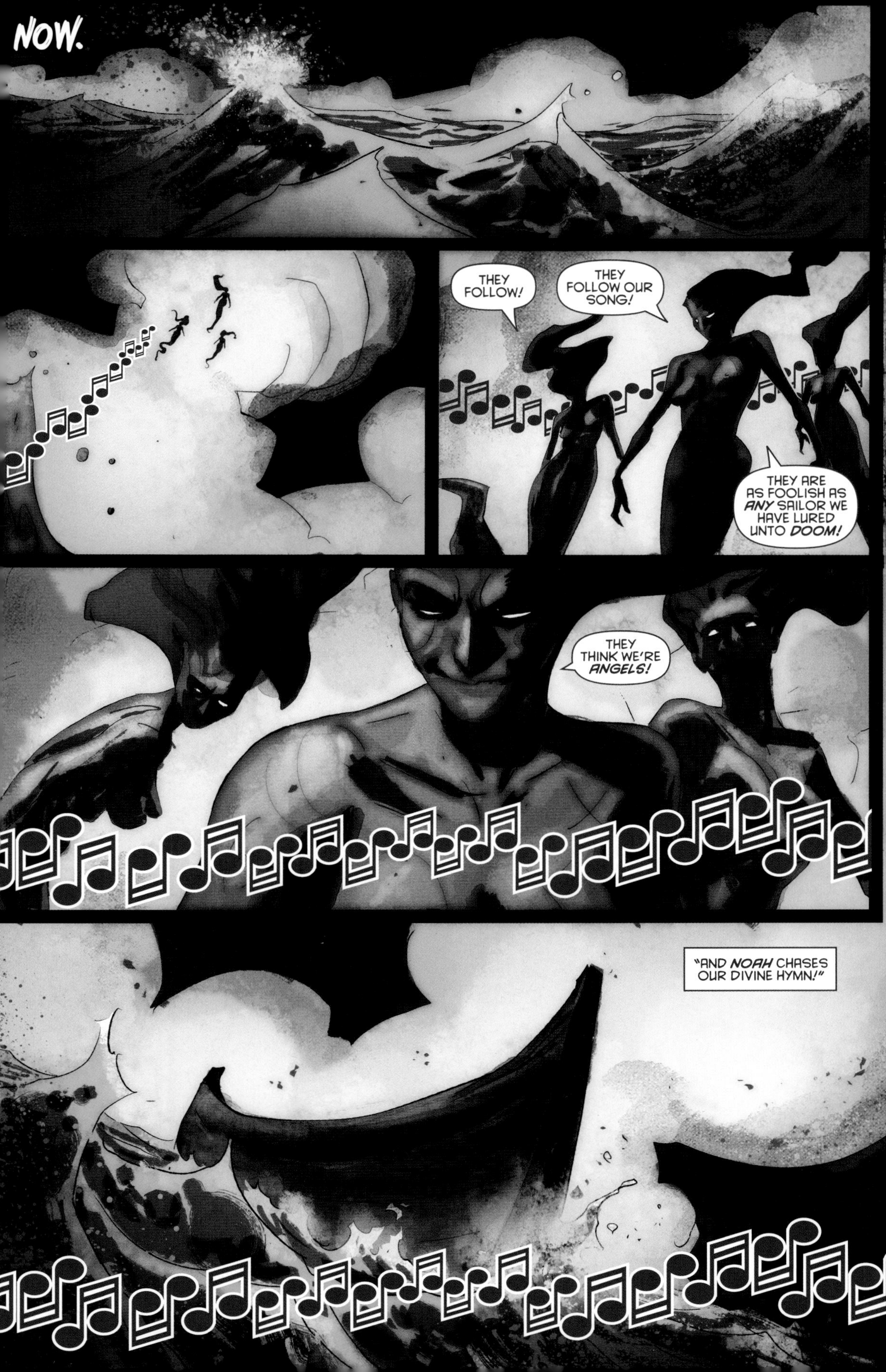
NOW.
THEY FOLLOW!
THEY FOLLOW OUR SONG!
THEY ARE AS FOOLISH AS ANY SAILOR WE HAVE LURED UNTO DOOM!
THEY THINK WE'RE ANGELS!
"AND NOAH CHASES OUR DIVINE HYMN!"

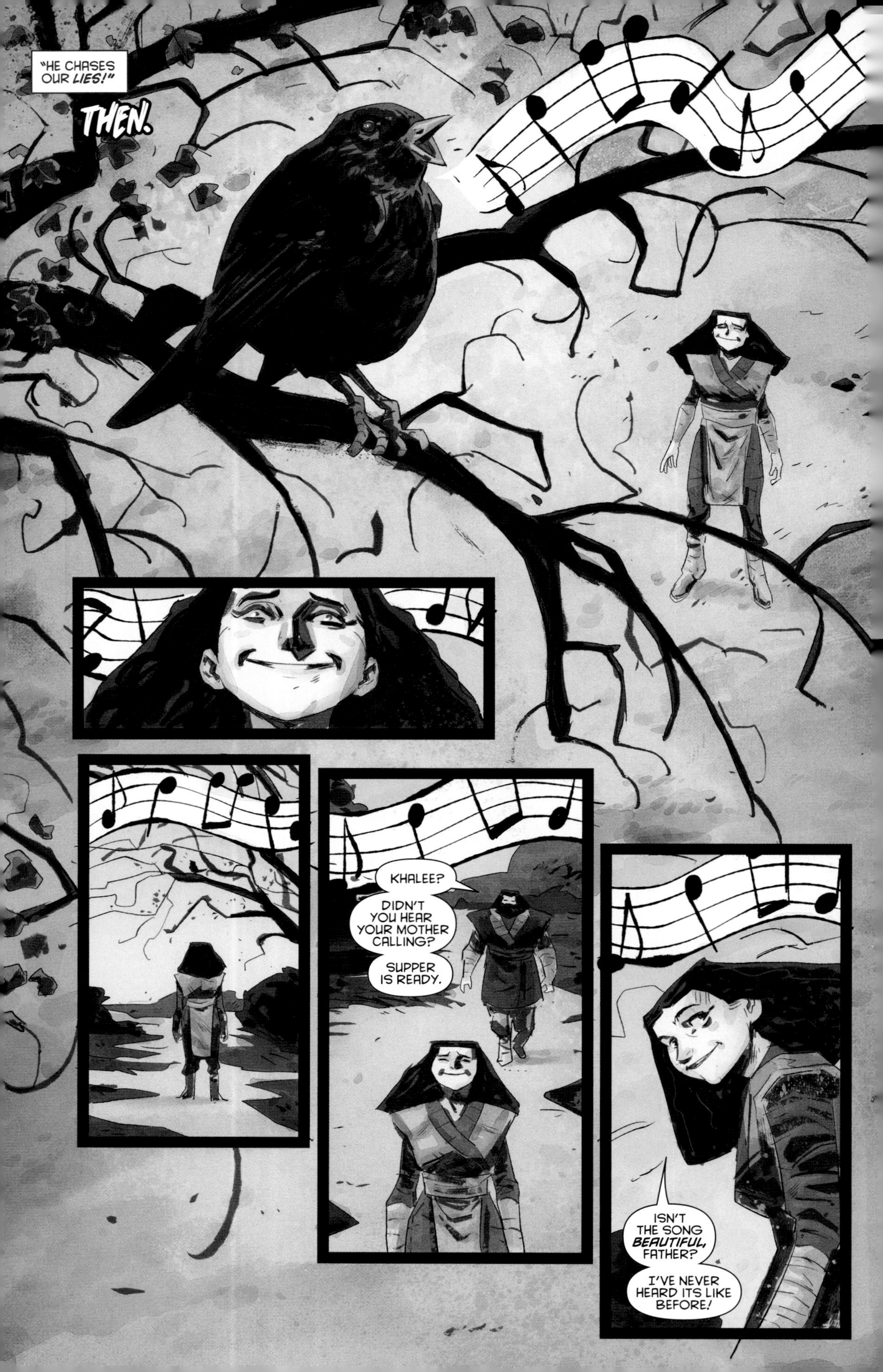

"HE CHASES OUR *LIES!*"
THEN.
KHALEE?
DIDN'T YOU HEAR YOUR MOTHER CALLING?
SUPPER IS READY.
ISN'T THE SONG ***BEAUTIFUL,*** FATHER?
I'VE NEVER HEARD ITS LIKE BEFORE!

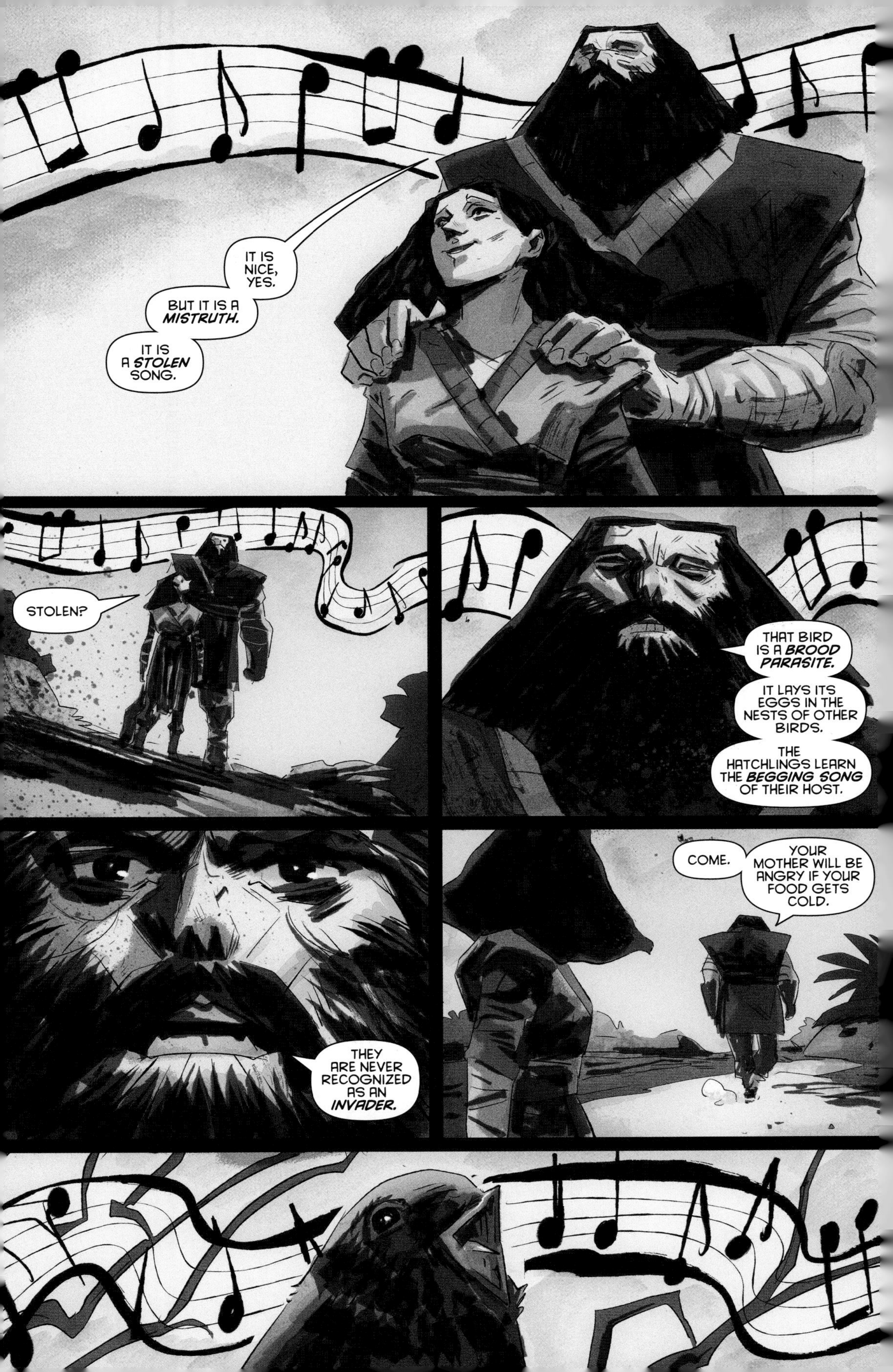
IT IS NICE, YES.
BUT IT IS A *MISTRUTH.*
IT IS A *STOLEN* SONG.
STOLEN?
THAT BIRD IS A *BROOD PARASITE.*
IT LAYS ITS EGGS IN THE NESTS OF OTHER BIRDS.
THE HATCHLINGS LEARN THE *BEGGING SONG* OF THEIR HOST.
THEY ARE NEVER RECOGNIZED AS AN *INVADER.*
COME.
YOUR MOTHER WILL BE ANGRY IF YOUR FOOD GETS COLD.

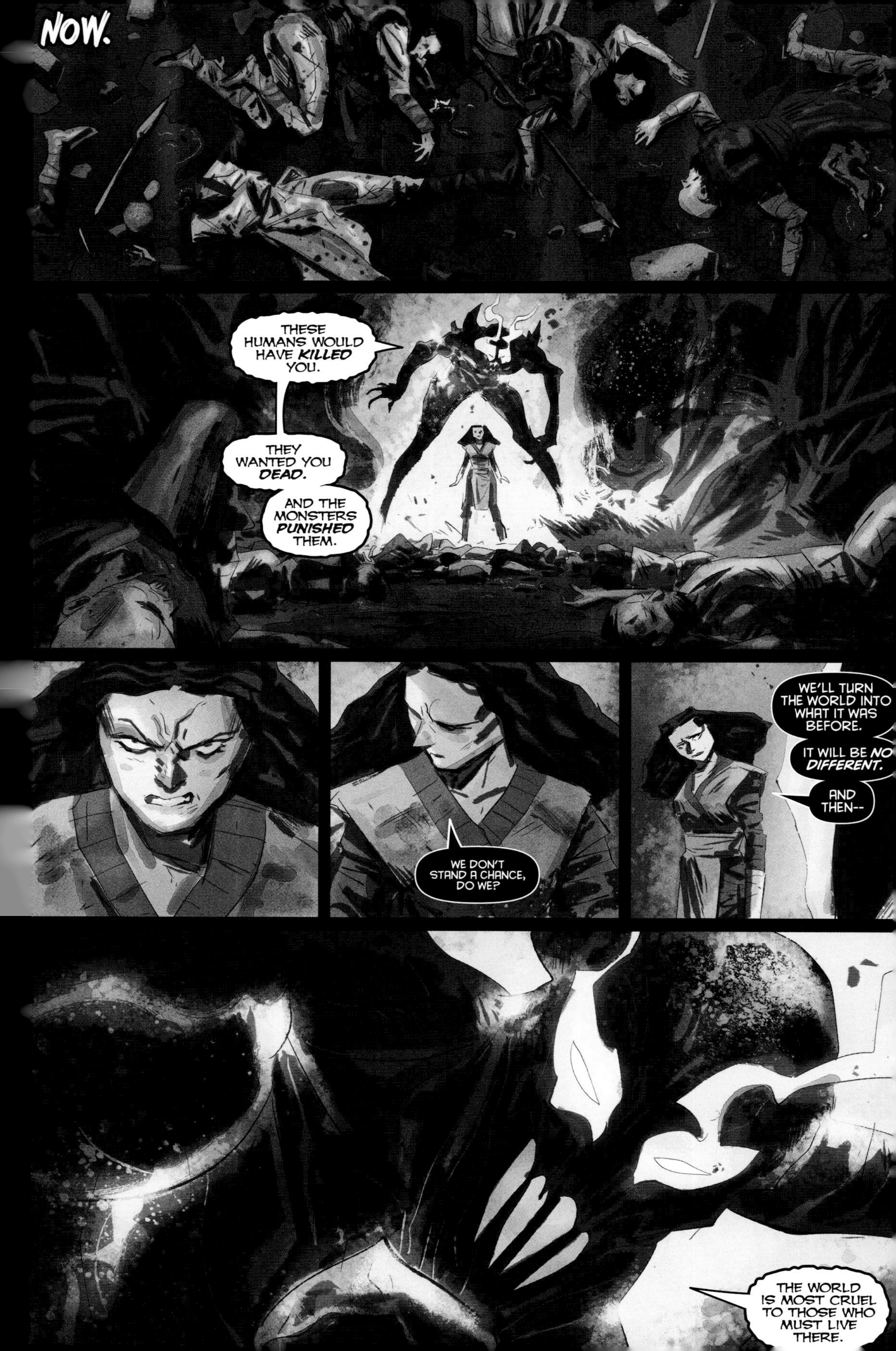
NOW.
THESE HUMANS WOULD HAVE KILLED YOU.
THEY WANTED YOU DEAD.
AND THE MONSTERS PUNISHED THEM.
WE DON'T STAND A CHANCE, DO WE?
WE'LL TURN THE WORLD INTO WHAT IT WAS BEFORE.
IT WILL BE NO DIFFERENT.
AND THEN--
THE WORLD IS MOST CRUEL TO THOSE WHO MUST LIVE THERE.

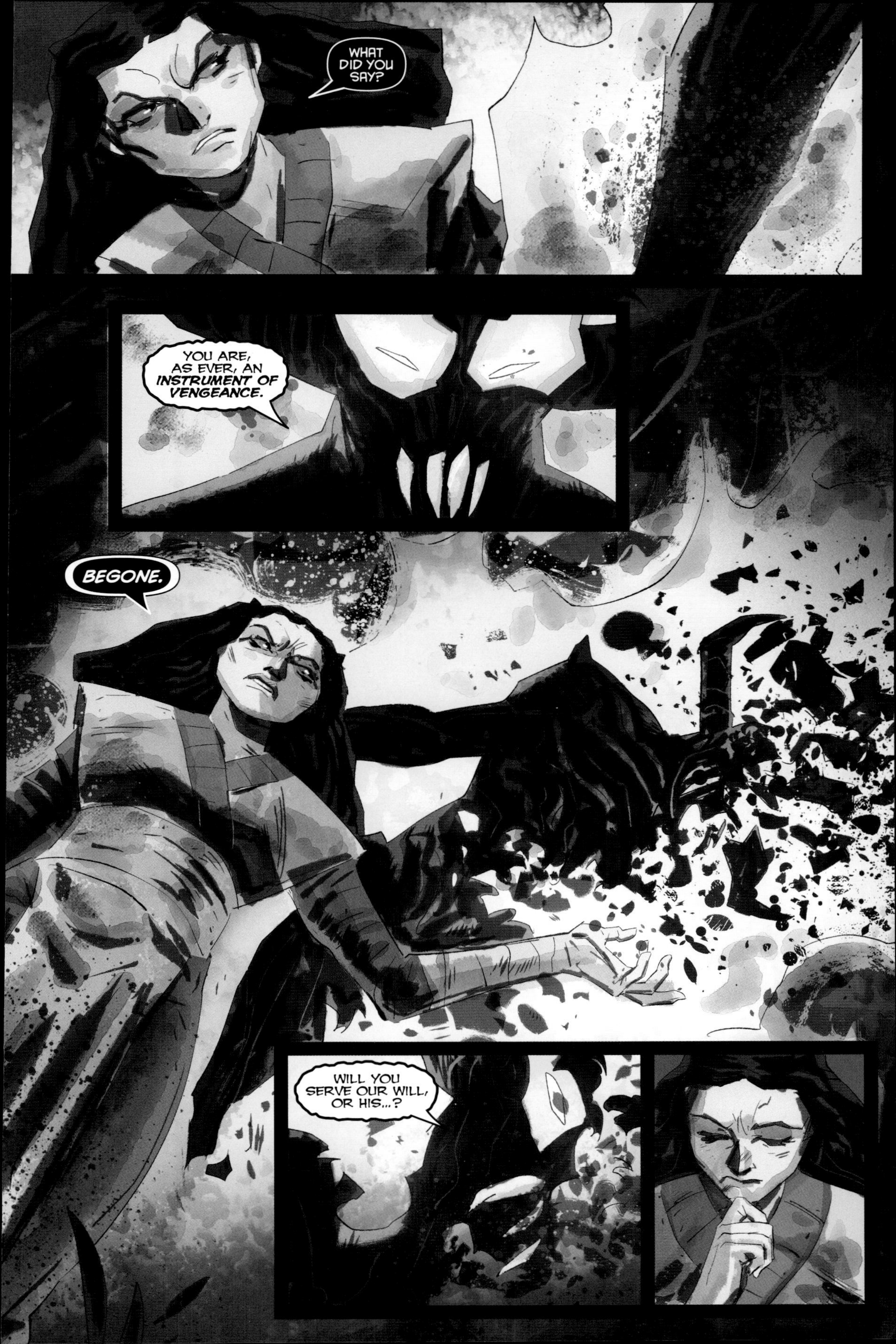
WHAT DID YOU SAY?
YOU ARE, AS EVER, AN *INSTRUMENT OF VENGEANCE.*
BEGONE.
WILL YOU SERVE OUR WILL, OR HIS...?

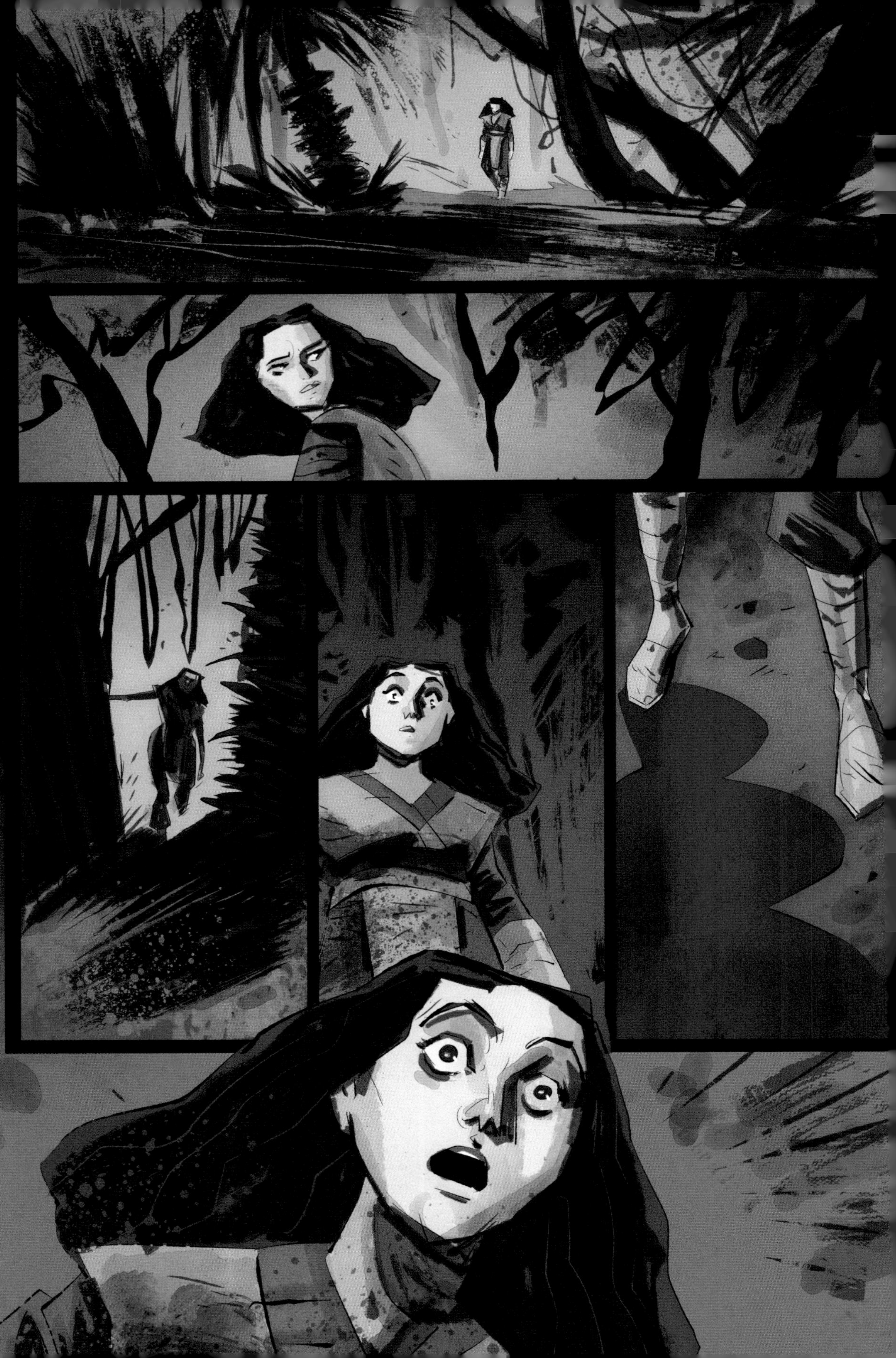

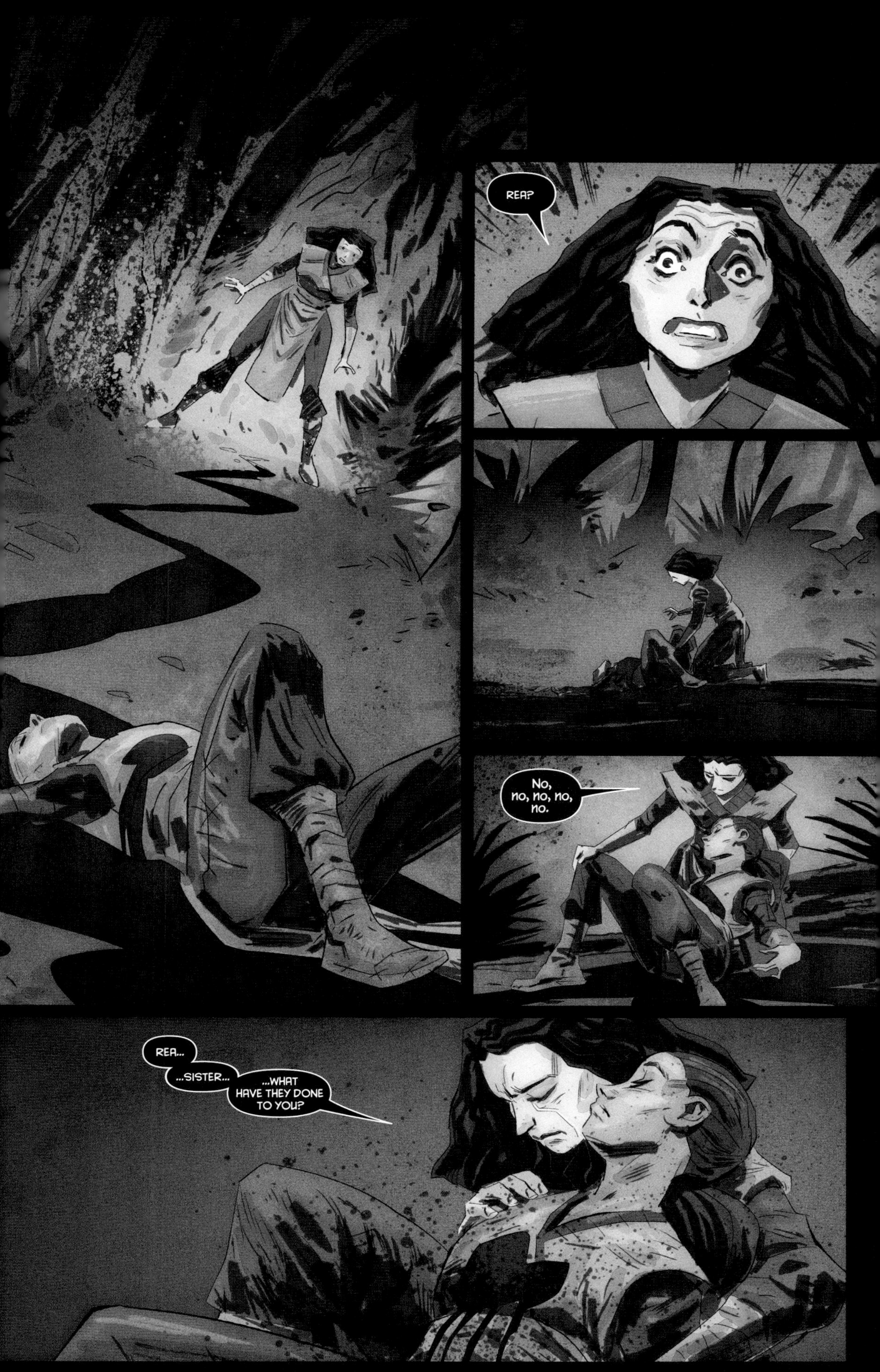
REA?
No, no, no, no, no.
REA...
...SISTER...
...WHAT HAVE THEY DONE TO YOU?

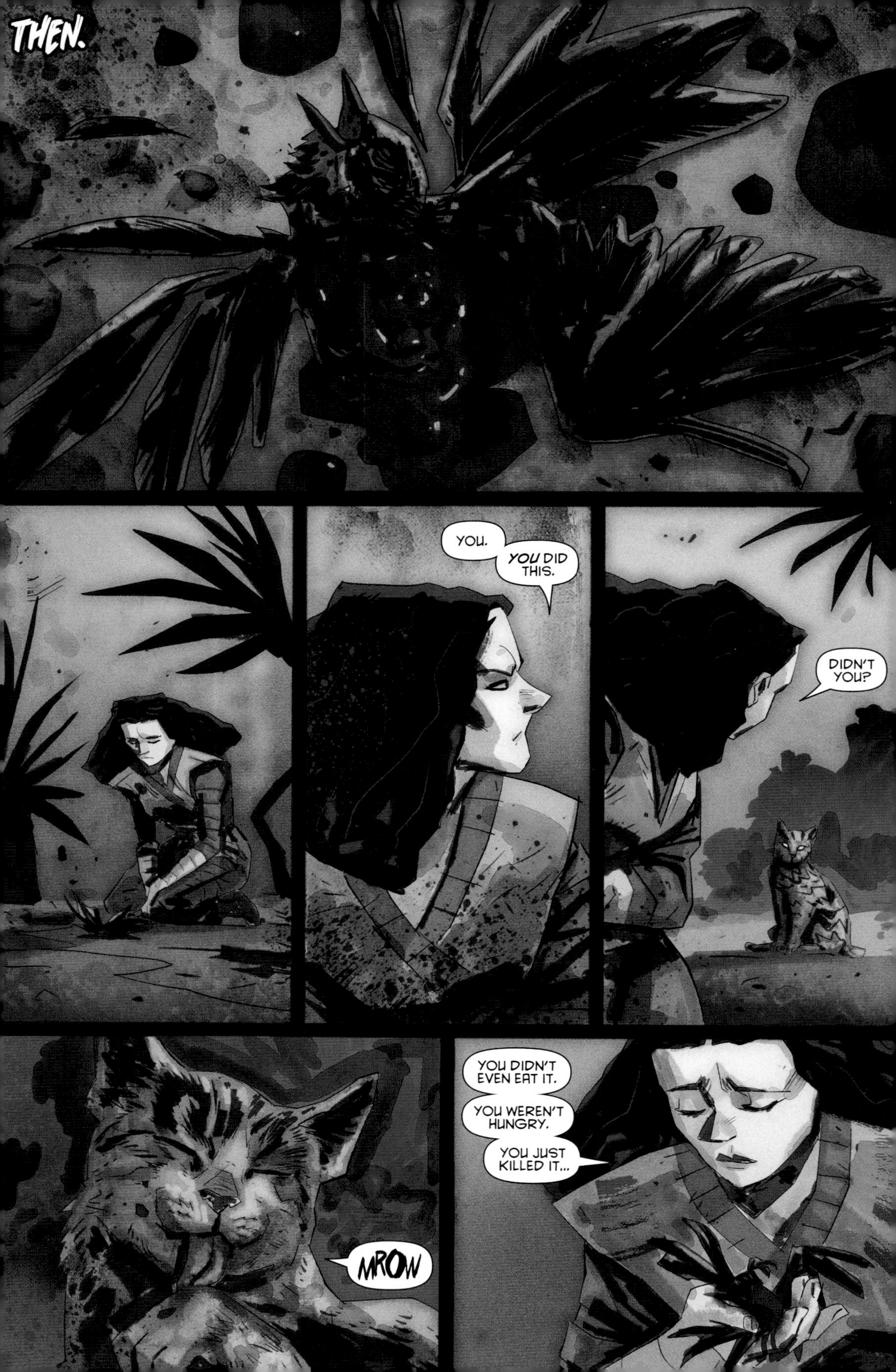
THEN.
YOU.
YOU DID THIS.
DIDN'T YOU?
MROW
YOU DIDN'T EVEN EAT IT.
YOU WEREN'T HUNGRY.
YOU JUST KILLED IT...

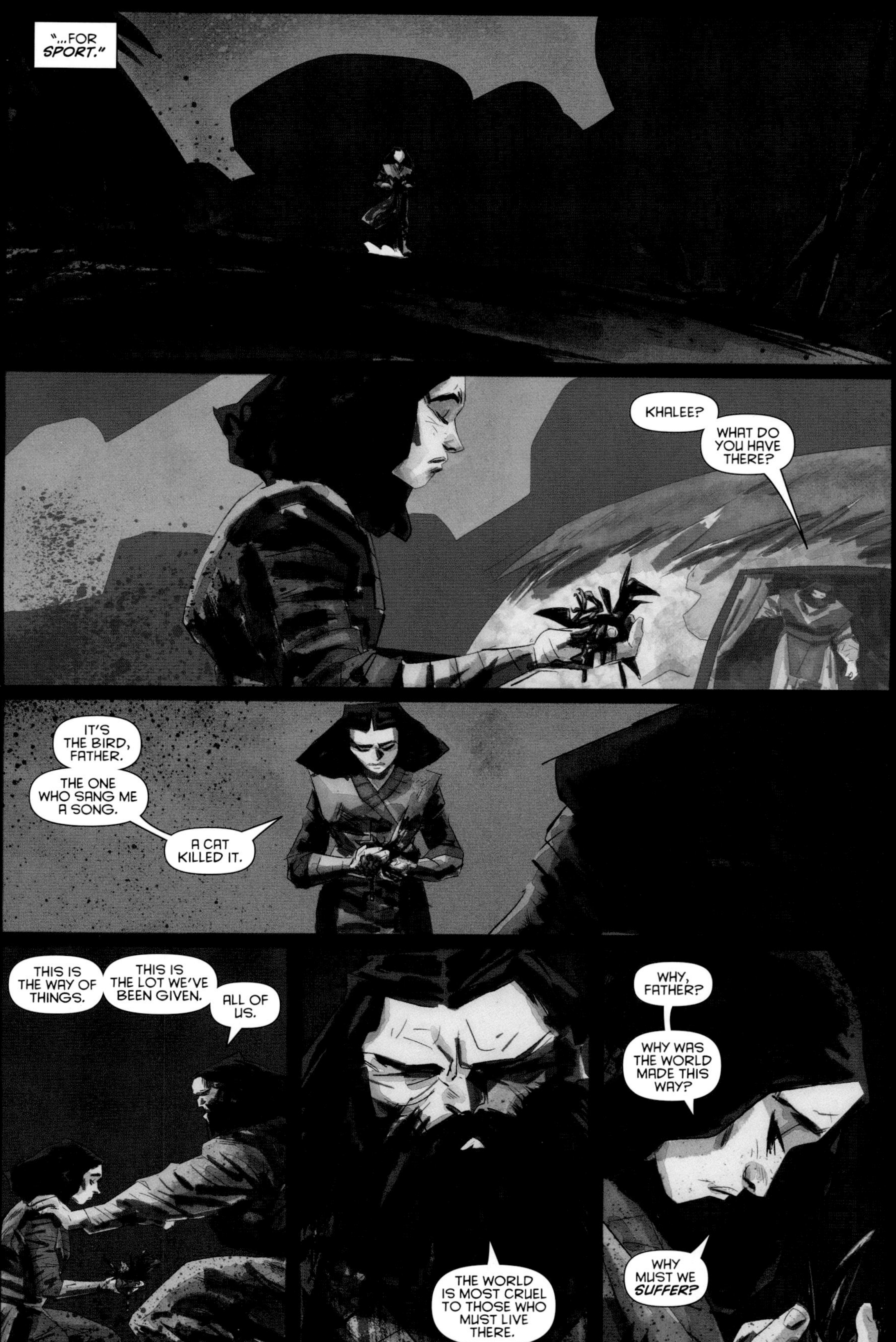
"...FOR SPORT."
KHALEE?
WHAT DO YOU HAVE THERE?
IT'S THE BIRD, FATHER.
THE ONE WHO SANG ME A SONG.
A CAT KILLED IT.
THIS IS THE WAY OF THINGS.
THIS IS THE LOT WE'VE BEEN GIVEN.
ALL OF US.
WHY, FATHER?
WHY WAS THE WORLD MADE THIS WAY?
WHY MUST WE SUFFER?
THE WORLD IS MOST CRUEL TO THOSE WHO MUST LIVE THERE.

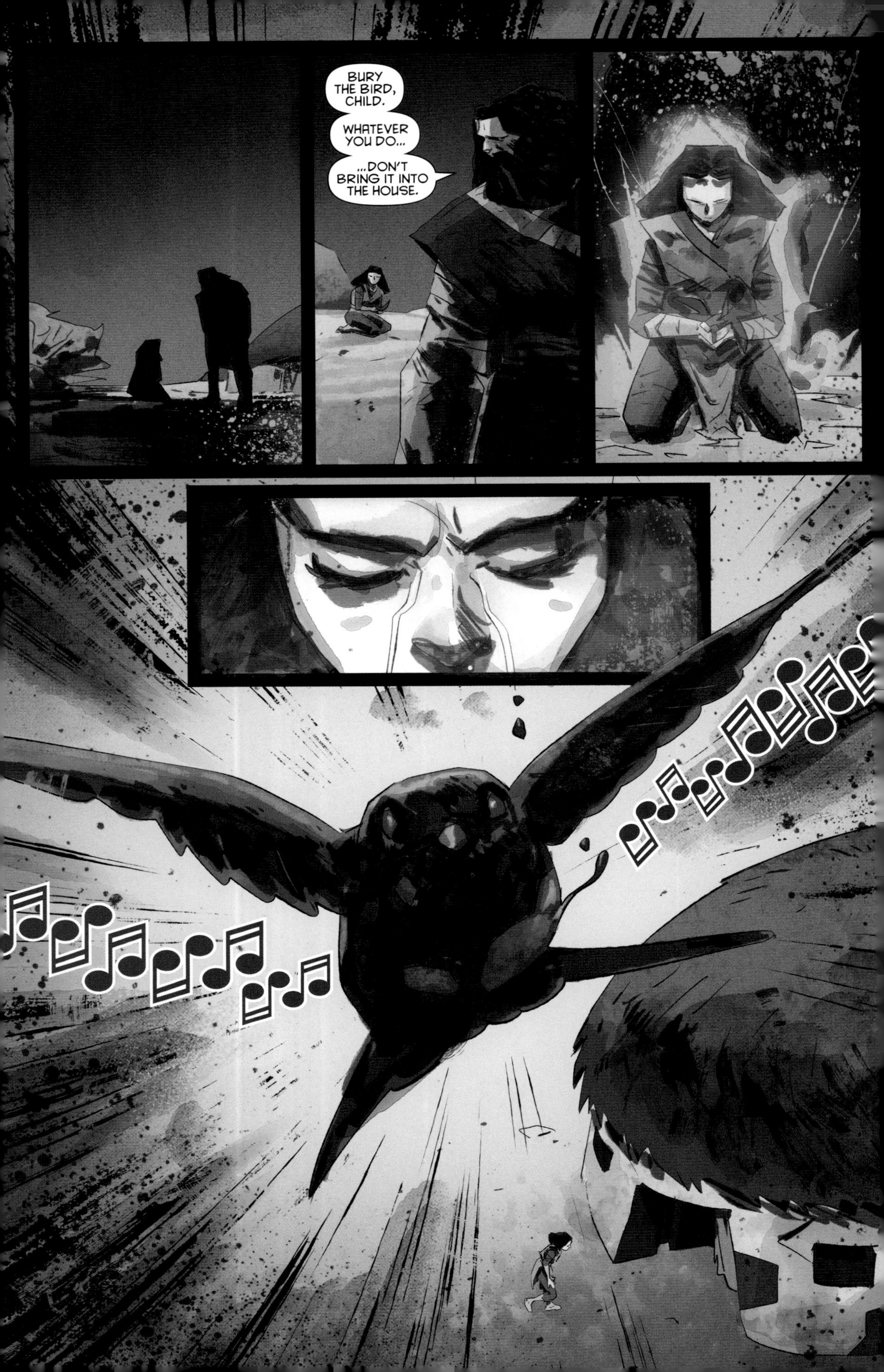
BURY THE BIRD, CHILD.
WHATEVER YOU DO...
...DON'T BRING IT INTO THE HOUSE.

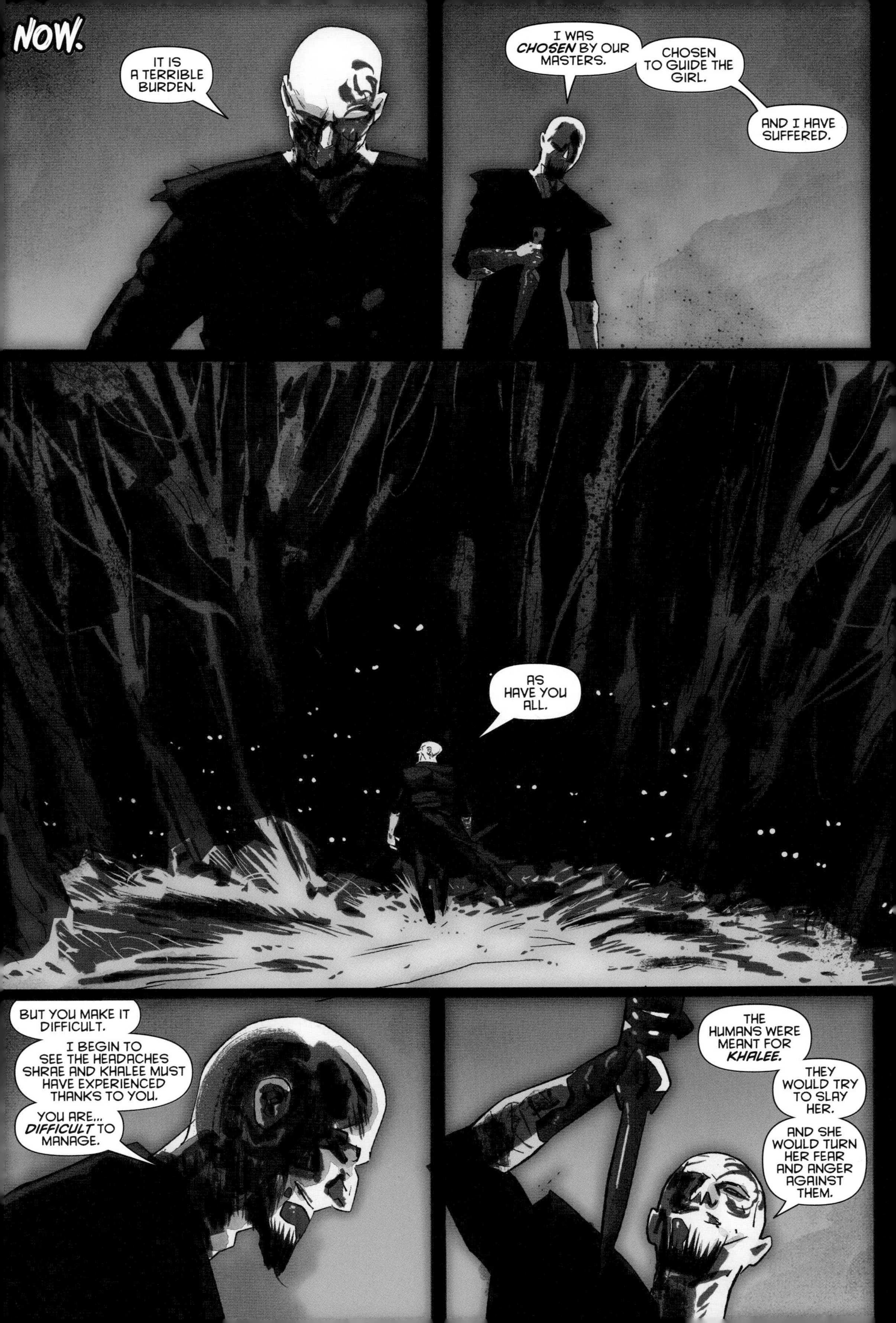
NOW.
IT IS A TERRIBLE BURDEN.
I WAS *CHOSEN* BY OUR MASTERS.
CHOSEN TO GUIDE THE GIRL.
AND I HAVE SUFFERED.
AS HAVE YOU ALL.
BUT YOU MAKE IT DIFFICULT.
I BEGIN TO SEE THE HEADACHES SHRAE AND KHALEE MUST HAVE EXPERIENCED THANKS TO YOU.
YOU ARE... *DIFFICULT* TO MANAGE.
THE HUMANS WERE MEANT FOR *KHALEE.*
THEY WOULD TRY TO SLAY HER.
AND SHE WOULD TURN HER FEAR AND ANGER AGAINST THEM.

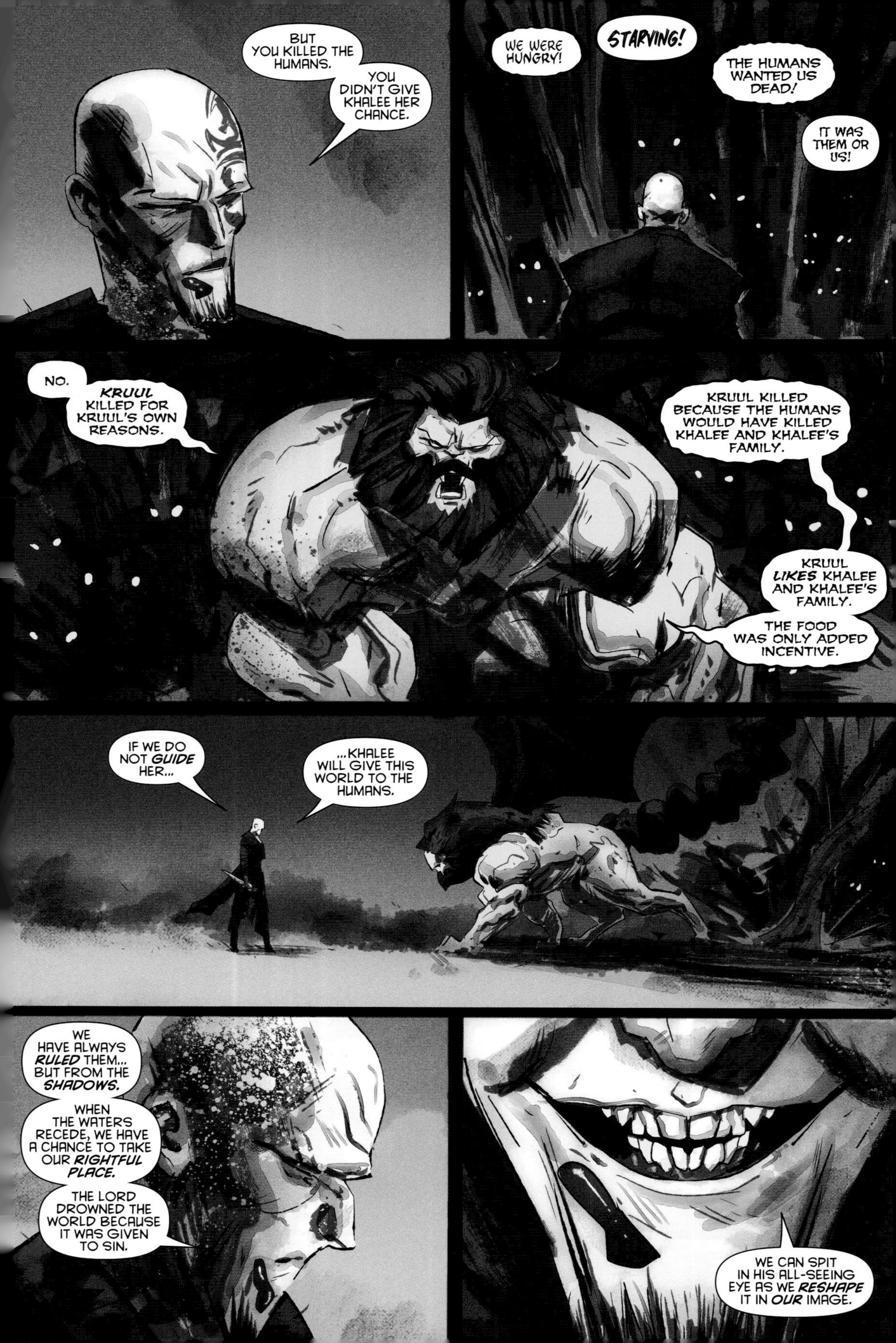
BUT YOU KILLED THE HUMANS.
YOU DIDN'T GIVE KHALEE HER CHANCE.
WE WERE HUNGRY!
STARVING!
THE HUMANS WANTED US DEAD!
IT WAS THEM OR US!
NO. KRUUL KILLED FOR KRUUL'S OWN REASONS.
KRUUL KILLED BECAUSE THE HUMANS WOULD HAVE KILLED KHALEE AND KHALEE'S FAMILY.
KRUUL LIKES KHALEE AND KHALEE'S FAMILY.
THE FOOD WAS ONLY ADDED INCENTIVE.
IF WE DO NOT GUIDE HER...
...KHALEE WILL GIVE THIS WORLD TO THE HUMANS.
WE HAVE ALWAYS RULED THEM... BUT FROM THE SHADOWS.
WHEN THE WATERS RECEDE, WE HAVE A CHANCE TO TAKE OUR RIGHTFUL PLACE.
THE LORD DROWNED THE WORLD BECAUSE IT WAS GIVEN TO SIN.
WE CAN SPIT IN HIS ALL-SEEING EYE AS WE RESHAPE IT IN OUR IMAGE.

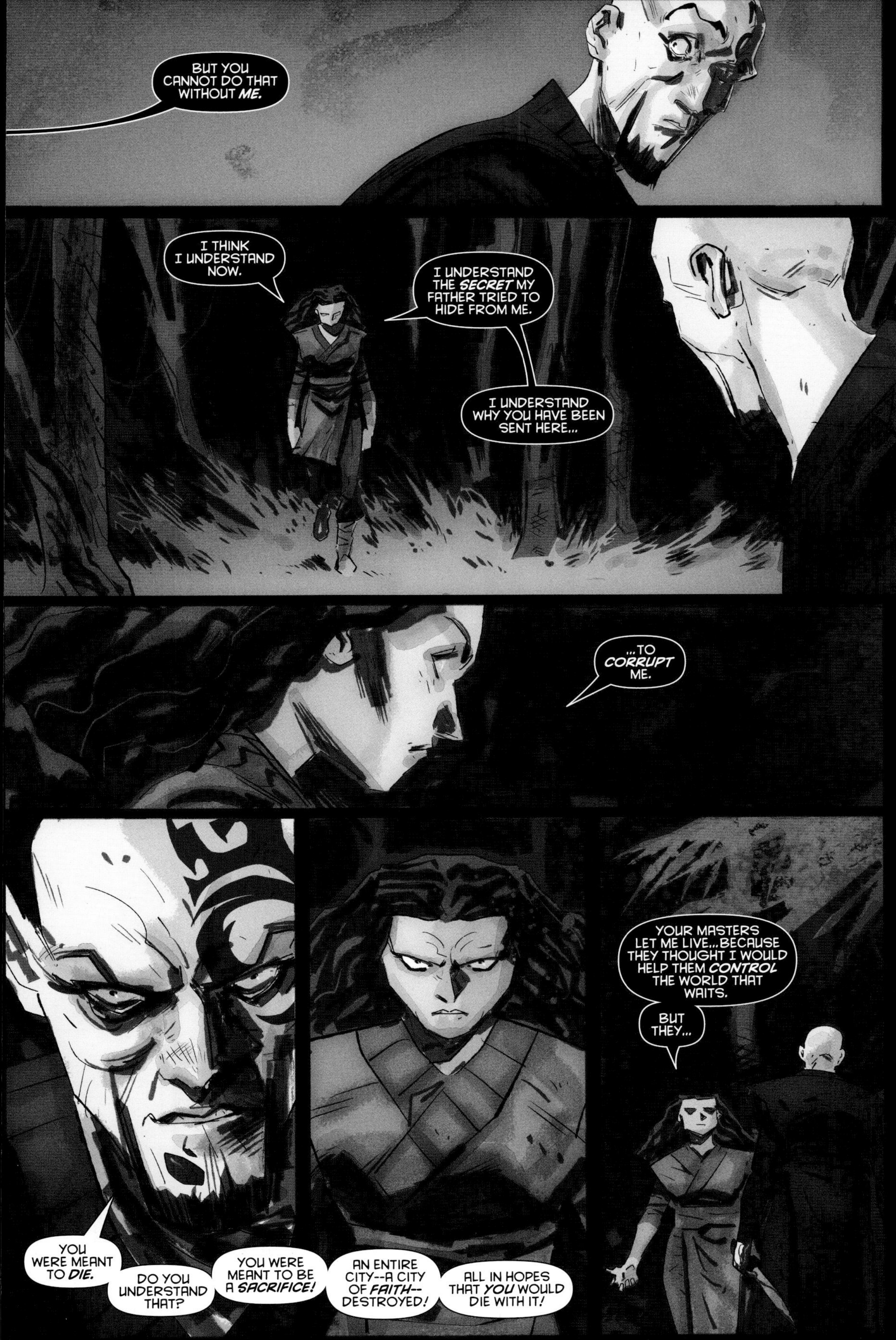
BUT YOU CANNOT DO THAT WITHOUT ME.
I THINK I UNDERSTAND NOW.
I UNDERSTAND THE SECRET MY FATHER TRIED TO HIDE FROM ME.
I UNDERSTAND WHY YOU HAVE BEEN SENT HERE...
...TO CORRUPT ME.
YOU WERE MEANT TO DIE.
DO YOU UNDERSTAND THAT?
YOU WERE MEANT TO BE A SACRIFICE!
AN ENTIRE CITY--A CITY OF FAITH--DESTROYED!
ALL IN HOPES THAT YOU WOULD DIE WITH IT!
YOUR MASTERS LET ME LIVE...BECAUSE THEY THOUGHT I WOULD HELP THEM CONTROL THE WORLD THAT WAITS.
BUT THEY...

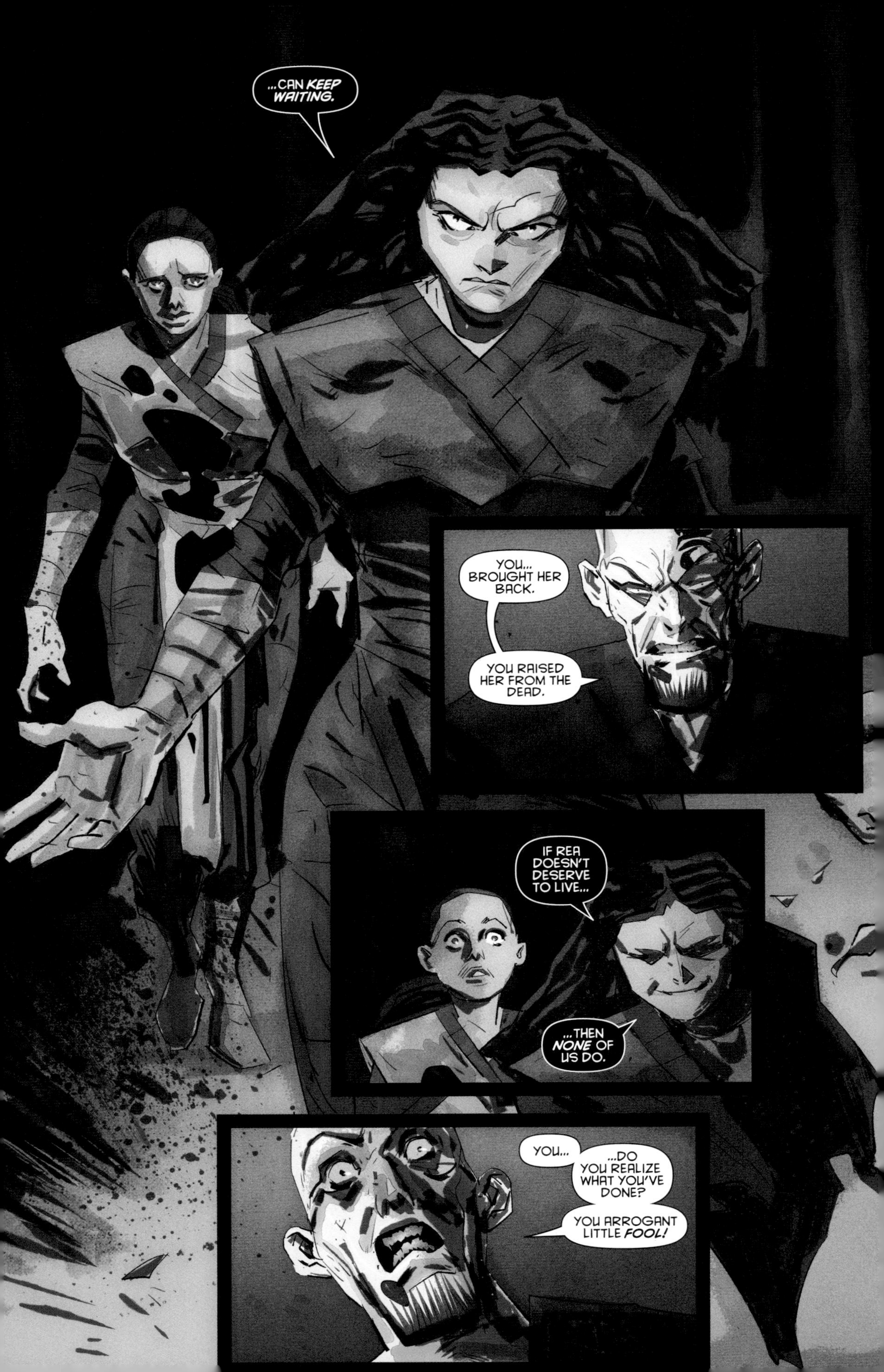
...CAN *KEEP WAITING.*
YOU... BROUGHT HER BACK.
YOU RAISED HER FROM THE DEAD.
IF REA DOESN'T DESERVE TO LIVE...
...THEN *NONE* OF US DO.
YOU...
...DO YOU REALIZE WHAT YOU'VE DONE?
YOU ARROGANT LITTLE *FOOL!*

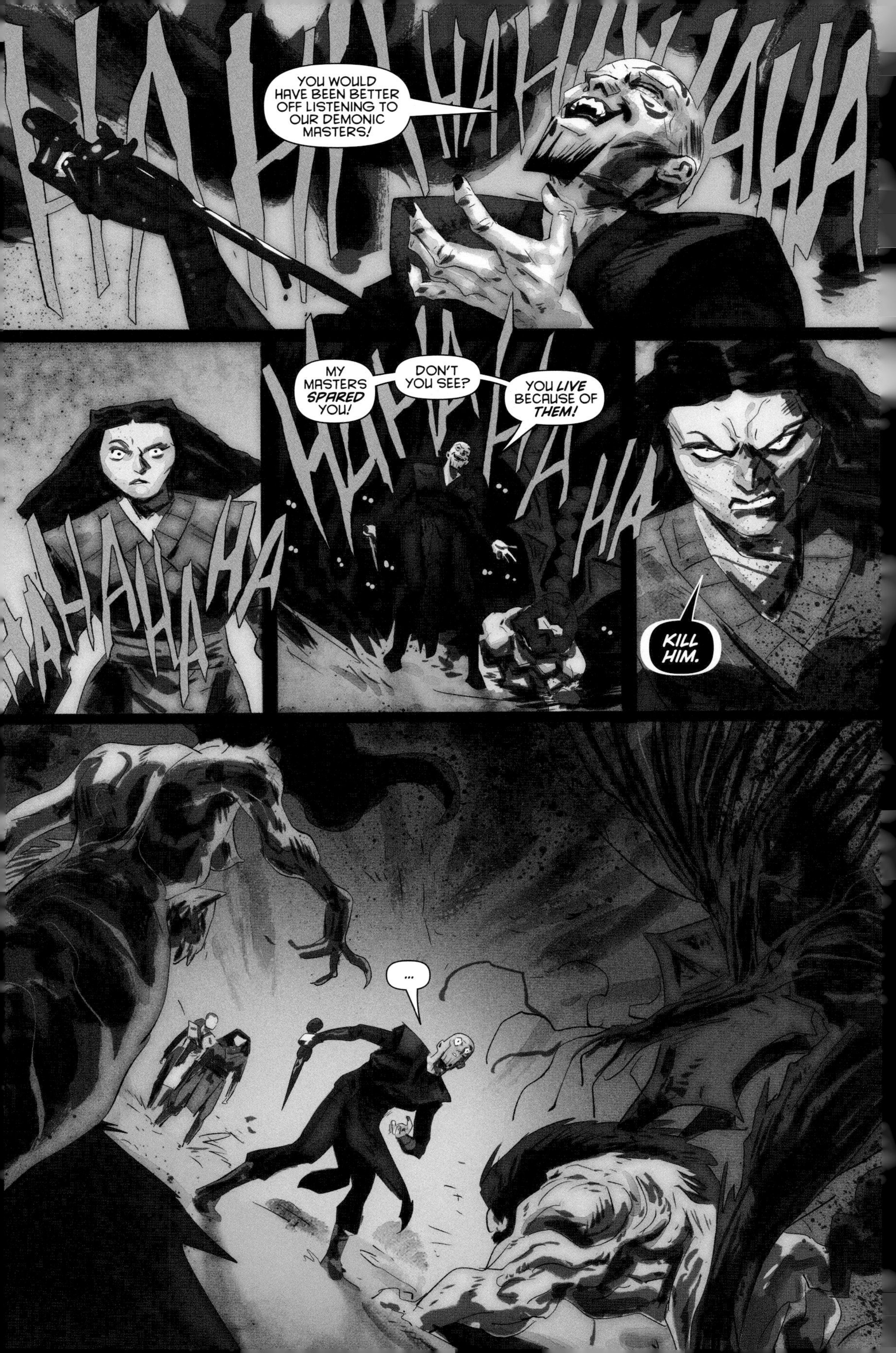
HA HA HA HA HA HA HA HA
YOU WOULD HAVE BEEN BETTER OFF LISTENING TO OUR DEMONIC MASTERS!
HA HA HA HA
MY MASTERS SPARED YOU!
DON'T YOU SEE?
YOU LIVE BECAUSE OF THEM!
HA HA HA HA
KILL HIM.
...

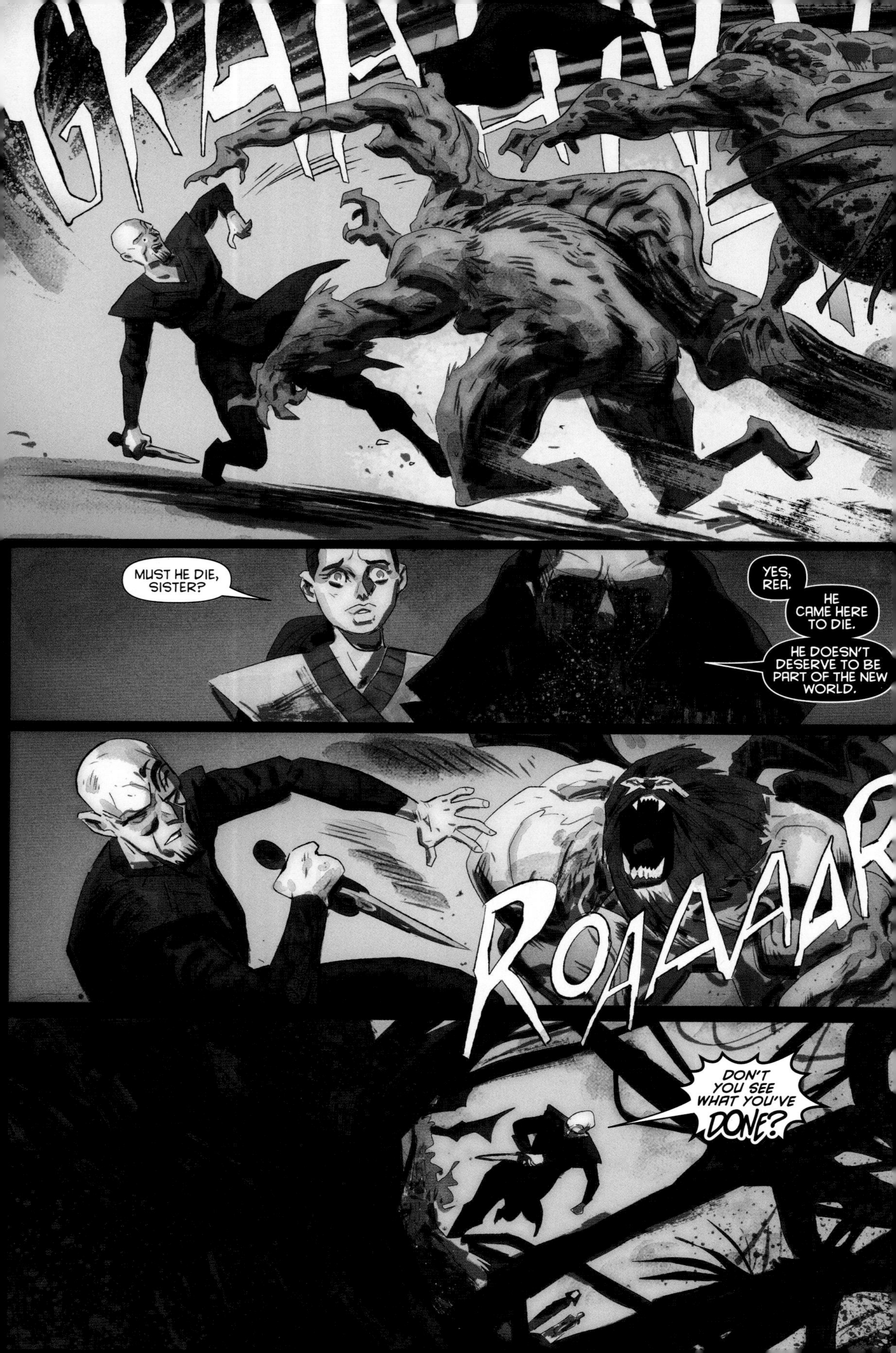
GRAAAAAAH
MUST HE DIE, SISTER?
YES, REA.
HE CAME HERE TO DIE.
HE DOESN'T DESERVE TO BE PART OF THE NEW WORLD.
ROAAAAR
DON'T YOU SEE WHAT YOU'VE DONE?

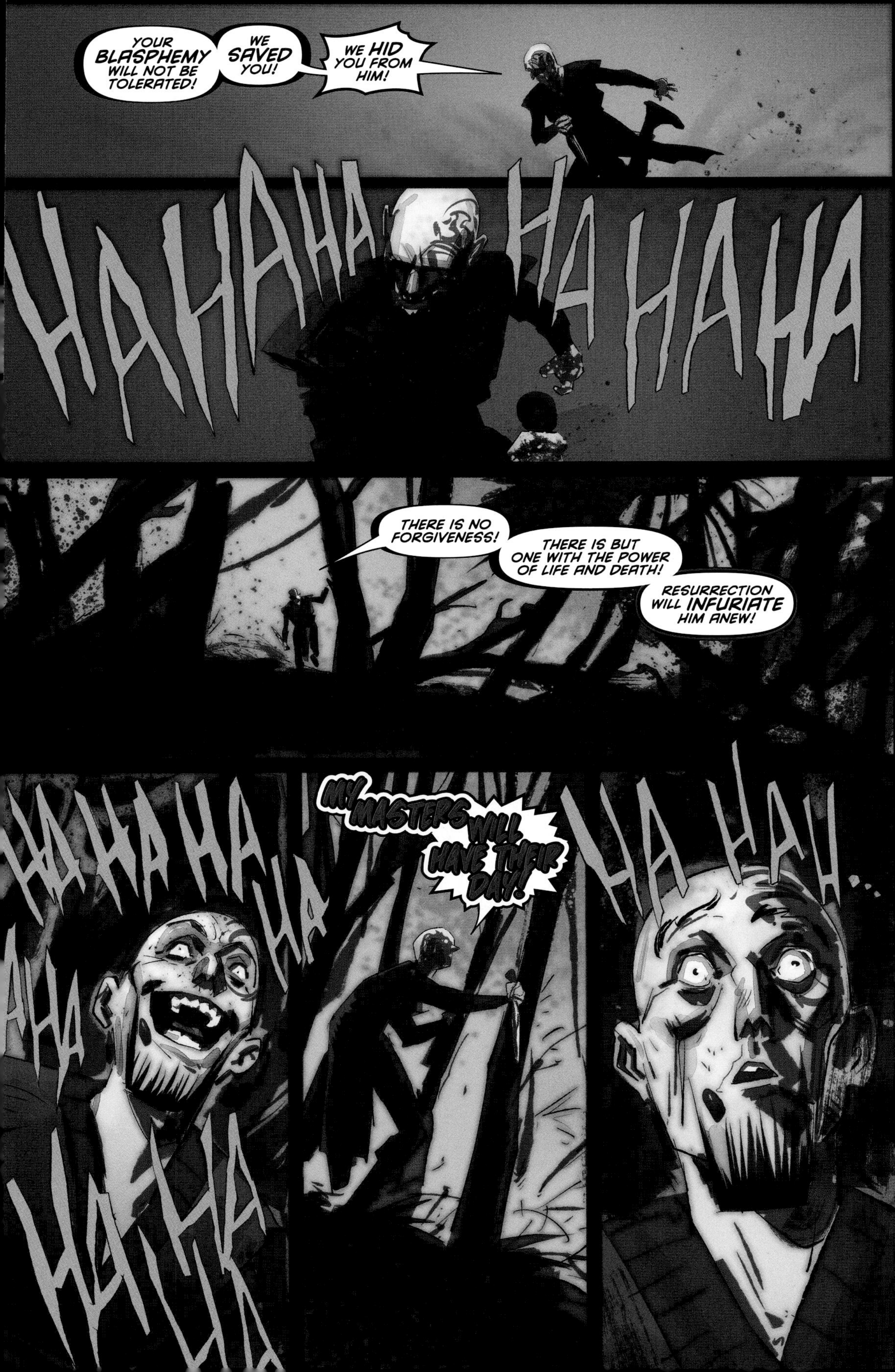
YOUR BLASPHEMY WILL NOT BE TOLERATED!
WE SAVED YOU!
WE HID YOU FROM HIM!
HAHAHAHA HA HA HAHA
THERE IS NO FORGIVENESS!
THERE IS BUT ONE WITH THE POWER OF LIFE AND DEATH!
RESURRECTION WILL INFURIATE HIM ANEW!
HA HA HA HA HA HA HA HA
MY MASTERS WILL HAVE THEIR DAY!
HA HA HA HA HA
HA HAH...

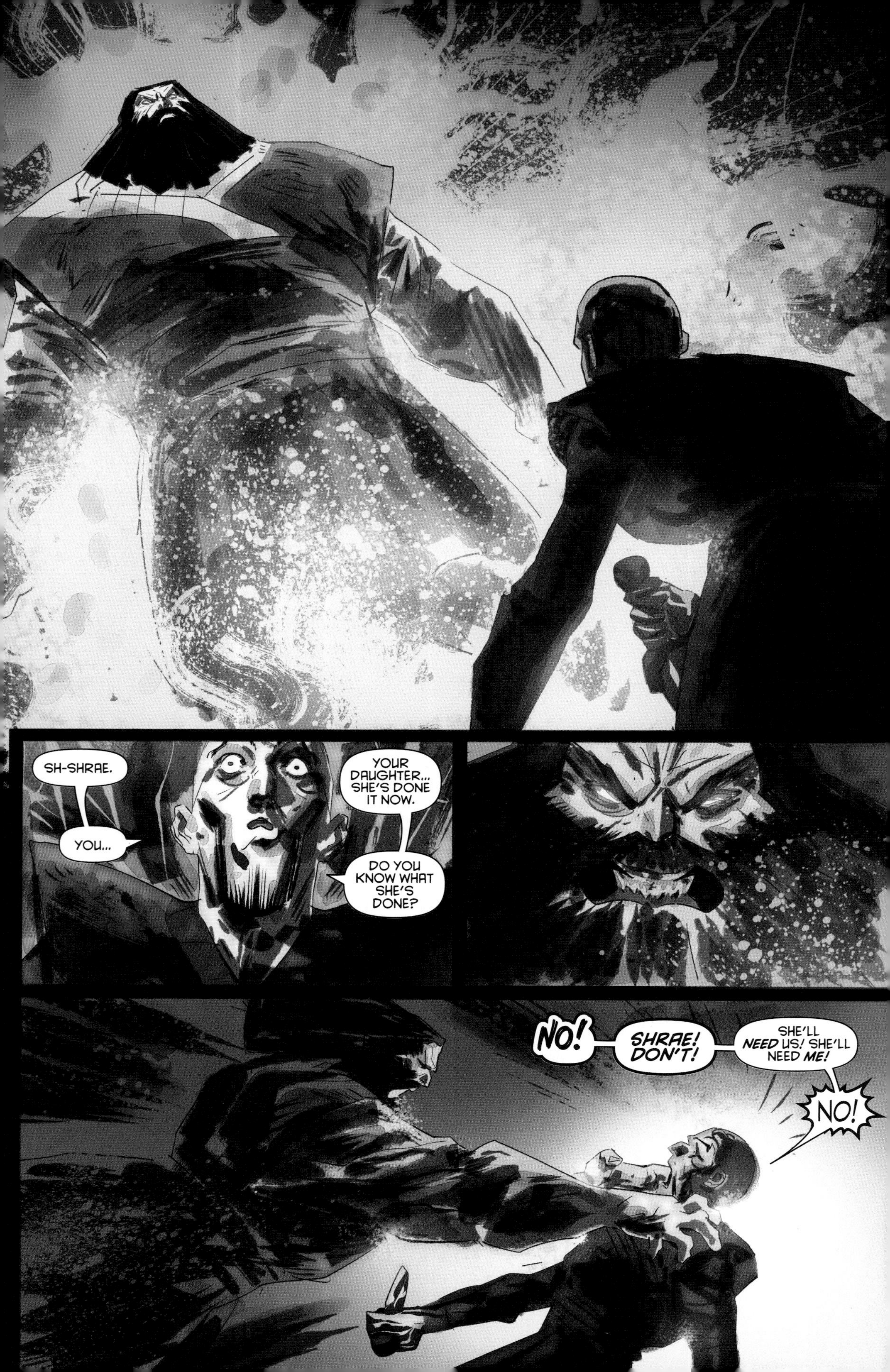
SH-SHRAE.
YOU...
YOUR DAUGHTER... SHE'S DONE IT NOW.
DO YOU KNOW WHAT SHE'S DONE?
NO!
SHRAE! DON'T!
SHE'LL NEED US! SHE'LL NEED ME!
NO!

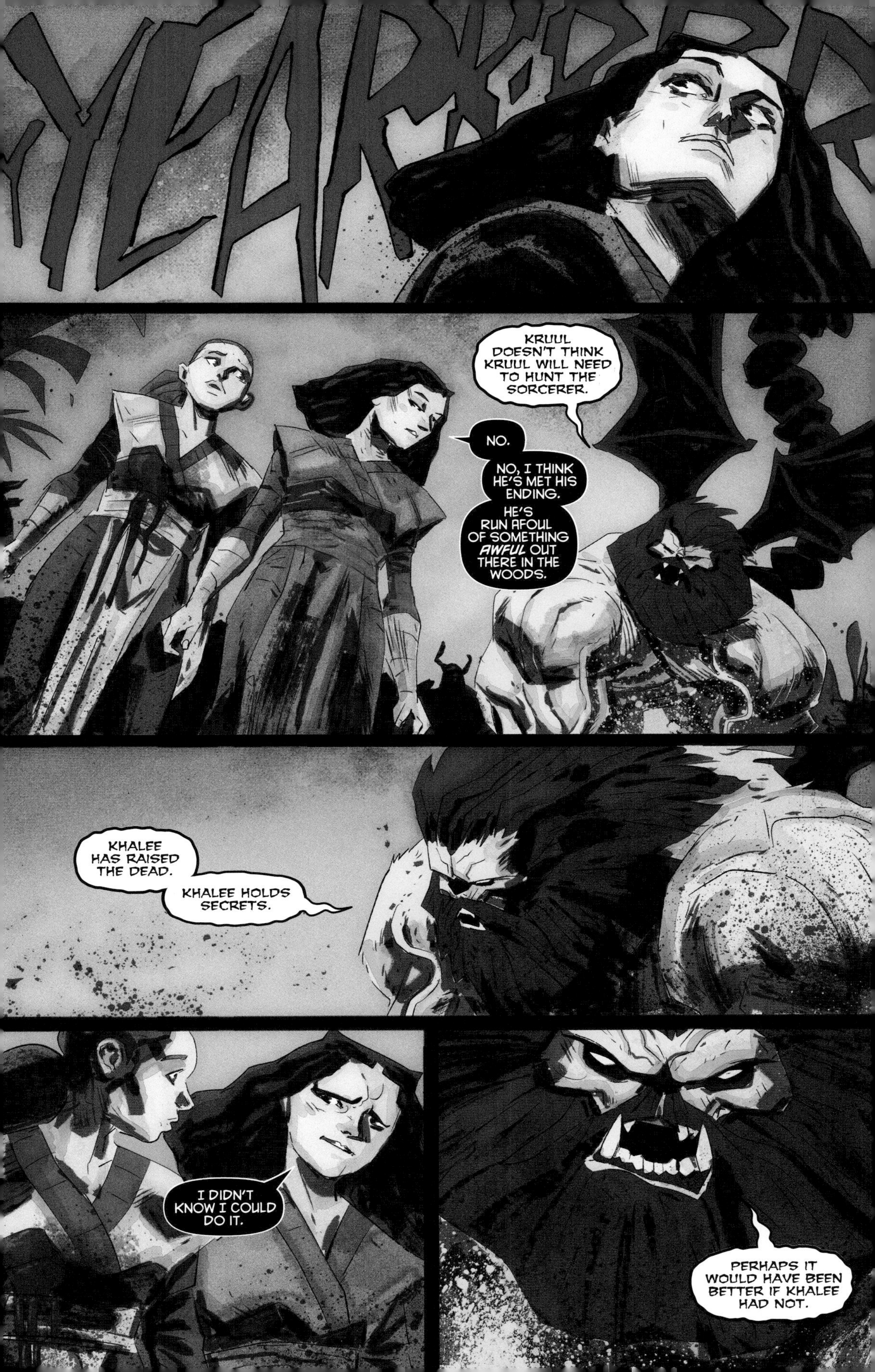
KRUUL DOESN'T THINK KRUUL WILL NEED TO HUNT THE SORCERER.
NO.
NO, I THINK HE'S MET HIS ENDING.
HE'S RUN AFOUL OF SOMETHING *AWFUL* OUT THERE IN THE WOODS.
KHALEE HAS RAISED THE DEAD.
KHALEE HOLDS SECRETS.
I DIDN'T KNOW I COULD DO IT.
PERHAPS IT WOULD HAVE BEEN BETTER IF KHALEE HAD NOT.

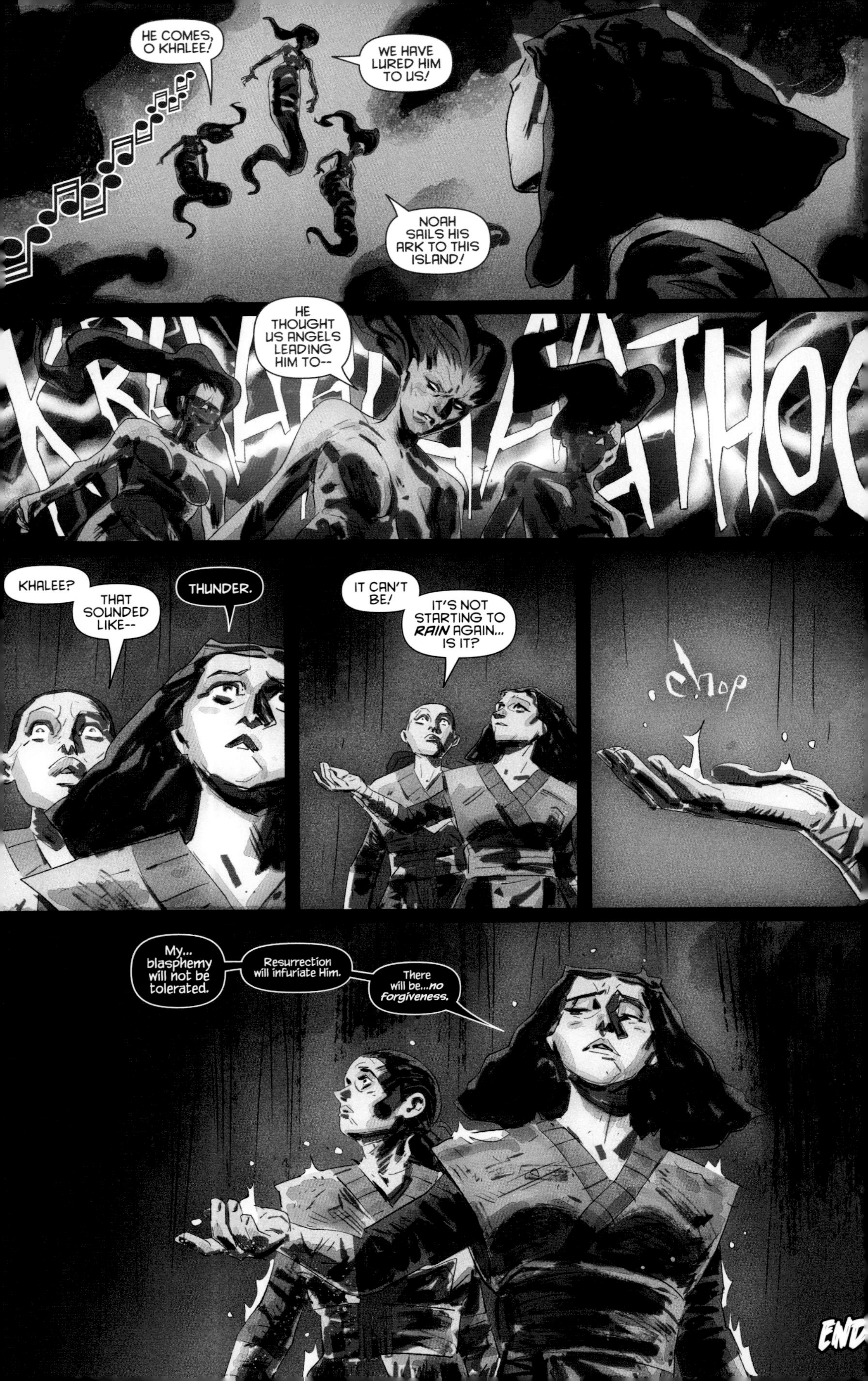
HE COMES, O KHALEE!
WE HAVE LURED HIM TO US!
NOAH SAILS HIS ARK TO THIS ISLAND!
HE THOUGHT US ANGELS LEADING HIM TO--
THOC
KHALEE?
THAT SOUNDED LIKE--
THUNDER.
IT CAN'T BE!
IT'S NOT STARTING TO *RAIN* AGAIN... IS IT?
drop
My... blasphemy will not be tolerated.
Resurrection will infuriate Him.
There will be...*no forgiveness.*
END

DARK ARK™
AFTER THE FLOOD

COVER GALLERY

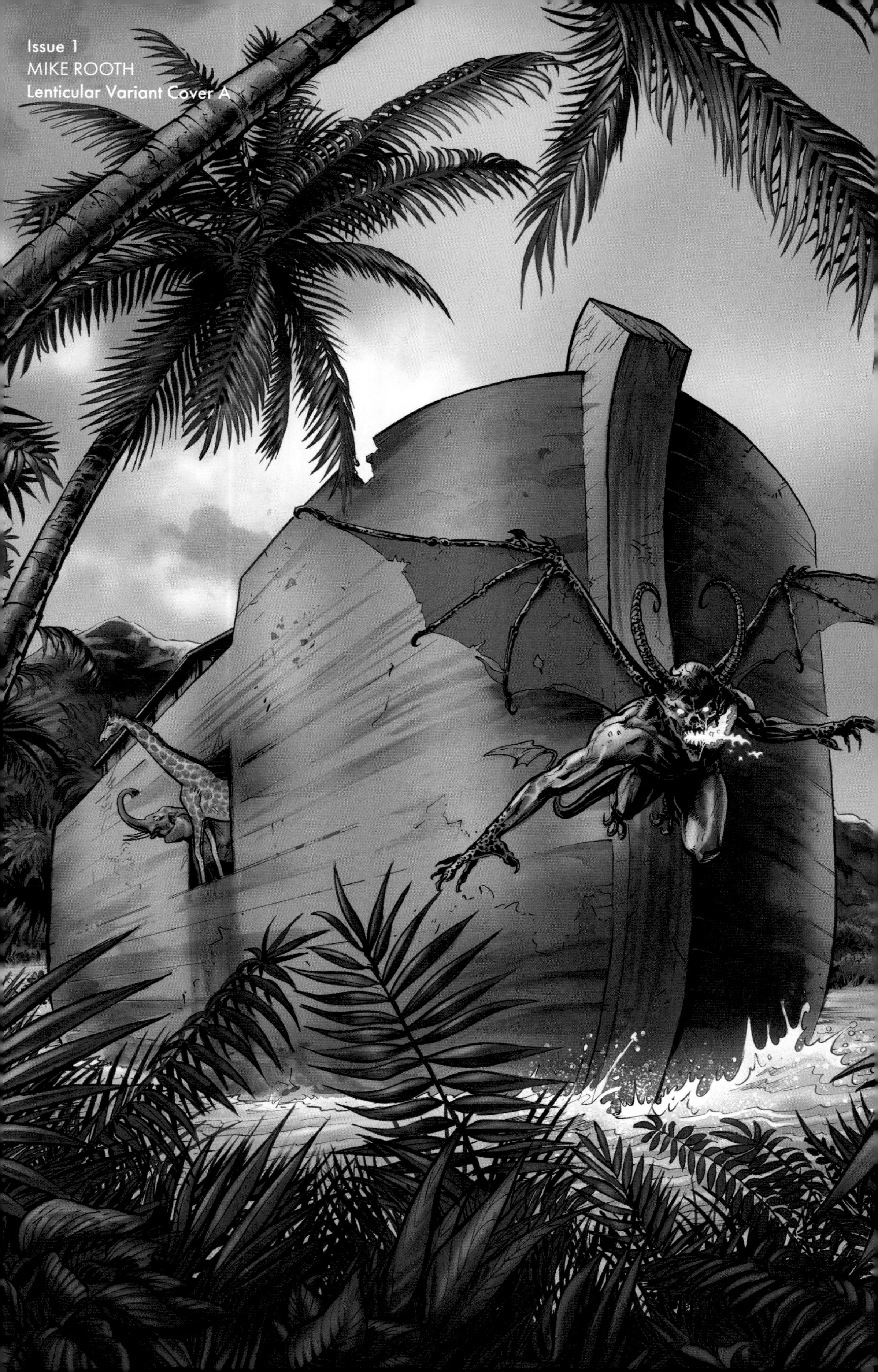
Issue 1
MIKE ROOTH
Lenticular Variant Cover A

Issue 1
MIKE ROOTH
Lenticular Variant Cover B

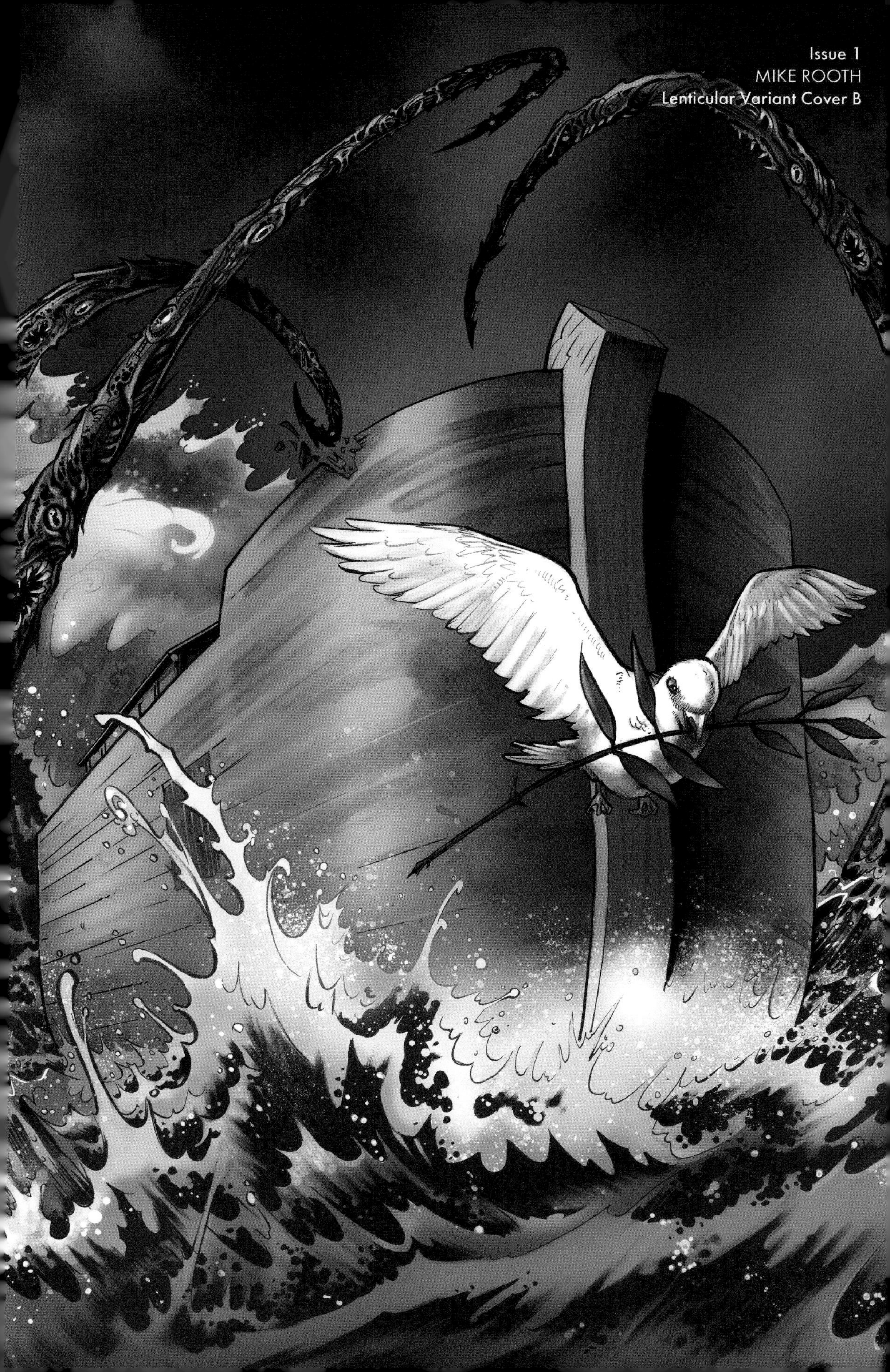

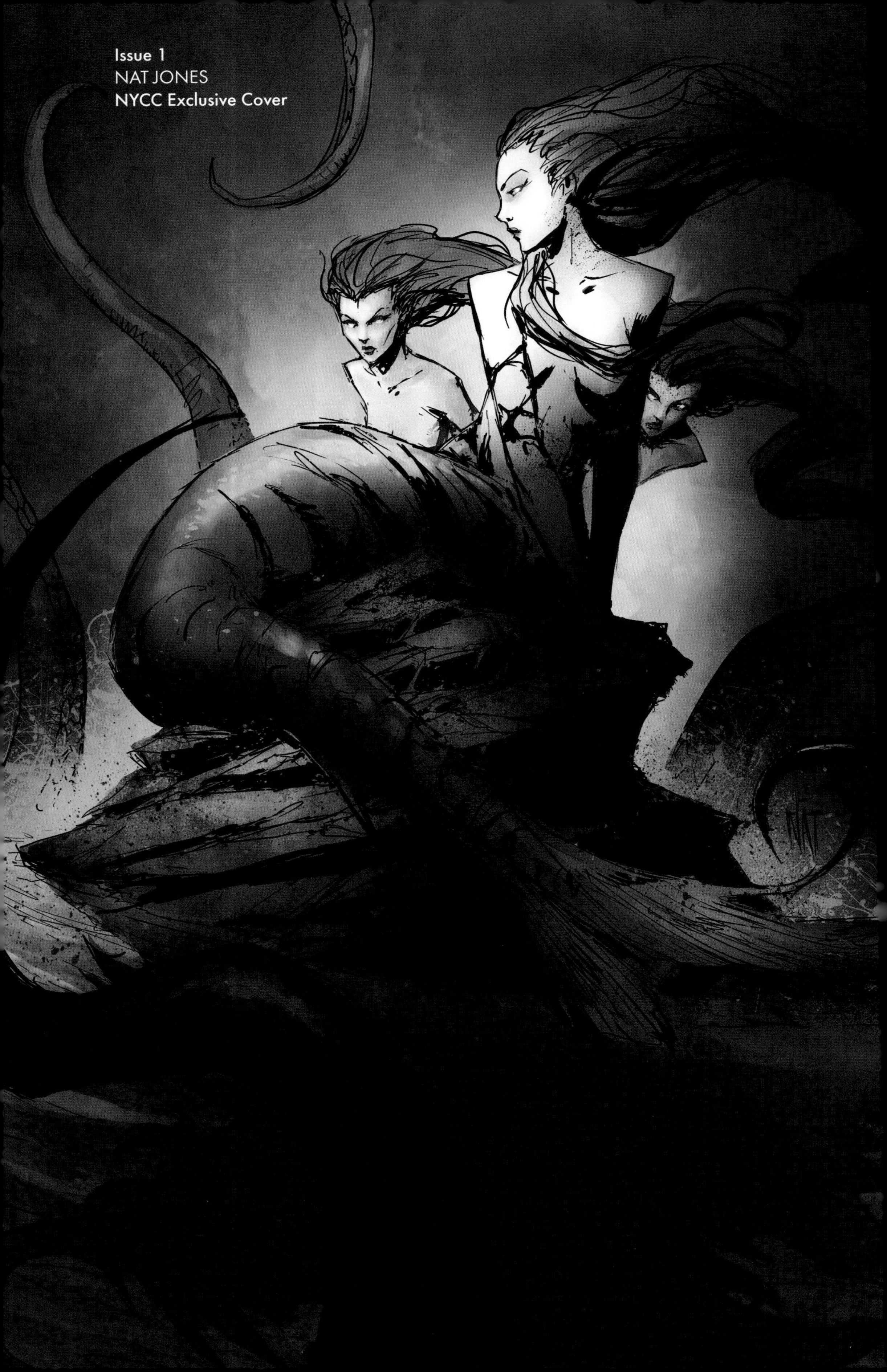

Issue 1
NAT JONES
NYCC Exclusive Cover

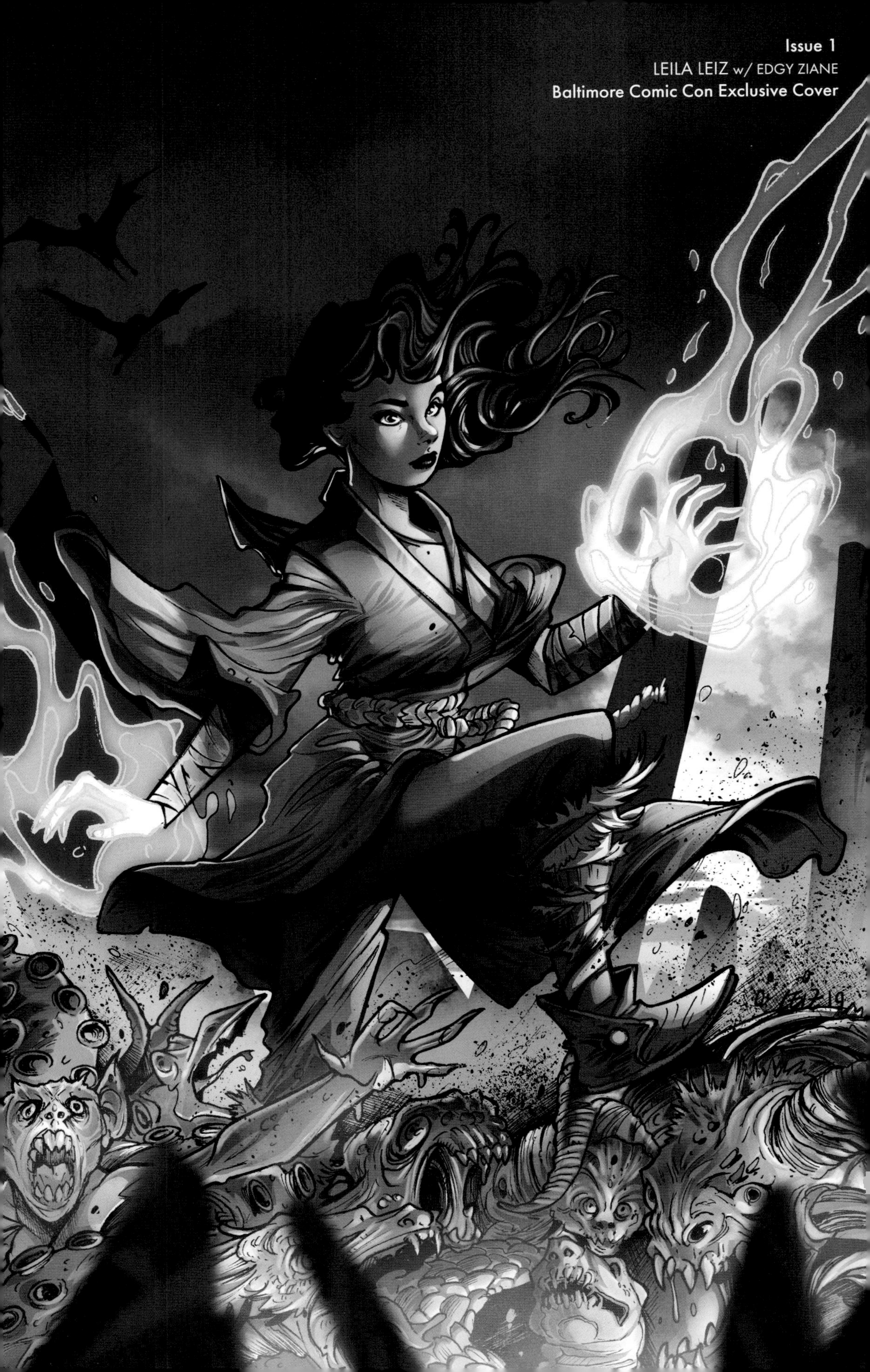
Issue 1
LEILA LEIZ w/ EDGY ZIANE
Baltimore Comic Con Exclusive Cover

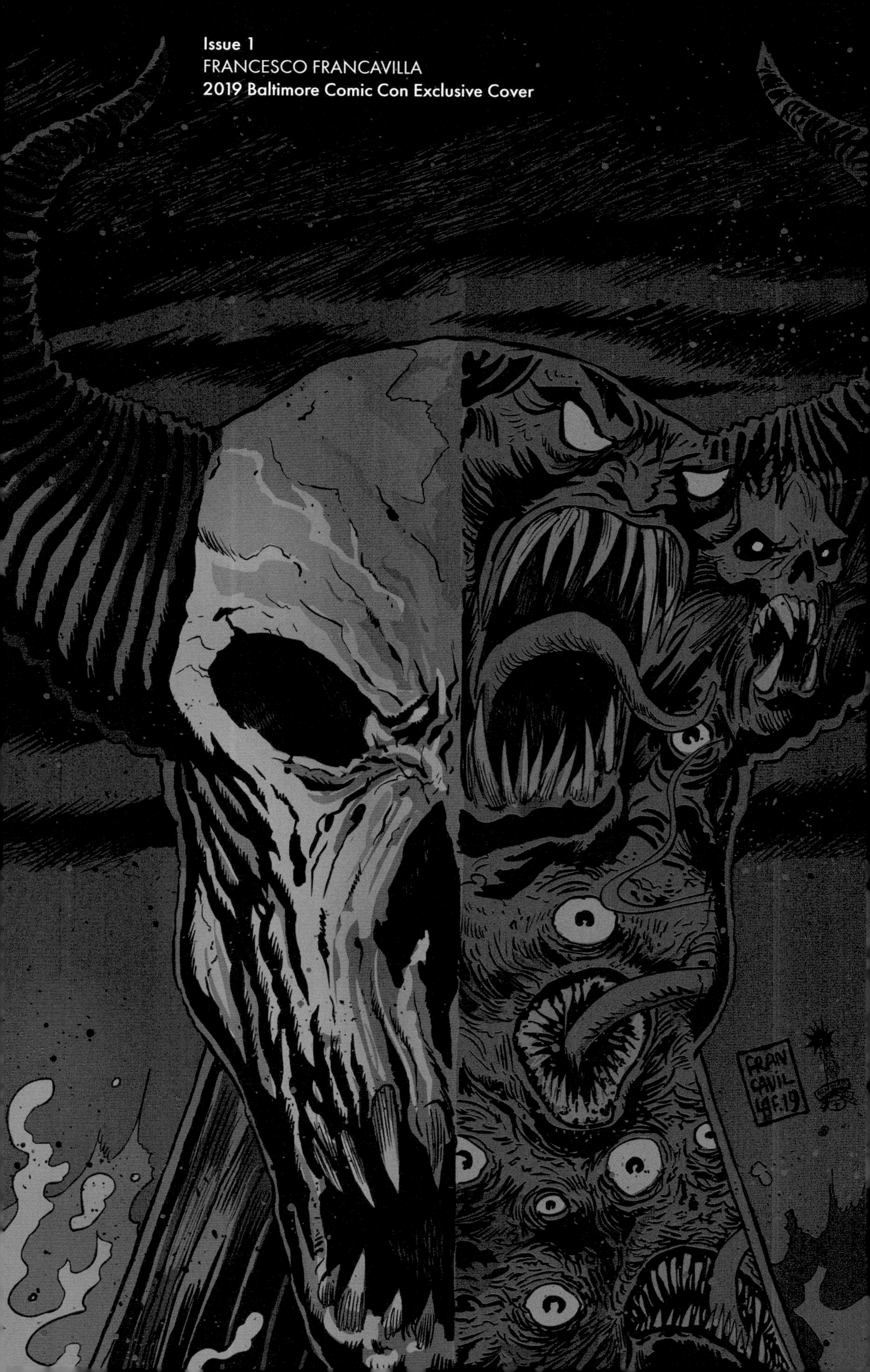

Issue 1
FRANCESCO FRANCAVILLA
2019 Baltimore Comic Con Exclusive Cover

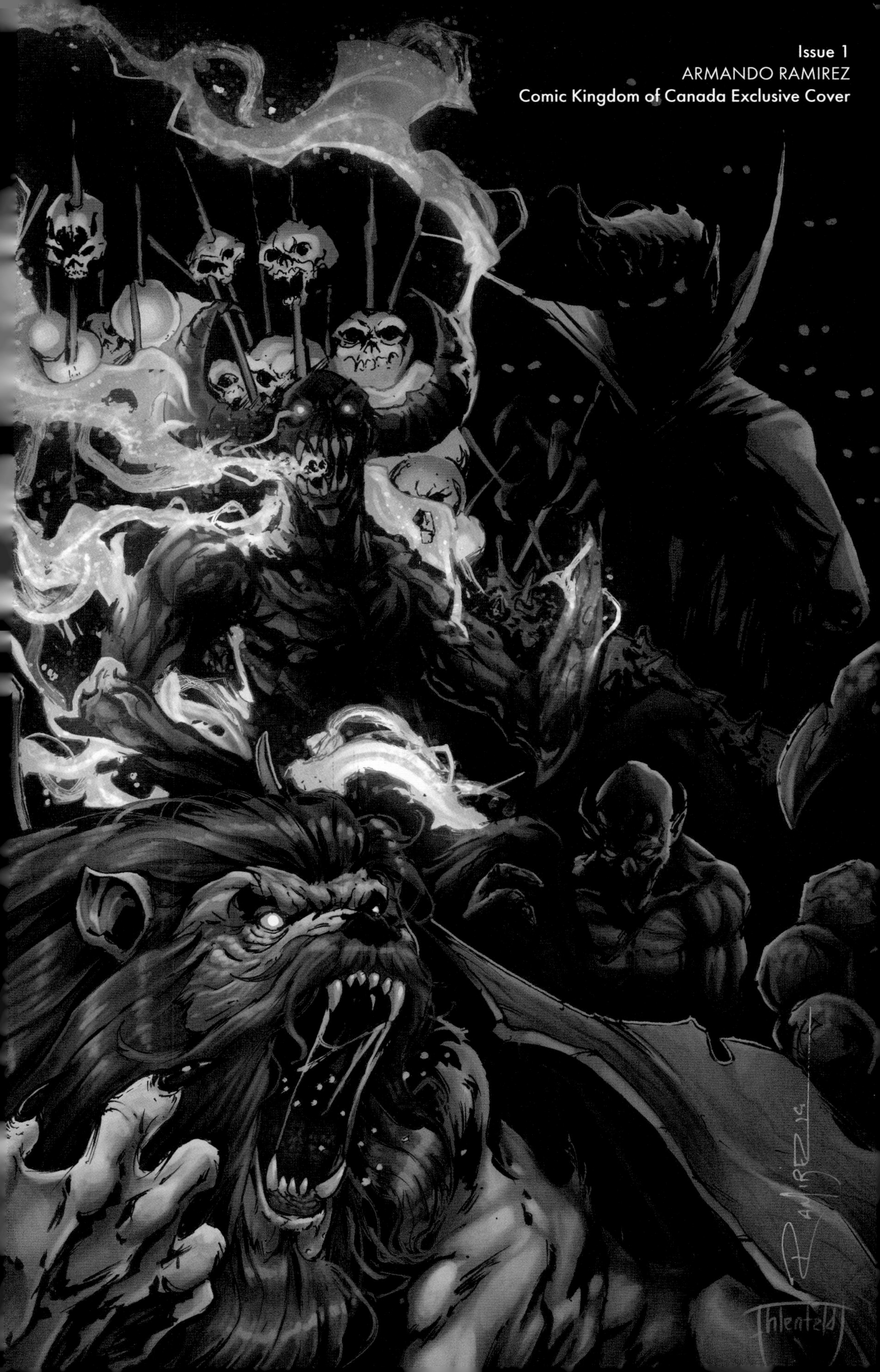

Issue 1
ARMANDO RAMIREZ
Comic Kingdom of Canada Exclusive Cover

Issue 1
MIKE ROOTH
Exclusive Wraparound Cover

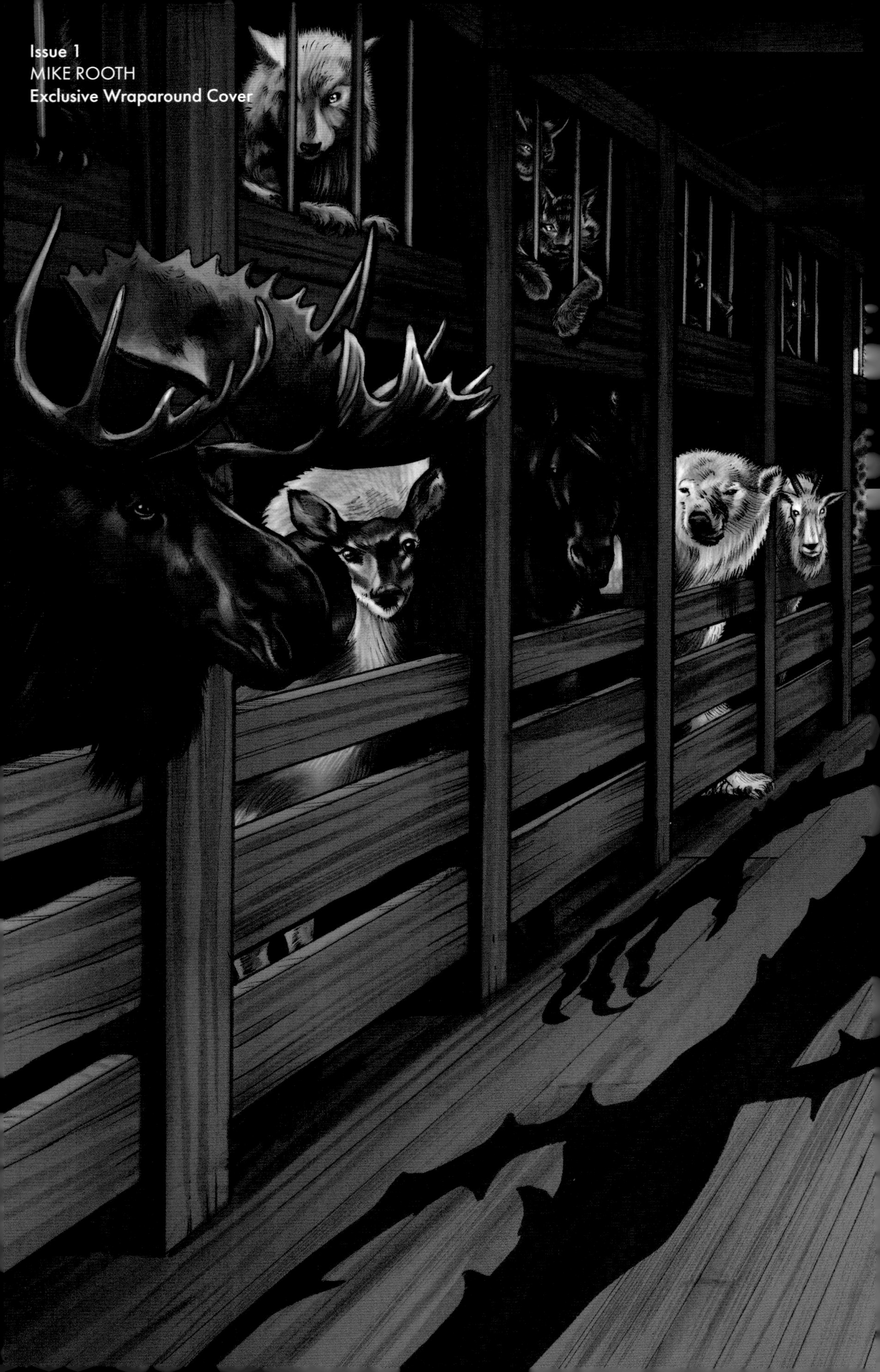

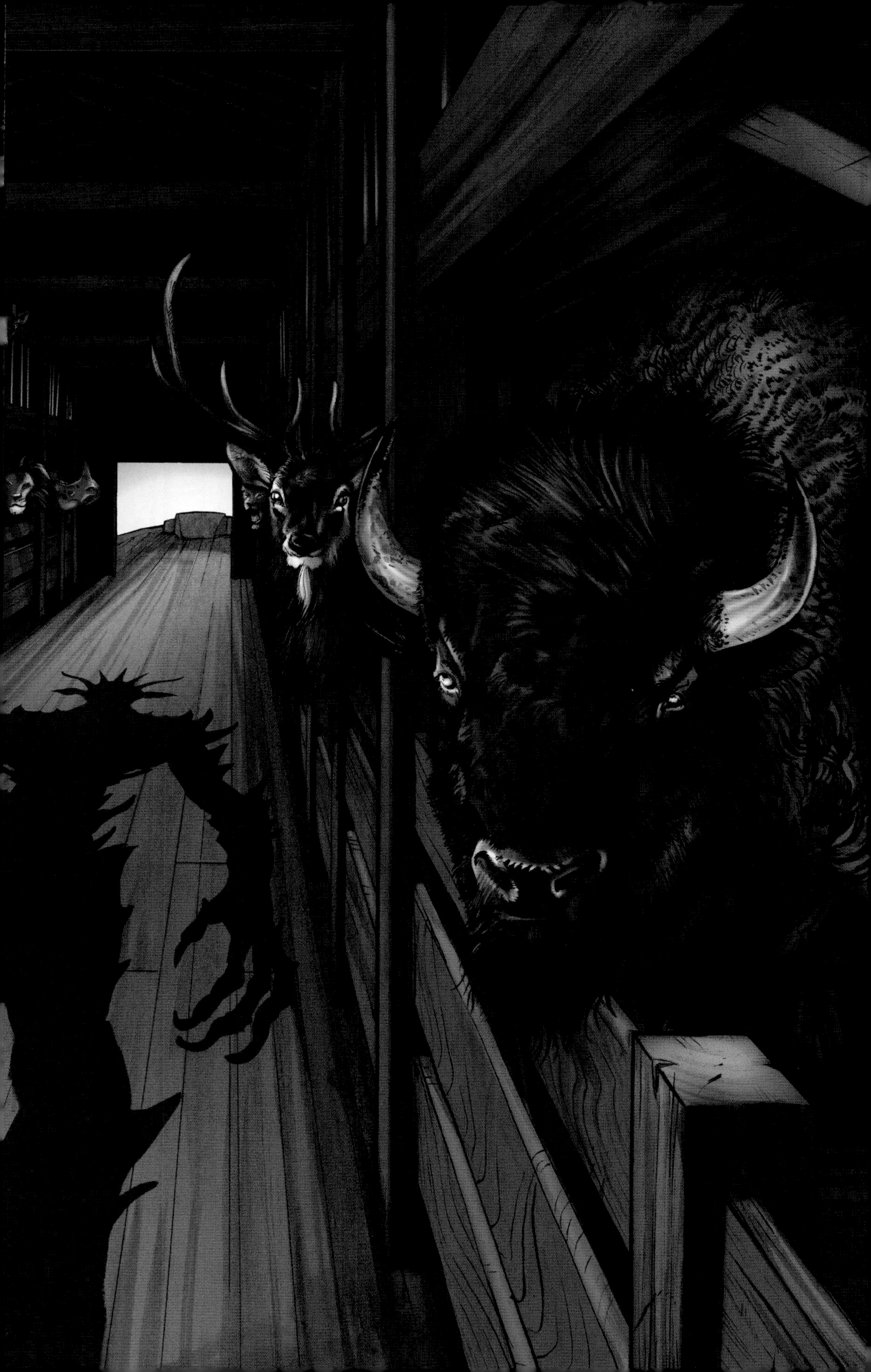

Issue 1
MIKE ROOTH
Exclusive Wraparound Cover (B/W)

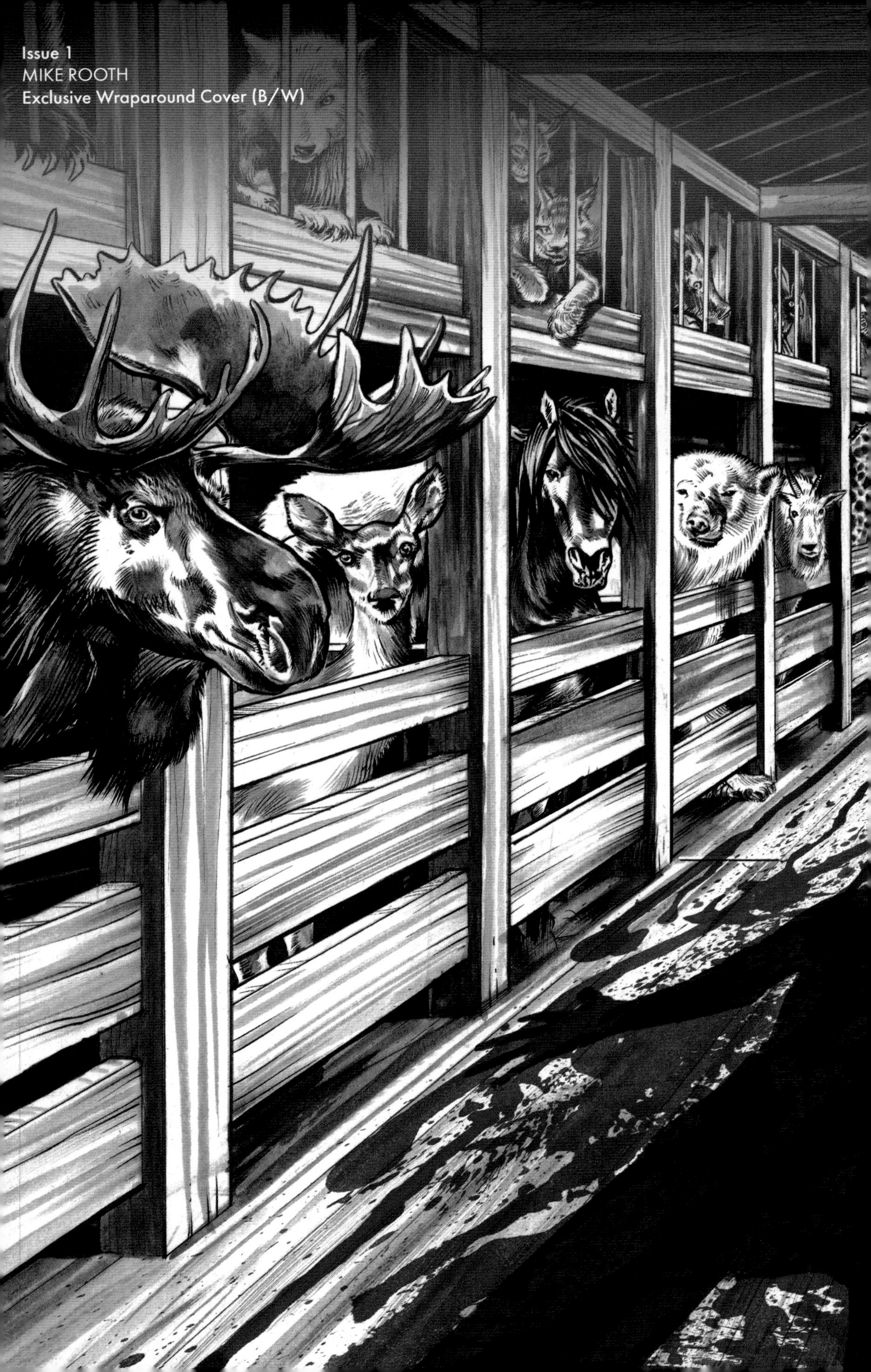

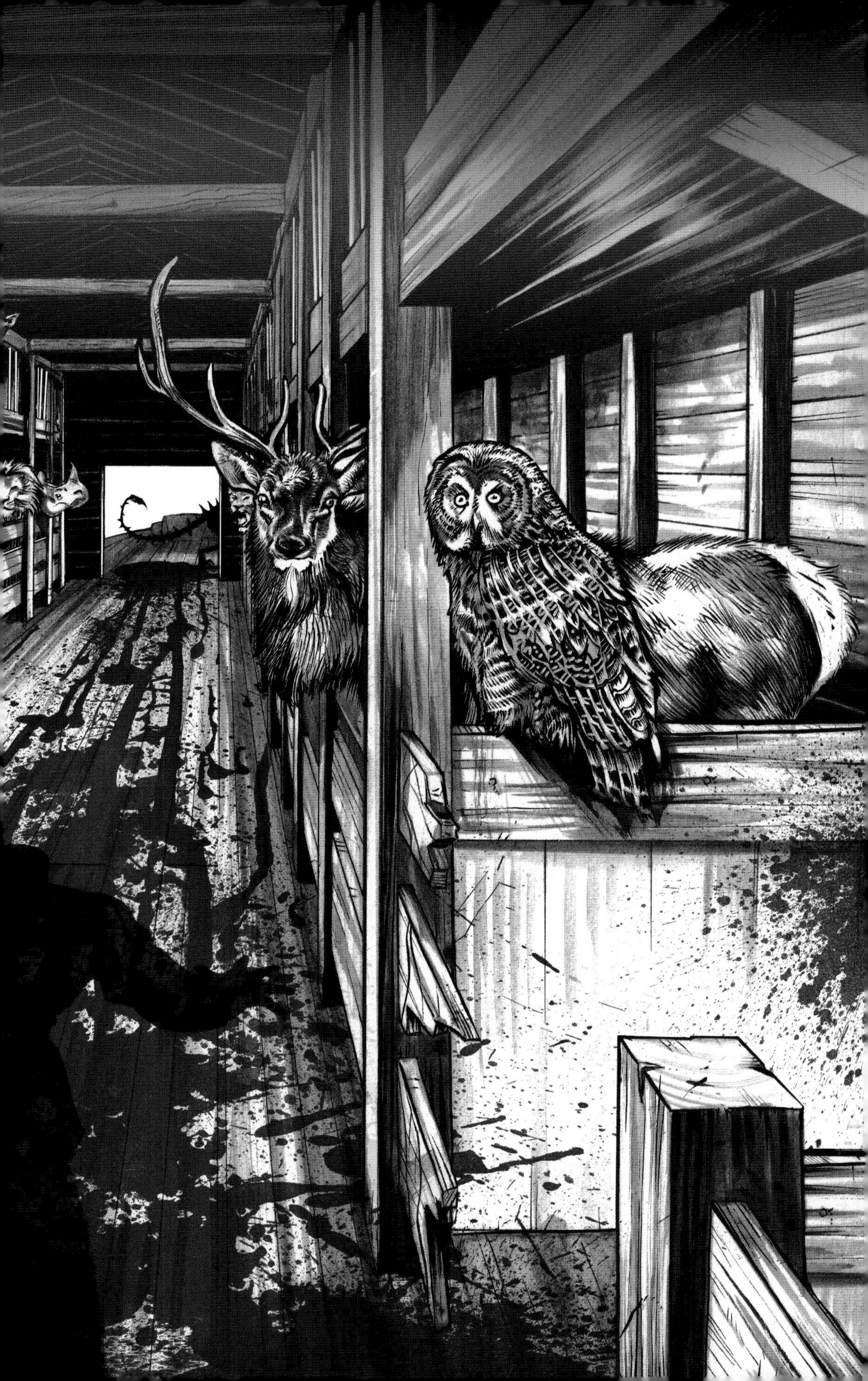

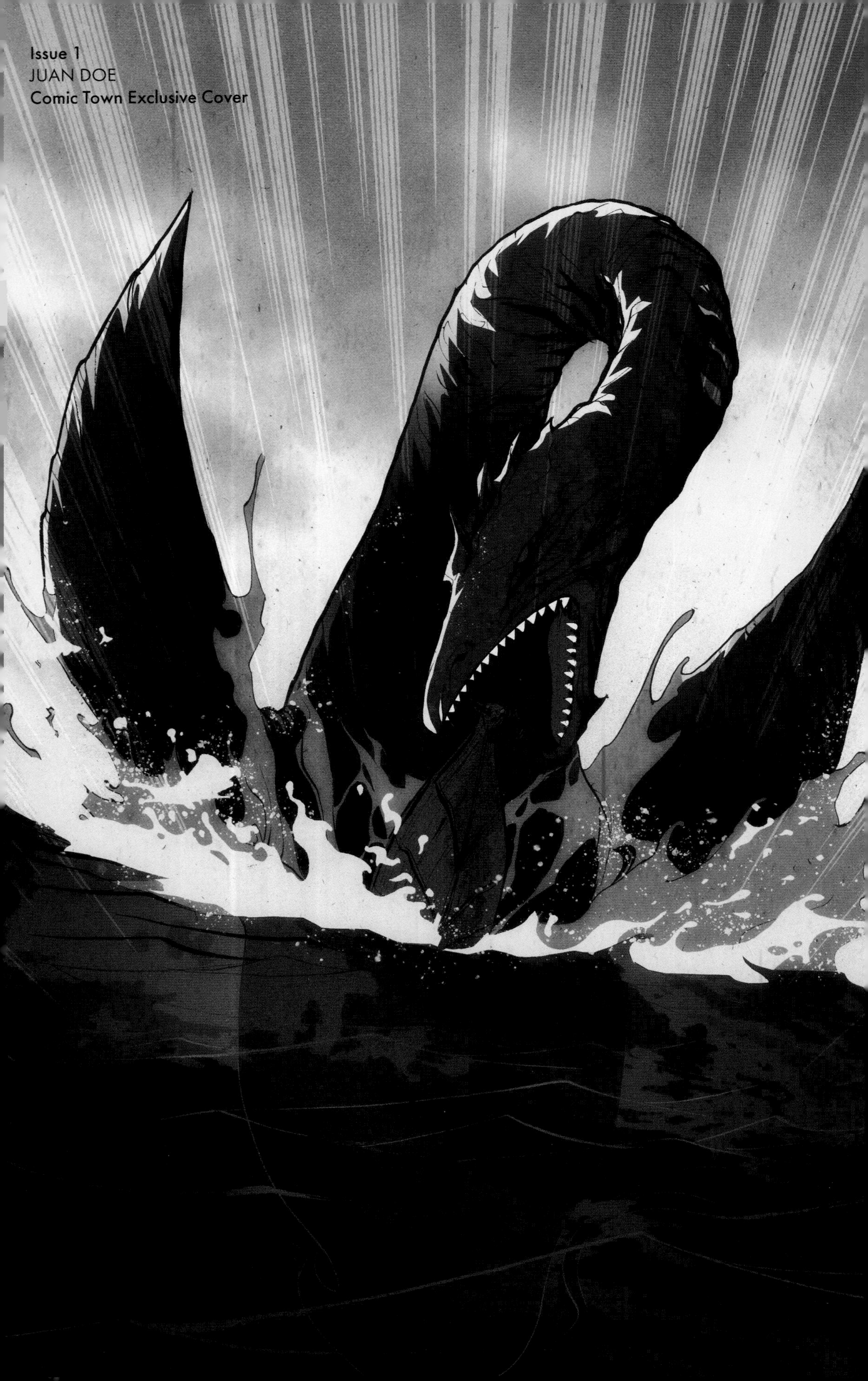

Issue 1
JUAN DOE
Comic Town Exclusive Cover

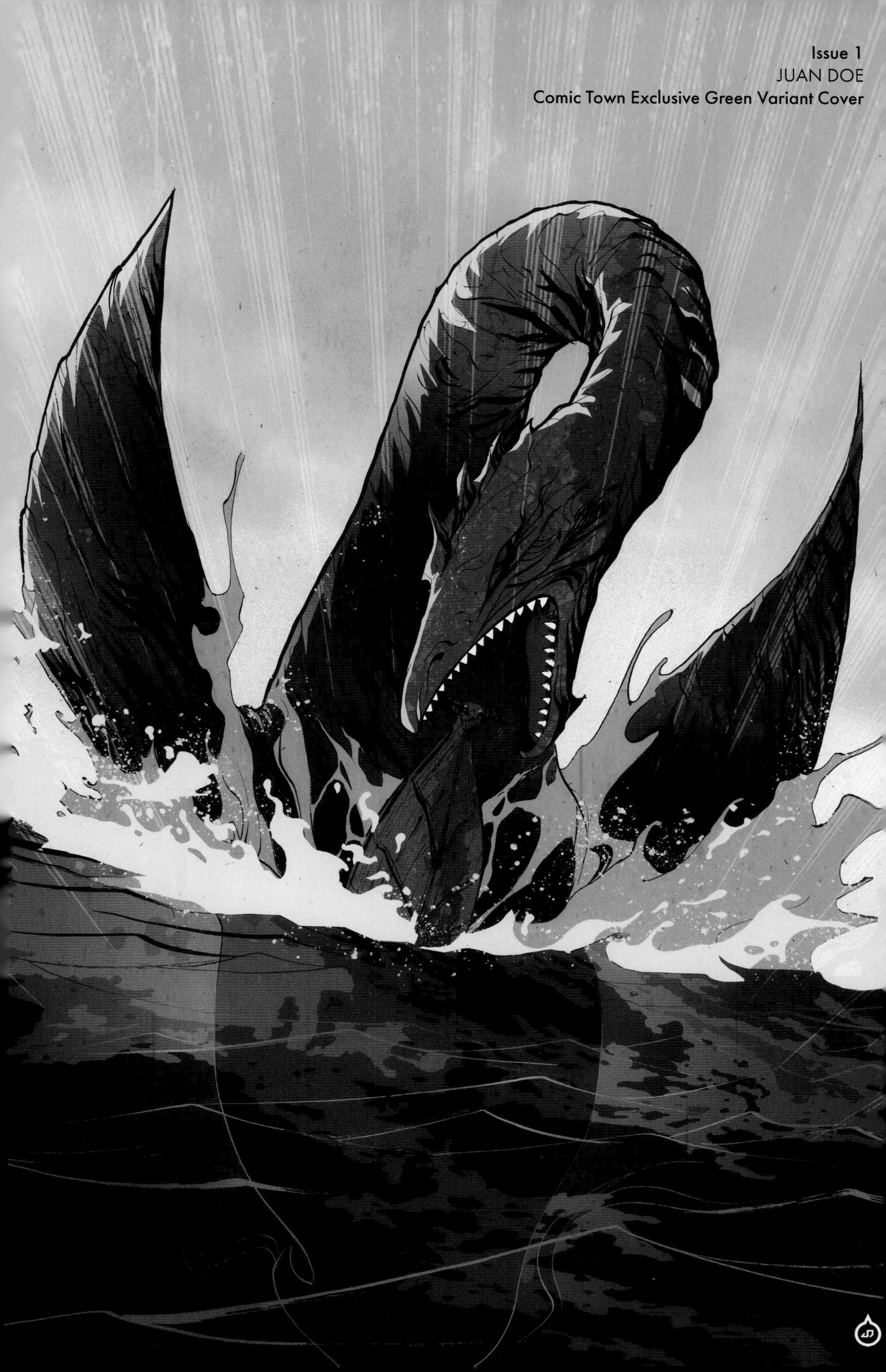

Issue 1
JUAN DOE
Comic Town Exclusive Green Variant Cover

Issue 1
ANDREI BRESSAN
Variant Cover

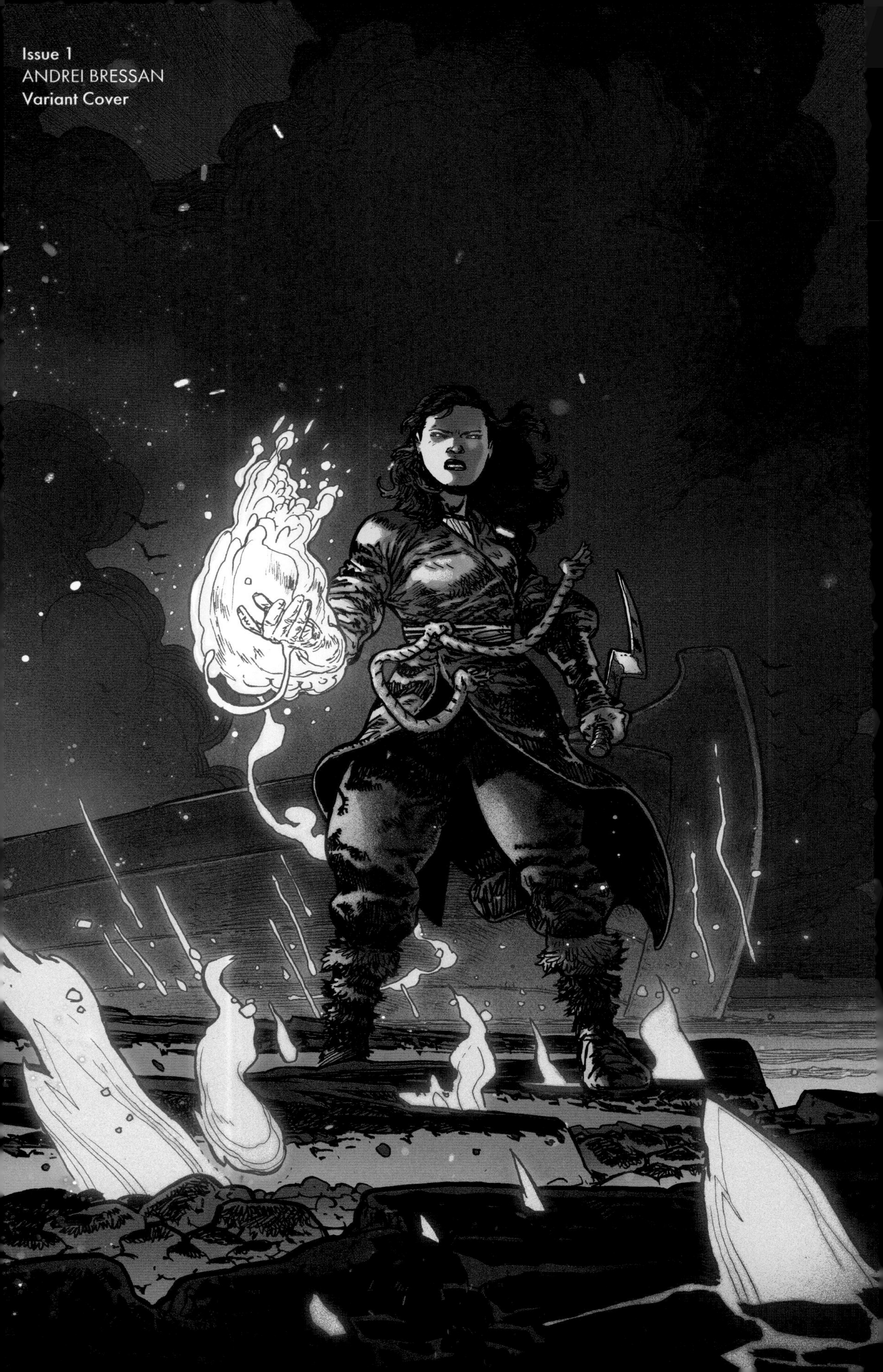

DARK ARK
AFTER THE FLOOD

BEHIND THE SCENES

DARK ARK
AFTER THE FLOOD

#3

DARK ARK: AFTER THE FLOOD
Issue 5
Written by Cullen Bunn

PAGES SIX AND SEVEN (Three panels, Double-Page Spread with two insets)
We're cutting to the here and now!

PANEL 1 (Inset of panel 2, upper left) – Close on Khalee, her brow furrowed, as she speaks, casting her arms out. It is Day.

CAPTION:
Now.
KHALEE:
All of you!
Listen to me!
You must remain calm!

PANEL 2 – Huge panel. We are behind Khalee as she stands before the monsters. Here, we should see all sorts of monsters—from small goblins to hulking ogres. Kruul and his cub are here. We might see some werewolves, maybe some PREYTONS (https://en.wikipedia.org/wiki/Peryton) and some LAMIA (https://en.wikipedia.org/wiki/Lamia) and some TREE CREATURES (https://en.wikipedia.org/wiki/Treant) and some GIANT SPIDERS. Really, whatever you like here. We just want a variety. The ruins of Shrae's Ark are in the background, beached. From within a hole in the hull, we see the shadowy shape of Ada (now here vampire self) watching. Maybe we only see her glowing eyes. Standing off to the side, we might see Orin and Janris and Selah (holding her baby) and Rea. In addition, we should see a small group of humans—the former prisoners of Shrae's Ark—standing in the background, watching, afraid. There should be at least ten of them.

KHALEE:

I know you are restless!
I know you are uneasy!
But we must be smart!
Soon, the sirens will lure Noah's Ark to these islands!
I know what you will want to do when that happens!
You will want to feast!

PANEL 3 (inset of Panel 2, lower right) – Close on Ada, crouched in the shadows, watching gloomily, her eyes aglow.

ADA (Small):
Wonderful things.

script by
CULLEN BUNN

PAGES
6-7
PROCESS

greyscale by
JUAN DOE

colors by
JUAN DOE

lettering by
DAVE SHARPE

DARK ARK
AFTER THE FLOOD

#5

DARK ARK: AFTER THE FLOOD
Issue 5
Written by Cullen Bunn

PAGE THREE (Five Panels)
Flashback continues.

PANEL 1 — SHRAE stand s next to YOUNG KHALEE, his hand on her shoulder. They are both looking in the same direction (toward the tree, OP).

> SFX (Music):
> >>>Musical notes<<<
> SHRAE:
> It is nice, yes.
> But it is a mistruth.
> It is a stolen song.

PANEL 2 — YOUNG KHALEE looks towards her father, confused.
> YOUNG KHALEE:
> Stolen?
> SFX (Music):
> >>>Musical notes<<<

PANEL 3 — Close on SHRAE.
> SHRAE:
> That bird is a brood parasite.
> It lays its eggs in the nests of other birds.
> The hatchlings learn the begging song of their host.
> SFX (Music):
> >>>Musical notes<<<

PANEL 4 — Closer on SHRAE.
> SHRAE:
> They are never recognized as an invader.
> SFX (Music):
> >>>Musical notes<<<

PANEL 5 — On YOUNG KHALEE turning to watch as SHRAE walks away.
> SHRAE:
> Come.
> Your mother will be angry if your food gets cold.
> SFX (Music):
> >>>Musical notes<<<

PANEL 6 — Close on the BIRD, singing.
> SFX (Music):
> >>>Musical notes<<<

script by
CULLEN BUNN

PAGE
3
PROCESS

greyscale by
JUAN DOE

colors by
JUAN DOE

lettering by
DAVE SHARPE

CREATORS OF DARK ARK AFTER THE FLOOD

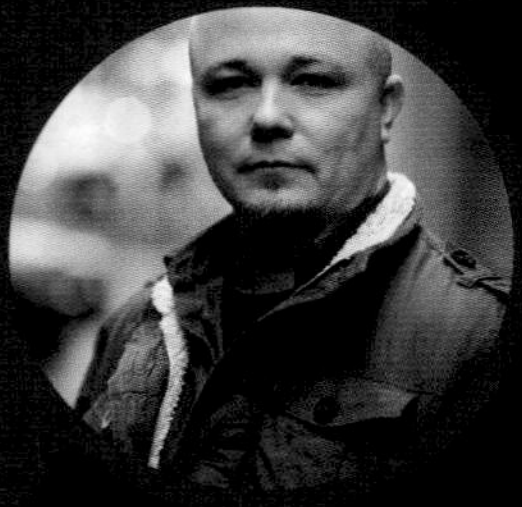

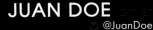

CULLEN BUNN writer

@CullenBunn

Cullen is the writer of such creator-owned comics as *The Sixth Gun, The Damned, Harro County* and *Regression*. In addition, he writes *X-Men Blue, Monsters Unleashed* and numerou *Deadpool* comics for Marvel. For AfterShock Comics, Cullen has written DARK ARK, UNHOL GRAIL, THE BROTHERS DRACUL, WITCH HAMMER and KNIGHTS TEMPORAL.

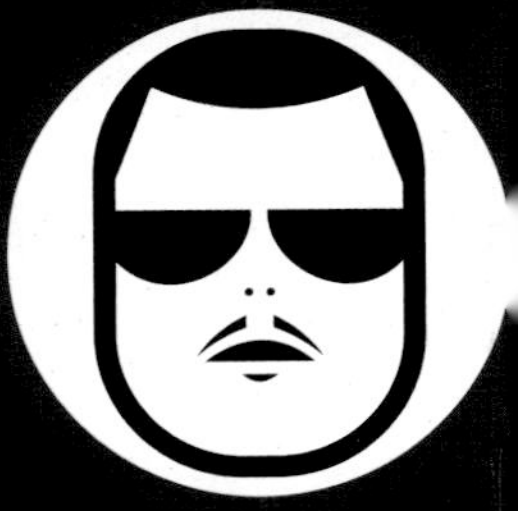

JUAN DOE artist

@JuanDoe

uan Doe is a professional illustrator with over ten years experience in the comic book industry. He has produced over a hundred covers and his sequential highlights include the *Fantastic Four in Puerto Rico* trilogy, *The Legion of Monsters* mini-series for Marvel and *Joker's Asylum: Scarecrow* for DC. He has illustrated AMERICAN MONSTER, WORLD READER, ANIMOSITY: THE RISE, DARK ARK, and BAD RECEPTION for AfterShock Comics.

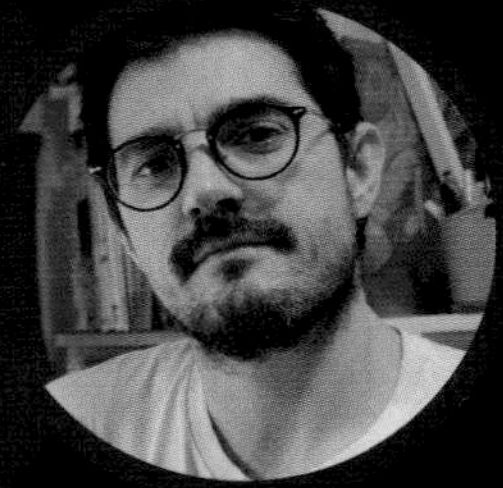

JESUS HERVAS artist

Jesus is a self-taught cartoonist who originally studied to become a forest engineer. Hailir from Madrid, Spain, Jesus first found work at the French publisher Soleil, where he illustrate series like *Deluge* and *Androides*. He then went on to work for several various Americ publishers, on titles such as *Hellraiser, Sons of Anarchy, Lucas Strand, Penny Dreadful,* and h first collaboration with writer Cullen Bunn, Boom!'s *The Empty Man*.

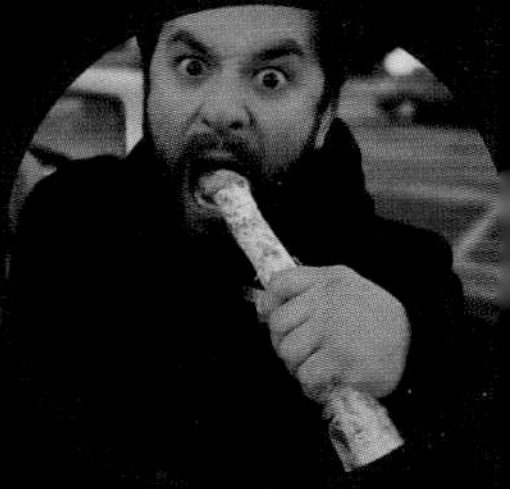

JUANCHO! colorist

uan Ignacio Vélez, aka JUANCHO! is comic book colorist/illustrator from Bogotá, Colombia and a Kubert School graduate. His past comic book experience stretches all the way from North American to European publishers. He currently lives in Barcelona, Spain, where he splits his time between eating fuet with guacamole and freelance color duties.

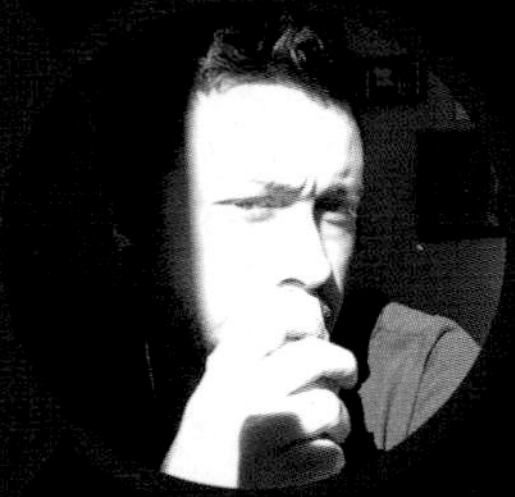

ANTONIO FUSO artist

@Antonio_Fuso

Antonio Fuso is an Italian comic book artist based in Rome. Among titles he has contributed are *Fear Agent, Judge Dredd, G.I. Joe: Cobra, Zombies Vs. Robots, Drive, Torchwood, Jam Bond 007, Survival Fetish* and the graphic novel adaption of Stieg Larsson's *Millennium Trilog* Antonio has also produced covers and illustrations for Boom! Studios, Valiant, IDW Publishin Archie Comics, Titan, Vertigo and the Belgian rock band dEUS. He is an interior design lov as well as coffee addicted.

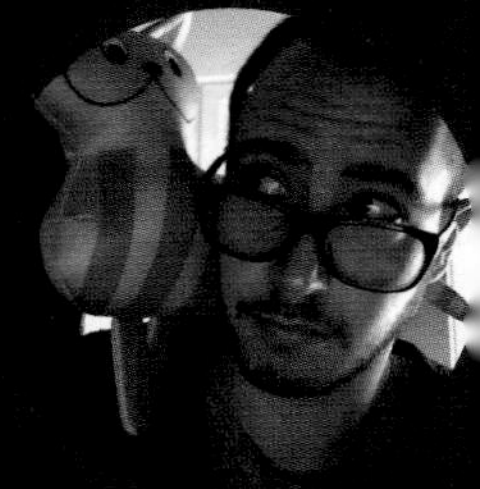

STEFANO SIMEONE colorist

@stefano_simeone

An Italian-born comic book artist and illustrator, Stefano has published four award-winning graphic novels in Italy for Tunué and Bao Publishing. He has also drawn *Cars 3, Rogue One: A Star Wars Story*, and *Star Wars: The Last Jedi* comics for Disney and LucasFilm. Stefano has also worked for a number of comic book publishers, including IDW, Image Comics, Boom! Studios and Archaia.

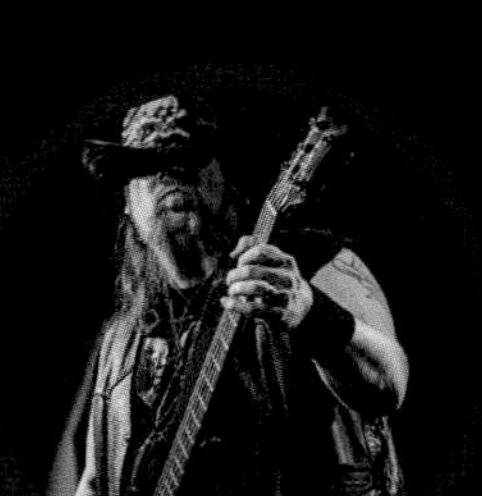

DAVE SHARPE letterer

@DaveLSharpe

Dave grew up a HUGE metalhead, living on Long Island, NY while spending summers Tallahassee, FL. After reading *Micronauts* (and many other comics), Dave knew he had to ha a career in the business. Upon graduating from the Joe Kubert School in 1990, he went on work at Marvel Comics as an in-house letterer, eventually running their lettering departme in the late 90s and early 00s. Over the years, Dave has lettered hundreds of comics, su as *Spider-Girl, Exiles, She-Hulk* and *The Defenders* for Marvel, and *Green Lantern, Harle Quinn, Sinestro* and *Batgirl* for DC Comics. Dave now works on both *X-O Manowar* and *Fa* for Valiant Comics in addition to his lettering duties on AfterShock's *The Revisionist*. Dave al plays bass and is way more approachable than he looks.